SPIRAL GUIDES

Travel with Someone You Trust®

P9-BJV-288

AMSTERDAM

Contents

the magazine 5

Finding Your Feet 35

Medieval Amsterdam 49

Canal Ring – West 79

Written by Simon Calder

Where to sections by Fred Mawer

Copy edited by Nia Williams
Page layout by Nautilus Design (UK) Limited
Verified by Colin Follett
Indexed by Marie Lorimer

Edited, designed and produced by AA Publishing
© Automobile Association Developments Limited 2001
Maps © Automobile Association Developments Limited 2001

Published in the United States by AAA Publishing,
1000 AAA Drive, Heathrow, Florida 32746
Published in the United Kingdom by AA Publishing

ISBN 1-56251-413-X

Color separation by Leo Reprographics
Printed and bound in China by Leo Paper Products

10 9 8 7 6 5 4 3 2 1

the magazine

In the family of great European cities, Amsterdam is the youngster. A millennium ago, it was nothing but a marsh, a short way inland from where the Rhine spills into the North Sea.

The first inhabitants set about modifying the swampy surroundings, establishing the pattern for the growth of the city. Adaptability and change are the watchwords of the Dutch – virtues that enabled them to survive against considerable natural and man-made adversity, then use the upsurge in world trade to fund the Golden Age of the 17th century. The profit center then, as now, was Amsterdam, the city that lives by its wits.

packed into not quite enough space. Yet it is also the most cosmopolitan city on the Continent, with large communities from Indonesia, the Caribbean and North Africa, and groups such as artists and gays, who revel in the liberal climate.

Amsterdam's celebrated tolerance has helped

Amsterdam a Capital

In many ways, the city still resembles the village that the original inhabitants created by damming the Amstel River. Compared with other European capitals, Amsterdam is tiny – just three-quarters of a million people

make it superlative in terms of art, architecture and culture. It's also made possible the blatant merchandising of sex and drugs. Even visitors with the noblest of intentions cannot ignore the marijuana dens and highly visible prostitution. Yet the chief civic characteristic is humanity, not sleaze.

Metropolitan Makeover

Type in www.amsterdam.nl on an internet terminal. You will be greeted by a stylish and snappy site boasting that the city is "home to offices of more than 1,000 foreign companies," and was "recently voted top of the list as a location for European HQ," and claiming that one in three visitors is attending a convention. The "re-branding" of Amsterdam is part of the campaign by Dutch prime minister Wim Kok's center-left coalition to shake off the undeserved image as a haven for anarchists and junkies. The city is being repositioned as a clean, efficient venue fit for business in the Euro-economy of the 21st century.

The articulate, animated community resides on the banks of a network of canals, whose geometric stubbornness has enabled Amsterdam to resist the architectural

of Humanity

outrages that have desecrated so many cities. The inky waters reflect a thousand bridges, and many more thousands of handsome houses overlooking cobbled streets, and seem to exert a calming influence that pervades the busy city life.

The sheer concentration of the cerebral rather than the physical is unmatched in other European capitals. Add a gratifying supply of relaxed bars and imaginative restaurants and the result is a city that manages to remain as civilized as it is diverse.

So Where's the Parliament?

The Netherlands is unusual in that the parliamentary capital is not found in the largest city. The Hague owes its position as seat of the Dutch government, and the location of many embassies, to its choice as the residence of Count Wilhelm II of Holland in the 13th century; the official name, 's-Gravenhage, means "the count's hedge." Later, the States-General of Holland was established there. Parliament still deliberates well away from the many temptations of Amsterdam – partly through tradition, but also because many Dutch people fret about the concentration of power in Amsterdam, a city that dominates commercially and culturally, yet is home to just one in 20 of the nation's population.

THE BEST of Amsterdam

A superlative selection from the best the city has to offer:

Bird's-eye view: from the tower of the Beurs van Berlage (➤ 67) the medieval core of the city is laid out beneath you.

Canal tour: the live commentary of Amsterdam Canal Cruises (➤ 84–87) makes it stand out from the rest.

Canal house: the Museum Amstelkring (➤ 64–65) is one of the most splendid 17th-century residences, with

Sound: the chimes of Westerkerk (➤ 92–93), ringing on the hour and half-hour.

Venue for people-watching (when raining): the Café Americain in the American Hotel (➤ 101) – bag a window for views across Leidseplein.

Venue for people-watching (when dry): place yourself outside the precariously leaning café of De Sluyswacht (➤ 72).

the added bonus of a chapel hidden in the attic.

New structure: the striking hulk of newMetropolis (➤ 69) has already become an essential component of the Amsterdam skyline.

Tram ride: number 20, from Centraal Station, circulates counterclockwise.

Church: the quiet, immaculate interior of Nieuwe Kerk (➤ 61–62) is a joy.

Water level is an ideal vantage point

Market: Noordermarkt (▶ 106), particularly the flea-market on Mondays.

Green space (free): the Begijnhof (▶ 54–55).

Green space (fee): Hortus Botanicus (▶ 144–145).

If you go to only one:

Art museum: the Van Gogh. The richness of Van Gogh's tragically short life becomes clear in this superb museum (▶ 124–127).

Specialty museum: clear winner in terms of the sheer opulence of its surroundings is the Theatermuseum (▶ 99).

Brown café: Café Papeneiland (▶ 101) – small, old and full of local characters.

Grand café: Café de Jaren (▶ 70), in the lofty premises of a former bank, with a fine water-side location.

Dinner venue: Café-Restaurant Amsterdam (▶ 103) – a jaw-dropping conversion of a power station with a menu to suit all budgets.

Hotel: Blakes (▶ 41) is not just the newest addition to the stock of superior hotels, it is also a theatrically designed boutique hotel par excellence.

Worth a peek even if you're not staying there.

Above: newMetropolis

Below: Vintage transportation

Amsterdam's Schiphol airport, one of the busiest in Europe, occupies a former lake bed

Unsuitable for Human Habitation?

From the pilot's point of view, the approach to Schiphol airport is an interesting one. The North Sea ends abruptly at a sturdy line of dunes, clearly augmented here and there by humans. As the plane turns above the city to line up with the runway, Amsterdam seems on the point of being overwhelmed by the water that surrounds and intrudes upon it. Next, the altimeter has to be checked to ensure that it can cope with the counter-intuitive reality of landing more than 12 feet beneath sea level.

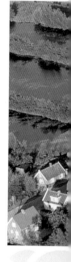

Unfit for human habitation? Much of the country is, at least in theory. Somewhere just north of Rotterdam, the Netherlands hits an all-time low: the land is nearly 20 feet below sea level. This is a country with a problem: one-third of the nation, including a substantial proportion of Amsterdam, lies beneath a line over which the North Sea would naturally flow were there no barrier. Sixty percent of the Dutch population, between the Schelde estuary near Belgium and the German border, lives beneath NAP – Normaal Amsterdams Peil, or Standard Amsterdam Level.

SHORE FOUNDATIONS

It was not always like this. Five hundred years before the birth of Christ, the sea level was lower and much of the coastline intact. By the end of the first millennium, the North Sea had encroached on large parts of what is now the Netherlands, with broad estuaries interspersed with precariously marshy land. The first settlers in Amsterdam started to make it habitable using a method that has served the Dutch well ever since: digging earth from the swamp to build up artificial islands, which

mation most notable in the former Zuider Zee ("South Sea"), now the IJsselmeer.

RESTLESS TIDES

There have been disastrous floods along the way, though, and the water that helped Amsterdam make its fortune is treated with great respect. Its significance and destructive potential was acknowledged more than three centuries ago, long before London became the location for the world's prime meridian: in 1684, Standard Amsterdam Level was estab-

One-third of Dutch territory lies below the level of the North Sea

gradually grew and became linked as human activity increased. The construction of robust dikes meant that the enclosed area, once drained, could be populated or farmed. Two great technological developments accelerated the process: the use of windmills to drive screw pumps, enabling larger areas to be drained and kept free of water; and the arrival of steam-powered pumps at the end of the 18th century. These added still more muscle, and enabled the large-scale recla-

lished. The zero point from which altitude is calibrated in much of northern Europe was located in the city, which at the time was connected with the North Sea, as the average high watermark of the Zuider Zee. Today, you can visit a replica of the original bronze marker in the City Hall/Opera complex. It is beneath ground level at that point, but not by very much. Alongside it are water columns that give a graphic representation of the problem. A digital link from the North Sea shows the current level of the tide at IJmuiden, the closest North Sea port to Amsterdam, and Vlissingen, in the far south-west. A third column shows the level reached by the sea in the most recent catastrophic floods: in 1953, much of it was inundated by a tide that reached about 15 feet above sea level in Amsterdam.

PILES OF PILES

Every Dutch schoolchild knows that the Royal Palace is supported on 13,659 wooden piles, to keep it from sinking into the swamp on which Amsterdam stands unsteadily. The technique of driving round wooden piles down to the first solid layer of sand, almost 40 feet below ground level, was widely employed during the building of the city – but not universally, as a number of dangerously teetering houses testify. The most notable, De Sluyswacht, is at the south end of Oude Schans, opposite the Rembrandthuis. It was built, not particularly well, in 1695 – barely a decade after the establishment of Standard Amsterdam Level showed the scale of the problem facing the city.

As long as the wooden piles are completely surrounded by water, they remain intact. But if air comes into contact with them they can start to rot, with unhappy consequences. Modern building techniques use square concrete piles, driven down to the second

The town-houses of Amsterdam are built on deep foundations

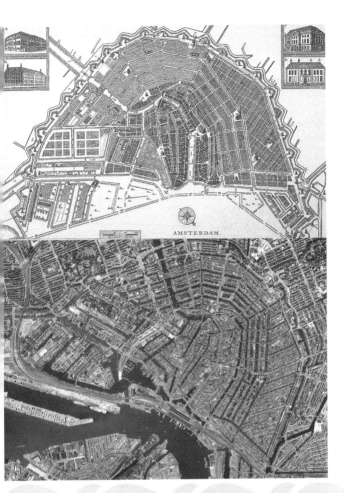

layer of sand at 130 feet, or even lower. One aesthetic benefit of the challenge to builders is the absence of more than a handful of high-rise buildings.

AN ITALIAN CONNECTION?

Amsterdam is often described by travel writers short of a cliché as "The Venice of the North." Numerically, there are clear similarities: both cities were built on around 100 islands, crossed by about 150 canals and linked by several hundred bridges. Both used their maritime connections to develop economic and cultural links that placed them well ahead of rival cities, and are now heavily dependent upon tourism. But the comparison stops there. Venice may slowly be sinking, but at least the first settlers had *terra firma* to start with. The Italians have not filled in many of their canals, as Amsterdam has; and Venice is unsullied by the automobiles that clog the narrow streets of the Dutch city. It could be some time before Venice finds itself described as "The Amsterdam of the South."

A present-day aerial view of Amsterdam (above) shows how true it has remained to the original 17th-century plan (top)

Gable Vision

Amsterdam is coy about architecture. There are few extravagant flourishes – nothing to match the dramatic structures of London, Paris or Berlin. Even the Royal Palace is just the old City Hall. The swamp on which Amsterdam sits simply doesn't lend itself to grand designs. So instead of a single icon, the defining image of Amsterdam is much smaller in scale: the elaborate gable that tops many canalside buildings.

ORNAMENTAL ORIGINS

To cope with the all too frequent rain, roofs need to be sharply raked. Elsewhere in northern Europe, these steep roofs are unadorned, but in Amsterdam, during the Golden Age of the 18th century, it became *de rigueur* to decorate and hide the unlovely inverted V.

In keeping with the city's spirit of diversity, gables are individual and distinctive. Most, though, fall into one of four categories. The most basic version is a spout gable, like an upside-down funnel, which adheres closely to the shape of the roof, and is only a modest embellishment to the shape of the front wall. There are plenty

The finest gables are those on the main canals, such as Herengracht (bottom)

of examples among the warehouses in the Jordaan area of Amsterdam. Next is the step gable, like two staircases meeting at the top; the prettiest examples can be found on the Bartolotti House on Keizersgracht (➤ 99). The neck gable was a move toward a more classical design, with a tall rectangular screen, called a variant, perching on the cornice like a head on shoulders; the elevated neck gable involved an intermediate step. There are plenty of examples around the canals of Prinsengracht, Keizersgracht and Herengracht.

Most visually appealing of all is the bell gable, where delicate arcs sweep up to a narrow center. This style can be found in profusion throughout the city. All gables are ornamented to a greater or lesser degree, and the elaborate and imaginative designs, each seeking to outdo their neighbors, are among the greatest treats in Amsterdam.

THE LEANING HOUSES OF AMSTERDAM

Many Amsterdam houses are inclined at angles other than 90 degrees to the horizontal. When the house leans to the left or right, the reason is structural weakness, probably caused by rotting piles. If the wooden posts that were pushed down to the first firm layer of sand come into contact with air as well as water, they begin to decay and the building starts to sag.

A forward lean, however, is usually a deliberate policy. Before proper drainage became common, the upper floors of a housefront were often intended to project outward so that water dripped on to the street (and passing pedestrians), not lower floors. And there's another good reason: the

steep, narrow staircases in canal houses don't lend themselves to the movement of bulky pieces of furniture. Removable windows and a pulley that is looped through the beam projecting from the top of the house allow the furniture to be hoisted from the outside. Tilting the facade forward reduces the risk of damage should the load start to sway.

KNOWN AT THIS ADDRESS

"Gable stones" are the often beautifully designed tablets that embellish many old houses. In the days when many could not read or write, these signified the owner or purpose of the premises. The best collection is on a wall in the southwest corner of the Begijnhof (➤ 54–55), where gable stones from a number of demolished properties are embedded.

Above: Residents ring the changes beneath a bell gable

Below: Gable stones on Zandhoek, a street in the Western Islands

Trading Places

On paper, Dutch economic prospects appear bleak. Europe's most densely populated major country possesses some natural gas reserves, dwindling fishery potential and an agricultural sector that accounts for just one-thirtieth of the economy. Yet the Dutch enjoy wealth out of all proportion to their natural resources. The Netherlands is among the richest countries in the world, and Amsterdam is one of the wealthiest cities in Europe.

The Dutch secret is an open one: matching supply with demand, and taking a cut in the process. Trade itself is as old as humanity, but the Amsterdam trick has been to innovate – politically, technologically and commercially – and become the warehouse of the world.

The neutrality of the Netherlands in a turbulent continent allowed early traders to link Germany and Scandinavia with southern Europe. Inexpensive lumber from the Baltic region was used to build large cargo ships that carried much more than those from rival countries. A vessel called the "cog," carrying 100 tons or more, was the juggernaut of the Middle Ages. And the financial insti-

tutions, from banks to the stock exchange, became established early enough to lubricate commerce during the expansionism of the 17th century – the Golden Age, economically as well as culturally.

Damrak is one of the main commercial arteries

KEEPING GOOD COMPANIES

Amsterdam came to dominate the global economy by devising corporatism the likes of which the world had never seen. The model was established by the United East India Company (VOC – Verenigde Oost-Indische Compagnie), formed at the start of the 17th century for the purpose of exploiting Asia. This first multinational

Notable Currency

The first single European currency originated in Amsterdam. In the 17th century, bankers in the city would accept any currency and exchange it for the gulden florijn (golden florin). That's why the national currency is Anglicized as "guilder," a corruption of gulden, yet is written Fl – short for florijn.

In the 1960s, De Nederlandsche Bank revolutionized graphic design for bank notes. Images of cultural figures were imposed on strong, simple typography; some, particularly the 10-guilder note, featuring artist Frans Hals, are still in circulation. The culmination was the 10-guilder note in 1997. On one side, imagery from electronic circuitry is used to shocking effect, while on the reverse is an underwater masterpiece complete with figurative fish and a poem, *Ijsvogel*, by Arie van den Berg.

brought together wealthy backers from Amsterdam and other Dutch towns to spread the heavy risks – and share the bumper profits – of trading with territories from Java to Japan. The VOC's great strength was its focus on money alone. Unlike the Spanish and Portuguese, the Dutch had no interest in converting locals to Christianity, and were therefore more acceptable to foreign rulers.

The same model was used to great effect by the West India Company, which traded with the Caribbean and South America and played a significant part in the slave trade. Meanwhile, the Greenland Company concerned itself with exploiting the northern seas. By the end of the 17th century, 4,000 vessels were trading with more than 600 ports around the world. Protectionism and military incursions by more powerful nations eventually sent the Dutch economy into decline, but the spirit of enterprise continued – Amsterdam made the first loan to the new U.S. government after the American War of Independence.

A meeting of the United East India Company

THE PROFIT PRINCIPLE

The principles of global wheeling and dealing remain intact. Rotterdam is the world's second-busiest port, just behind Singapore. The KLM airline carries more passengers each year than would make up the entire population of the Netherlands. Amsterdam begins the 21st century with a massive building project around Schiphol, with office buildings being acquired for European headquarters of global corporations eager to use the highly educated, multilingual workforce. Today, two-thirds of the national economy is in the service sector. While others make their goods, the Dutch buy, sell and move.

Building a new
Jerusalem

"One day this terrible war will be over," wrote a 15-year-old girl on April 9, 1944. "The time will come when we will be people again and not just Jews! We can never be just Dutch, or just English, or whatever, we will always be Jews as well. But then, we'll want to be."

THE FIRST JEWISH COMMUNITY

From the 16th to the 20th century, Amsterdam became a place of sanctuary for thousands of Jewish people forced from their homes in eastern and southern Europe. Sephardic Jews were expelled from Spain and Portugal, while Ashkenazic Jews faced persecution in Poland and Germany. Even in liberal Amsterdam, they faced restrictions for 200 years, forbidden from owning shops and barred from many skilled trades. At the end of the 18th century, in a tide of egalitarianism following the French Revolution, the Act of Civil Equality ended such discrimination.

FASCISM AND WAR

When Adolf Hitler's National Socialist Party seized power in Germany in 1933, the Netherlands was a natural place of refuge for Jews – among them the family of Otto Frank, a successful merchant living in the city of Frankfurt, where Anne Frank had been born on June 12, 1929. Otto re-established his business in Amsterdam and the family lived relatively comfortably.

War broke out in Europe on September 1, 1939. The following May, the Nazis occupied the Netherlands, and the persecution of Jews began. By October, Dutch civil servants had to sign a declaration of Aryan (non-Jewish) descent, and Jewish people faced compulsory registration. The Jewish community responded by forming a self-protection force. During a clash in February 1941, a member of the Dutch Nazi party died. In retribution, the Germans rounded up 400 Jews. This in turn triggered a call from the Dutch trade union movement for a general strike in protest against the persecution. This action is still celebrated each year.

From May 3, 1942, Jews had to wear a yellow star.

Below: After Hitler seized power in Germany in 1933, fascism swept across Europe

Left: A statue of Anne Frank stands outside the Westerkerk

Jewish-owned businesses were requisitioned by the administration of the occupiers. By 1943, Jews were being rounded up by the thousands and sent east to take part in "work projects" in Germany.

Of the 140,000 Jews who resided in the Netherlands at the time of the Nazi invasion, 107,000 were deported to concentration camps. Only a very few survived the experience.

GOING UNDERGROUND

The Frank family was among those Jews who went underground, which often involved hiding in an attic or basement (their Dutch name, *onderduikers*, means "divers," because they literally dived out of sight). Some Dutch people performed heroic acts to protect them; but half the 16,000 who found hiding places were captured and sent to death camps. Most were traced through informers, who received a reward of 7 guilders.

No-one is sure how the Frank family was found, but when the Nazis and their Dutch collaborators raided the house at Prinsengracht 263 (► 94–97) they went straight to the bookshelf that concealed the entrance to the secret annex. Only Otto Frank survived the Nazi death camps to which they were dispatched. He published Anne's diary, and the Anne Frank House has become a shrine to the human spirit.

Above: The Anne Frank House has become one of the most visited venues in Amsterdam

PORTRAIT OF THE ARTIST AS AN OLD MAN

On July 15, 2006, Amsterdam will celebrate the 400th anniversary of the birth of its most famous citizen. Yet when Rembrandt Harmenszoon van Rijn died in 1669, he was a penniless outcast, shunned by the wealthy Amsterdammers who had previously bankrolled one of the world's great artists.

Rembrandt was born in Leiden, south of Amsterdam, in 1606 and spent the first 25 years of his life there. His father was a miller with big plans for his son. At the tender age of 14, Rembrandt won a place at Leiden's university, but left to study painting. At the time, the world of art was dazzled by the Italian baroque – notably the work of Caravaggio, itself influenced by early Flemish work. Rembrandt found a local teacher, Jacob van Swanenburch, and later studied in Amsterdam for six months under Pieter Lastman. It was under Lastman's tutelage that Rembrandt strengthened the intense humanity that characterizes so much of

Above: The Rembrandt House contains many of the artist's curios

Top left: Statue of Rembrandt on Rembrandtplein

Left: The artist's living room and bedroom

his work. He returned to Leiden and began to give lessons, but the city soon proved insufficiently dynamic to satisfy his ambition.

Dr Tulp, which now hangs in the Mauritshuis in The Hague. This was a classic example of a profession – in this case the Guild of Surgeons – banding

TO AMSTERDAM

In 1631, Rembrandt moved to Amsterdam. Thanks in no small part to the mercantile adventures of the United East India Company (► 16–17), the economy was booming, and rich merchants were commissioning biblical paintings and portraits. Always pragmatic, Rembrandt used members of his family as models: his depiction of his mother as the Prophetess Anna hangs in the Rijksmuseum (► 114–117). A year after his arrival in Amsterdam, he won the contract for *The Anatomy Lesson of*

together to pay for a group portrait. Rembrandt also became adept at etching; most of his expressive and detailed works are on display in the Rembrandt House (► 66).

FAME AND FORTUNE

Besides his own creative work, which broke new ground in combining dynamism with rationalist restraint, Rembrandt traded in the efforts of others. As an art dealer, he made a profit of 100 guilders buying and selling *Hero and Leander* by Rubens. Rembrandt wed, no doubt for love, but his marriage in 1634

Rembrandt worked with an eye for profit, using his family as models. This is his son, Titus

to Saskia van Uylenburgh was commercially fortuitous. She was from a well-to-do family and was the cousin of a leading art dealer. By means of such networking, Rembrandt built up a profitable portfolio of commissions. Many of his works used Saskia as a model, and it was in the 1630s that he produced some of his most expressive self-portraits.

Rembrandt became sought-after as a teacher, and his pupils helped keep pace with the demand for portraits, religious paintings and secular landscapes. Even today there is dispute over the authorship of some of the works attributed to him.

In 1639, the couple moved into a fine house in the Jewish quarter, a purchase around six times more expensive than the average Amsterdam dwelling at the time. The choice of location was partly because the Canal Ring, with its beautiful houses, was far from completion. A possibly stronger motive was Rembrandt's interest in Judaism and Jewish society.

THE EVENTFUL FORTIES

During the 1630s, Rembrandt and Saskia had three children who died in infancy. In 1641 Saskia gave birth to a son, Titus, who survived – but she died the following year. Her will left her fortune to her son, but entrusted the management of the inheritance to Rembrandt – as long as he did not remarry. The following year Rembrandt completed

The Waag once housed an operating theater, scene for one of Rembrandt's most celebrated works

his most celebrated work. *The Shooting Company of Captain Frans Banning Cocq* shows a band of civil guardsmen looking casual and cocksure. Darkened with age, it became known as *The Night Watch* and it now hangs in the Rijksmuseum.

Rembrandt was not a great traveler, though to see some of the landscapes he created at this time you would imagine that he had seen much of Europe and the Bible lands. He used some of his income to buy all manner of exotic artifacts from Asia and the Americas, which are displayed at the Rembrandt House.

DECLINE AND FALL

In 1649 the artist hired a housekeeper, Hendrickje Stoffels, who soon became his lover. Amsterdam society gossiped about Rembrandt's mistress, but most tolerated his affair. He continued to produce some fine work – much of which, such as *Nathan Admonishing David*, hangs in overseas galleries.

Rembrandt's extravagant lifestyle – and increasing disdain for deadlines – proved his financial downfall. In 1656 he was declared bankrupt and his collection of art and antiquities was auctioned to pay off his creditors. Not entirely by choice, he continued to work. His 1661 depiction of *The Syndics of the Cloth Guild*, hanging in the Rijksmuseum, shows his talents undimmed. In 1663, Hendrickje died, followed five years later by Titus. Poor and alone, Rembrandt died on October 4, 1669. His place of burial is not known, but his legacy lives on.

A REMBRANDT TRAIL

A substantial part of the life of Rembrandt has been concealed by the years. Along Nieuwe Doelenstraat, at No 20, De Jaren café now stands on the site where Rembrandt lived when he first married Saskia. A Scottish pub – the Balmoral, part of the Doelen Hotel – stands where, in 1642, he painted *The Night Watch*.

Moving north along Kloveniersburgwal, the Trippenhuis was the original home of the Rijksmuseum, and at the north end, the Waag is the bulky gatehouse that is now home to a café. It was in an upper room here, then used as an operating theater, that Rembrandt painted *The Anatomy Lesson of Dr Tulp*.

Going southeast from here, through some uncomfortably modern surroundings, you reach the Rembrandt House, miraculously preserved in an area in which much has been desecrated. It shows the contrast between Rembrandt's highly successful (for a time) commercial management and the poverty of Vincent van Gogh.

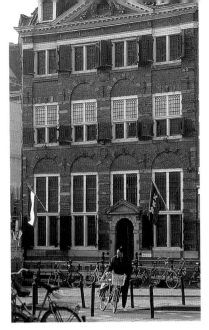

The Rembrandt House has survived four turbulent centuries

You Don't Have to Ride a Bike But ...

The bicycle mirrors Amsterdam perfectly: it is human-scaled, often elegant and mostly gentle. It's also the best way to get around. The city is flat and compact, making cycling easy, while narrow streets and bridges give cyclists an edge on motorized transportation. Between them, the nation's three-quarters of a million people own 400,000 bikes – Europe's highest concentration.

RISKS AND REWARDS

Typical bikes are rusty old sit-up-and-beg models – deterrents to thieves who openly use heavy cutting gear to break locks and steal the more appealing bikes to sell on the streets or at markets, or ship out of the city. On the plus side, the city is made for cyclists. Bike lanes are almost everywhere, often separated from traffic and pedestrians, and so are bike racks. As car parking becomes tougher, more people are swapping the car for the bike. A number of new roads through the city have been abandoned, such as the underpass at the northern end of Weesperstraat, or grassed over, like the dual carriageway that ran through the middle of Museumplein until 1999.

Amsterdam, a city made for two wheels

A bicycle made for four

LAW AND SAFETY

In theory, cyclists must obey all traffic regulations and must not cycle under the influence of drink or drugs. In practice, the term "organized chaos" best describes the cycling in the city. One-way streets are seen as an inconvenience by some, as a challenge by others and as an infringement of cyclists' rights by the more militant two-wheelers. Accidents between bikes take place fairly frequently, but a bigger danger is of a pedestrian straying in to the path of a fast-moving cyclist.

Perhaps the toughest trick is keeping wheels from getting caught in tram tracks. Cross them at a wide angle and take special care around Dam Square and Centraal Station, where there is a profusion of tracks.

FREE BIKES FOR ALL

In the 1960s, the city distributed hundreds of free "white bikes" around Amsterdam. You picked one up, rode it to your destination and left it for the next rider. The bikes disappeared within days. Many ended up in the canals; others were stolen by residents and clumsily repainted. In 1999 the idea resurfaced – this time abetted by technology. Now 250 bikes, painted white and with solid wheels and tires (to make them less attractive to thieves), are in circulation. A fee of 1 guilder a time is charged to free the electronic lock. The problem for visitors is that this can be paid only with a "smartcard" that is used mainly by Amsterdammers.

The average Amsterdam bike is cheap and cheerful

Renting a Bicycle

Dutch railways ban bikes from most trains, making access difficult, and any decent bike will become an instant target for thieves. So instead of bringing your own bike, rent one.

Typically you pay around 5 guilders an hour or 25 per day for a reasonable bike. Check the brakes before you set off and make sure the seat and handlebars are firm. Borrow or rent a helmet. At most places, you have to leave a deposit (some prefer cash to credit cards), and sometimes a passport too.

Bike City
Bloemgracht 68–70, Jordaan ☎ 020 626 3721; www.bikecity.nl 13, 14, 17, 20 to Rozengracht

Damstraat Rent-a-Bike
P Jacobszdwarstraat 7–13, southeast corner of Dam ☎ 020 625 5029; www.bikes.nl 4, 9, 14, 16, 20, 24, 25 to Damrak

Feets Bike Rentals and Tours 3e Looierdwarstraat 75, Jordaan ☎ 020 625 1855 7, 19, 17, 20

Holland Rent-a-Bike
Damrak 247 ☎ 020 622 32 07 4, 9, 16, 20, 24, 25

Mac Bike
Marnixstraat 220, southwestern Jordaan ☎ 020 626 6964; www.macbike.nl 10, 17, 20; also
Mr Visserplein 2, close to Waterlooplein ☎ 020 620 0985 9, 14, 20

Café Society

For many visitors, sight-seeing in Amsterdam is something to do to fill the time between hanging out in a selection of the city's 1,400 cafés. Amsterdammers regard their cafés almost as second living rooms – places to meet up with friends or just to chill out for an afternoon reading the newspapers. The best examples epitomize *gezelligheid*, which loosely translates as an infectiously cozy and sociable atmosphere that is almost part of the national psyche.

The Dutch use of the term "café" is confusing for foreigners. It describes not only a place where you might have a cup of coffee or snack, but also where drinking is the focus of activity – in other words, what Americans would call a bar and the British a pub. Even establishments that are virtually restaurants can, in Dutch parlance, be called cafés. To complicate matters further, many cafés perform a number or all of these roles.

BROWN CAFÉS

These are the archetypal Amsterdam cafés: the oldest, dating from the 1600s, look as if they could be lifted from Rembrandt or Vermeer paintings. They are rather like old-fashioned British pubs, but have a more intimate, parlor-like feel. The "brown" in the title comes from the tobacco-stained ceilings and walls (more mustard-colored, in fact), and the wood paneling and floorboards. You may also find little Persian rugs on tables, frilly net curtains on windows, newspapers on racks, flickering candles and gleaming brass taps on a worn old bar, and a cat snoozing on a shabby chair. Usually, the barman is deep in conversation with a local, and the male customers outnumber the women.

Brown cafés are essentially bolt-holes used to escape from the biting Amsterdam winter, but many post a bench or table or two outside during fine weather. As well as alcohol, they always serve coffee. In terms of food, basic sandwiches, croquettes, nuts, cheese, boiled eggs (oddly

displayed in a stand on the bar) and perhaps apple pie may be available.

Best brown cafés:
Café Papeneiland (➤ 101),
Café 't Smalle (➤ 102),
't Doktertje (➤ 70),
Hoppe (➤ 71),
Oosterling (➤ 156),
In de Wildeman (➤ 72).

TASTING HOUSES

In previous centuries, customers visiting *jenever-* (Dutch gin) and liqueur-distillers were given free

have anywhere to sit) before heading home.

Best tasting houses: De Drie Fleschjes (➤ 71), Wynand Fockink (➤ 72).

GRAND CAFÉS

Airier, brighter, modern alternatives to brown-café nostalgia began appearing in the 1980s. Some, often referred to as designer bars, are late-night haunts for a desperately hip crowd, with thumping music and challenging modern art. But the so-called "grand

Below: One of the best brown cafés – Papeneiland

samples before purchasing a bottle or keg. Only a handful of *proeflokalen*, or tasting houses, still exist, and now they charge for drinks. Nonetheless, a visit is highly recommended, for they are some of the most civilized and atmospheric bars in the city, decorated with old wooden casks and stone bottles. Amsterdammers treat them as places where you pop in for a quick *jenever* or three (few

cafés" have a wider appeal, attracting everyone from businesspeople to shoppers and students. While some fail to live up to their name, the best – with their lofty ceilings, striking bar displays and library-style reading tables piled high with magazines and newspapers – capture something of the style of Viennese coffee houses and more fashionable Parisian cafés. Most offer meals ranging from lunchtime snacks to three-course dinners.

Best grand cafés:
Café Américain (► 101),
Café de Jaren (► 70),
Café Luxembourg (► 70),
De Kroon (► 156).

EETCAFÉS

These encompass both brown and more modern cafés where, even though people can come just to drink, the emphasis is primarily on the food (some call themselves *petits restaurants*). They used to concentrate on inexpensive traditional Dutch dishes, but many now offer more adventurous, high-quality fare.

With most of the city's restaurants only open in the evening, *eetcafés* make good lunchtime options.

Best *eetcafés*:
Café de Prins (► 102),
Land van Walem (► 102),
Spanjer & Van Twist (► 102),
't Gasthuys (► 71).

The Internet

Many coffee shops have an Internet terminal or two. A more salubrious option is easyEverything at 22 Reguliersbreestraat: with 650 PCs, it claims to be the world's largest Internet café. It is open daily, 24 hours a day.

TEA ROOMS

Amsterdam has its fair share of cafés that might also be called tea rooms – that is, daytime places that serve sandwiches, cakes and pastries, tea and coffee. Some are attached to department stores, others are tiny salons at the rear of pastry shops.

Best tea rooms:
Backstage (► 155),
Pompadour (► 105),
Villa Zeezicht (► 72).

Above: Amsterdam even boasts Internet access on the street

Left: Most coffee shops have an imaginative menu

COFFEE SHOPS

Since the mid-1970s, the Dutch authorities have tolerated the sale and consumption of small amounts of soft drugs (hashish and marijuana), arguing that this keeps users separate from the criminal underworld. Other countries, however, are critical of this liberal attitude, claiming that it is a malignant influence on their drug problems and that the country exports more Ecstasy than cheese.

Whatever the case, Amsterdam's euphemistically named "coffee shops" not only are spots for coffee and sometimes alcohol, but also places officially licensed to sell soft drugs – even if the deliveries they receive from suppliers are technically illegal. Green-and-white stickers cling to the windows of each of the 150 such establishments.

Coffee shops vary enormously in atmosphere. Those in the city center – along Warmoesstraat for example – are often grungy, psychedelic dives, while outlets of the Bulldog chain are brash and commercial. More appealing options are:

Rusland, said to be the oldest in town (Rusland 16);

Barney's, which also does all-day breakfasts (Haarlemmerstraat 102);

La Tertulia, an innocent-looking daytime corner café run by a mother and daughter (Prinsengracht 312);

and **De Rokerij,** an exotic, candlelit den with an African/Oriental theme. It has the atmosphere of a good student party in the evenings (Lange Leidsedwarsstraat 41).

Registered coffee shops bear an official sticker

CAFÉ ETIQUETTE

In brown cafés and tasting houses, you're expected to go up to the bar to order: you can either pay for the drinks there and then, or set up a tab if you're staying for a while.

In grand cafés, take a seat and a waiter or waitress will come over and take your order.

In coffee shops, the drugs menu may not be overtly displayed: it will either be on or behind the bar, or in larger establishments the drugs will be sold from a separate booth.

snapshot of AMSTERDAM

Above: One of the fleet of sightseeing boats

Top left: Gables jostle for attention

Above: Statue of Vondel in Vondelpark

Left: The Oude Kerk, one of the city's earliest churches

Right: City of flowers

Below: Living on water

Above: Concentric city

Below: Brouwersgracht

Above: Spring blooms at Keukenhof

Left: Commemorative tankard at the Heineken Museum

Above (upper): The Amstel

Above (lower): Picasso in the Stedelijk

Herring
and Heineken

Fish and beer have played significant roles in Amsterdam's road to prosperity. In medieval times, its fishermen improved the way the ubiquitous herring was cured by gutting the fish before treating them with salt. This meant that they could be transported on long sea voyages. "The silver from the sea gave the Dutch the Golden Age," is how Holland's pre-eminent food writer, Johannes van Dam, poetically puts it.

Meanwhile, the fledgling city's coffers were further boosted by the Count of Holland. In 1323, he designated Amsterdam one of only two ports in his province allowed to import beer from Hamburg, the most important ale-producing town in northern Europe. It wasn't so much that 14th-century Amsterdammers were medieval lager louts – rather that beer was then far safer to drink than the local water.

DUTCH SUSHI

The Dutch are mad about herring, and some might say rather eccentric in the way they eat it: as *maatjes haring*, raw and salted, at street fish stalls. In Amsterdam, they

Tails of the unexpected: a fishy feast

Above: Soused herrings – an acquired taste

prefer to eat it in chunks on cocktail sticks; elsewhere in the Netherlands, they adopt the more flamboyant approach of holding the fish by the tail and letting it slip

in late May/early June of the freshest, youngest herring (*groene* or green herring).

Above: A simple snack – herring and pumpernickel

down the throat.

The uninitiated can reduce the likelihood of retching by masking the briny flavor with chopped onions or by opting for a herring sandwich. Whatever you choose, expect to be left with an aftertaste strong enough to savor for a few hours.

There used to be a lot of fuss about the annual arrival

However, legislation now stipulates that all cured herring has to be made from frozen fish to ensure that it is parasite-free. Therefore, whatever Amsterdammers tell you to the contrary, nowadays there is little difference in taste between *groene* and *maatjes* herring.

THE HEINEKEN STORY

Heineken started brewing lager in Amsterdam in 1864. Now the second largest brewery company in the world (after Anheuser-Busch) reaches an audience that other beers cannot reach: its beer is sold in 170 countries. It attributes much of its success to the cultivation of the Heineken A-Yeast in 1886: the yeast cell is still flown every month from its main brewery near Amsterdam to its 100 breweries abroad.

Clever marketing is another key ingredient. For example, the "e"s in the name lean back slightly in a kind of smile, to give the brand a subliminal feel-good factor. Though its Amsterdam brewery stopped production in 1988 (see page 141 for details about tours), Heineken's presence in the city is still unavoidable. Carthorses pull a Heineken dray loaded with barrels round the streets each day, and the company owns the famous De l'Europe hotel and the Heineken Hoek café, smack-dab in the middle of Leidseplein, the city's busiest square. (Cynics might suggest that their chief purpose is as props for the enormous advertizing signs on top of them: on the café, two glasses of neon yellow liquid are filled and then poured.)

If you order an unspecified beer (a *bier* or *pils*) in an Amsterdam café, the chances are you'll be given a Heineken Pilsener. It will be served in a half-pint flower-pot shaped glass, and will be presented with an inch or so of head (the barman always makes a great show of skimming off the extra froth with a plastic spatula). In brown cafés, you usually need to order at the bar, and can either pay on the spot or, if you're staying for a few, ask for a tab.

OTHER BREWS

If you fancy contributing to the funds of a company other than Heineken, don't order an Amstel. The Netherlands' second-best selling beer (named after the river that runs through Amsterdam) became a Heineken subsidiary in 1969, and is even produced in the same breweries as Heineken beer. Murphy's Irish Stout was also taken over by Heineken in 1986.

Several cafés make a point of offering an extraordinary range of beers, such as **In de Wildeman** (► 72). Civilized **Maximiliaan** (► 74), on the site of a medieval brewery at Kloveniersburgwal 6–8, just south of the Nieuwmarkt, was the Netherlands' first brew pub when it opened in 1992, and you can drink the very potent homemade beers of t' IJ on the premises, too.

Amsterdam's best liquor store for beer is **De Bierkoning** at Paleisstraat 125, near Dam square: it sells 850 varieties, including beer in champagne bottles, Belgian Trappist beers and the original Czech Pilsener beer.

Above: Heineken Pilsener is the standard tipple in Amsterdam's hostelries

Below: Amstel is now part of the Heineken empire

Finding Your Feet

First Two Hours

Amsterdam deserves the prize as Europe's most accessible city. It is easy to reach by train, boat and plane.

Schiphol Airport

Since the first commercial flights took off in 1920, Amsterdam's airport has grown to become one of the most important in Europe.

- **Schiphol,** 18km (11 miles) southwest of the city, is certainly the most passenger-friendly of the large airports, with effectively a single terminal and easy public transportation to the city center. It is also worth a visit in its own right (➤ 172).
- The tourism information office (open 7 a.m.–10 p.m.) in **Arrivals Halls 2** can help with advice for the whole of the Netherlands, but for Amsterdam specifics you could do better to wait until you arrive in the city center.

Best Bets for Airport Transfers

By train

- The **quickest and least expensive way** into Amsterdam is by rail from the station that is built into the airport concourse.
- There are at least five trains an hour between 6 a.m. and midnight, with hourly departures through the night. **Slow trains** to Amsterdam's Centraal Station take 20 minutes; non-stop expresses are a few minutes faster.
- You must **buy your ticket in advance** or risk a big fine on the train.
- **Be careful with your bags** – the run from Schiphol to the city center is a favorite with petty thieves.

By bus

- **KLM-branded airport buses** run from the the airport to a number of big hotels for a fare of 17.50 guilders (30 guilders round trip).
- There are departures **once or twice each hour** during the day.
- From 5:20–7 a.m., and 6–10 p.m., **you have to reserve a seat** by phoning 020 653 4975. The journey to and from the airport takes between 20 and 50 minutes, depending on where your hotel is located on the bus circuit of the city.

By taxi

- **Fares to the city center** are three or four times the amount charged on public transportation.
- It is **usually faster** to go by train to Centraal Station and take a taxi from there.

Centraal Station

Whether you arrive by air and take the train to town, travel by rail from elsewhere in Europe or take the sea-rail connection from Harwich in the U.K. via Hook of Holland, you end up in a station which is itself a historical monument (➤ 68). It is, however, best enjoyed when you are unencumbered by luggage.

- You descend from the platforms **to the main concourse,** basically a shopping center, which is usually crowded with travelers and loiterers.
- The station is the **most popular venue for pickpockets and hustlers** who make a point of targeting tourists.

- If you are using one of the automatic ticket machines, you may be **approached by someone trying to sell you a ticket.** Decline any such offer; at best you will end up with a dud or overpriced ticket, at worst you will be robbed during the transaction.
- For tourist information, **ascend to Platform 2A.**
- Most people head **straight out of the main (south) entrance,** to be confronted by a confusion of taxis, trams, vendors and hundreds of bicycles.
- The **main taxi stand is to the right,** as are the stands for trams 1, 2, 5, 13, 17 and 20 (counterclockwise).
- To the left, you will find the **stands for trams** 4, 9, 16, 20 (clockwise), 24 and 25, and the entrance to the Metro (subway).
- Beyond that is an imposing white-painted wooden building that was once a tram station but now functions as the **city's main tourist office;** note that it has shorter opening hours than the office in the station.
- To the right is the **GVB (public transportation) office,** where you can buy travel passes and check details of cruises.

Tourist Offices

- The information service in the Netherlands is known as the **VVV (Vereniging Voor Vreemdelingenverkeer).** It is part of the private sector and makes money from commission on hotel reservations and from selling tours, books, maps etc.
- If you have specific questions, they will be answered, but lines are long and responses brisk. **Offices may close their doors** for up to half an hour if lines are long.
- **Stationsplein** (opposite Centraal Station – main office) Daily 9–5.
- **Centraal Station** (Platform 2A) Mon.–Sat. 8–8, Sun. 9–5.
- **Leidseplein** Sun.–Wed. 9–5, Thu.–Sat. 9–7.
- In addition there is a **telephone information service** (tel: 0900 400 4040), offering advice Mon.–Fri. 9–5. Note: this is a premium-rate number.

Getting Around

Orientating Yourself

Amsterdam's layout still follows the basic pattern devised in 1609. The center, with most places of interest, is a collection of islands divided by canals and connected by bridges. It forms a semicircle, with the IJ River as the flat side and the major canals extending concentrically, like ripples in a pond.
- The main canals (going outward) are Herengracht, Keisersgracht and Prisengracht; **the suffix *gracht* means canal.** To these have been added a number of lesser canals that radiate out from the center or just cut randomly across the others.
- To confuse matters, the **most important post-1609 additions** are Singelgracht (beyond Prinsengracht) and Singel (without the *gracht*), inside Herengracht.
- To the east, **the system is disrupted** by the broad Amstel River.

Areas

Besides the divisions used in this book, there are a few smaller areas you should know about, again running clockwise from the IJ River:
- **De Wallen** – literally "the walls," which used to enclose the river: now it's Amsterdam's main Red Light District.

- **De Pijp** – due south of the center, a multicultural area with many immigrants from former Dutch colonies in Asia and Latin America.
- **Spiegelkwartier** – an upscale art and antiques shopping area, centered on Nieuw Spiegelstraat.
- **Spuikwartier** – the lively area around the southern half of Spuistraat, merging into the square named Spui.
- **9 Straatjes** – the three-block-square just west, literally "nine streets."
- **Jordaan** – west again, the city's most upwardly mobile quarter.

Streets

Going clockwise from the station, the most important streets are:

- **Prinshendrikkade** – running southeast to the docks area.
- **Zeedijk** – curving south past the Red Light District to Nieuwmarket.
- **Damrak** – running directly southwest to the city's main square, Dam.
- **Nieuwendijk** – shadowing Damrak, just to the west, and one of Amsterdam's main shopping streets.
- **Nieuwzijds Voorburgwal** – another street parallel to Damrak, and carrying the bulk of trams. It leads to many of the areas most popular with tourists.
- **Leidsestraat** – across Herengracht, the old road to Leiden leading to the busy tourist area of Leidseplein.
- **Haarlemmerstraat** – running west and dividing Jordaan from the Western Islands.

Public Transportation

Distances are short and many visitors never step on to a tram, bus or Metro train. But on a cold or wet day, you may be grateful for them – and a tram trip is an attraction in its own right. Amsterdam has an excellent public transportation system.

Trams

- Services **radiate out from Centraal Station.** Route 20 is the handiest, passing many places of interest.
- **Tram stops are usually easily identifiable,** and the busier ones have indicator boards showing when the next three services are due.
- **Ring the bell** a little ahead of the stop to guarantee that the driver will halt.
- Take care when getting off. Many stops are **in the middle of the road.**

Buses

- The main bus station is out west at **Marnixstraat** (where it meets Lauriergracht), but some services terminate at Centraal Station.
- Between midnight and 3 a.m. trams and the Metro are replaced by a skeleton service of buses on special *Nachtlijn* **("night line")** routes from Centraal Station.

Metro

Digging a subway presents special challenges in a city that is largely below sea level, which is one reason the network is small.

- **A single line runs southeast** of Centraal Station, with two branches extending into areas of dense housing where few tourists will venture.
- Two other branches **run around the periphery of the city,** one winding almost all the way around the perimeter to a point not far from Centraal Station.
- **A new line,** due to be completed in 2006, will connect Amsterdam Noord (north of the IJ) with central areas of the city and will be much more useful to visitors than the present network.

Tickets and fares

- A **common ticketing system** covers trams, Metro and buses throughout the whole country. The Netherlands is divided into hundreds of zones, of which central Amsterdam is one.
- There is a **uniform system of strip tickets.** Any single journey within the zone requires a two-strip ticket, while a three-strip ticket allows you as many rides as you can squeeze into an hour.
- Metro tickets **must be bought at the station ticket office,** but you can pay on board buses or trams – on the latter, board at the front and pay the driver unless there is a sign on the front saying Conductorstram, in which case board at the back and pay the conductor.

Discount tickets and passes

- If you plan to use public transportation a lot, **buy a 15-unit card** (called a *Nationale Strippenkaart*), which cuts costs by nearly 50 percent. You can get it from rail and Metro stations, VVV offices, newsstands, tobacco shops and supermarkets, but not aboard trams or buses.
- When you board a vehicle, **stamp the requisite strip** (usually two) in the machine provided.
- **An unlimited day pass** *(dagkaart)*, available from rail and Metro stations and tram and bus drivers, costs 12 guilders for one day and 5 guilders each additional day. Bear in mind that for the one-day pass you have to take five trips before you show a profit.
- The *Museumjaarkaart* (MJK), an annual pass, offers free admission to around 400 museums and discounts on other attractions. You will need a passport photograph. Even with a card, you have to line up at the cash desk for your visit to be registered; there, you will be provided with the ticket necessary to get in.

Taxis

- You may be able to hail a taxi in the street, but do not count on it: **most Amsterdammers summon one by telephone** (tel: 020 677 7777) or walk to a taxi stand.
- Taxi stands tend to be found at major intersections or outside big hotels.
- Most passengers **round up the fare,** but rarely give a more substantial tip.

Cycling

- No other city is **so well designed for cycling;** there are plenty of bike lanes and no hills. Distances are short. For details of where to rent a bike, ➤ 24.

Boat

Besides the regular canal tours operating on fixed routes (➤ 84–87), there are three more ways of getting around the city on water.

- **For the Canal Bus,** buy a ticket valid all day (a slightly more expensive version includes other forms of transportation). The route system is difficult to master and the schedules are not very frequent, but since almost everywhere is near a canal, it makes for a pleasantly different day out.
- **The Museumboot** (tel: 020 530 1090) operates from Centraal Station and stops at five points close to tourist sites: Anne Frank Huis, the Museum Quarter, the Flower Market, Waterlooplein and the Maritime Museum area. A day ticket allows you unlimited rides all day and gives discounts on admission for numerous museums. Boats run every 30 minutes in summer, every 45 minutes in winter.
- **Water taxis** must be booked in advance (tel: 020 622 2181) and fares are high.

Car

Driving is not an ideal way of getting around because of the scarcity and high cost of public parking and the Byzantine system of one-way streets.

- **Look out for cyclists,** many of whom ignore all known traffic rules, and beware of trams that do not hesitate to assert their priority.
- Where on-street parking is permitted, it works on a **pay-and-display system.** The few multi-story parking garages around the city charge even more.
- Seven **Park and Ride locations** ring the city. At the Sloterdijk facility (west of the city and adjacent to a rail station), the fee includes two return tickets for the five-minute train ride to Centraal Station.
- During the annual **Queen's Day celebrations around April 30,** many of the city's roads are closed to all motor traffic.

Car rental

- The biggest selection of companies and vehicles is available at **Schiphol airport.**
- For cut-price car rental **you could try easyRentacar** – but be warned that the location is out at Zaandam, about 20 minutes by train from Centraal Station. You must reserve in advance, on www.easyRentacar.com

Admission Charges

The cost of admission for museums and places of interest mentioned in the text is indicated by price categories

Inexpensive under 7 guilders **Moderate** 7–15 guilders **Expensive** more than 15 guilders

Children's reductions, and the ages at which they apply, vary wildly.

Accommodations

Virtually any hotel you might consider will be within walking distance of all the city's major attractions. The most appealing area to stay is the Canal Ring, where the old gabled buildings house dozens of hotels. The medieval center has some of both the grandest and the seediest establishments, while the Museum Quarter is convenient for culture-lovers, though the canal-free streets and the buildings have less character than those on the Canal Ring.

What to Expect

- **Most canal-front hotels are small** and offer only bed and breakfast. Public rooms may be limited to a breakfast room and possibly a bar or lounge. Stairs may be improbably steep (and there may be no elevator); bedrooms come in all shapes and sizes and the least expensive may not have its own bathroom.
- Breakfast – **usually a buffet of breads, fruit, meats and cheeses** – and the 5 percent city tax are normally included in rates at inexpensive establishments, but charged as extra in upscale hotels.

Reservations

Arguably, the single most important piece of advice to take is to reserve accommodations as far in advance as possible. Hotels, especially the most characterful ones recommended on the following pages, are booked solid, particularly on weekends and April through September. Even in low season (November through March, when rates drop by around a quarter), try to make plans well ahead.

- You can make reservations daily 9–4 through the **Amsterdam Reservation Centre** (tel: 777 000 888 – if calling from the U.S., add the prefix 011 31), or online on www.hotelres.nl
- Tourist offices (► 37) also make **on-the-spot reservations** for a small fee.

Hostels

Amsterdam's many hostels are an important element in the accommodations scene.

- The best is **City Hostel Vondelpark** (Zandpad 5, tel: 020 589 8996; www.njhc.org/vondelpark). Part of the Hostelling International group, it is set on the eastern edge of the Vondelpark (very convenient for the big museums and the nightlife around Leidseplein), and has a bar, bikes to rent and private rooms with bath as well as dormitory accommodations.
- If it's full (quite likely), consider **Ëben Haezer** (Bloemstraat 179, tel: 020 624 4717), a Christian youth hostel in the Jordaan which is smoke- and alcohol-free, and has a theoretical upper age limit of 35.
- Another option is **Hans Brinker** (Kerkstraat 136, tel: 020 622 0687), spartan but with a prime location near Leidseplein. It has everything from eight-bed mixed dormitories to single rooms.

Apartments

- **Amsterdam House** (Amstel 176a, tel: 020 626 2577) has 20 apartments, most along canals, and 10 houseboats on its books. There is a minimum stay of three nights out of season, a week in season. For more options, contact the tourist board (► 189).

Recommended Hotels

Accommodations prices
Expect to pay per standard double room per night:
Expensive (more than 600 guilders)
Mid-range (300–600 guilders)
Inexpensive (under 300 guilders)

Expensive

Amstel Inter-Continental Amsterdam

Lording it over the Amstel River, this is the most luxurious, most expensive hotel in the city: royalty, celebrities and businesspeople with generous expense accounts choose to stay here. Opened in 1867, it shut down for two years in the 1990s to undergo a complete restoration. The galleried main hall takes your breath away, and you can lap up the river views from a choice of restaurants, as well as from the conservatory lounge, the impressive indoor pool and open-air terraces. The ultra-swanky bedrooms come with such indulgences as completely stocked bars. Other than the price, which may also leave you breathless, the hotel's only drawback is that it is less central than the other luxury hotels recommended and most of the places you might want to visit will be a 15- to 30-minute walk away.

➕ 204 off B1 ✉ Prof Tulpplein 1, 1018 GX ☎ 020 622 6060; fax: 020 622 5808

Blakes

The grand old house – originally a theater that burned down, then offices for a Catholic charity – opened in 1999 as the city's most sumptuous small boutique hotel (it has just 26 bedrooms). The dramatic, oriental-influenced decor is the creation of interior designer Anouska Hempel. Bold color schemes in the bedrooms range from beige and cream to "elephant and raspberry," and mini-bars are stocked with healthy oxygen canisters. See also restaurants, ► 103.

➕ 202 C4 ✉ Keizersgracht 384, 1016 GB ☎ 020 530 2010; fax: 020 530 2030

De l'Europe

Fin de siècle opulence, in the form of chandeliers and frescoed ceilings in the public areas, acres of drapes over beds in bedrooms, and floor-to-ceiling marble in the bathrooms, rules at this landmark luxury hotel dating from the late 19th century. Its location – on the River Amstel, yards from the Flower Market – could hardly be better. Many bedrooms have private balconies overlooking the river, and in summer there is a waterside dining terrace.

🚇 203 E4 ✉ Nieuwe Doelenstraat 2–8, 1012 CP ☎ 020 531 1777; fax: 020 531 1778

The Grand Amsterdam

Built in the 17th century for the Admiralty, this classic "classic baroque" building served as the city hall until 1988. Now it is the most understated and peaceful of the city's luxury hotels, despite being just south of the Red Light District. The plush bedrooms overlook two beautiful courtyards and serene canals. Meals are taken in the refreshingly unstuffy Café Roux (▶ 73).

🚇 203 E4 ✉ Oudezijds Voorburgwal 197, 1012 EX ☎ 020 555 3111; fax: 020 555 3222

Pulitzer

A first-rate conversion of 25 17th- and 18th-century canal houses, all interconnected or adjoined via covered walkways through the hotel's large courtyard garden. Though a chain hotel (part of the Sheraton group), it doesn't feel like it. Quality art and tasteful modern furniture offset original features in bedrooms such as painted beams. The café/restaurant, with an iconoclastic version of a Frans Hals painting, is relaxing and fun.

🚇 202 C5 ✉ Prinsengracht 315–31, 1016 GZ ☎ 020 523 5235; fax: 020 627 6753

Seven One Seven

Dutch fashion designer and interior decorator Kees van der Valk has turned this early 19th-century canal house into a discreet, luxury B&B that has the feel of the private home of a wealthy family. Most of the eight bedrooms, themed after painters, authors and composers, are enormous. All are treasure troves of art – from African masks and Murano glass to modern paintings – and have cozy features such as colossal sofas and deep, sunken baths. Rates include afternoon tea and drinks.

🚇 203 E2 ✉ Prinsengracht 717, 1017 JW ☎ 020 427 0717; fax 020 423 0717

Mid-Range

Ambassade

Old-fashioned elegance is the name of the game in this hotel, which spreads through 10 17th-century canal houses. Chandeliers, rugs on parquet floors and ticking clocks characterize the lounge and breakfast room, while Louis XVI-style furniture creates a refined air in the bedrooms. The most distinctive, with vaulted, beamed ceilings, are under the gables. The Ambassade owns the Float and Massage Center just down the street.

🚇 203 D4 ✉ Herengracht 341, 1016 AZ ☎ 020 555 0222; fax: 020 555 0277

Canal House

This pair of 17th-century canal houses has been converted into a thoroughly civilized hotel with grand yet homey features. Its centerpiece is a stately breakfast room overlooking a pretty garden. Antique bric-à-brac – old dresses, hats, lamps, mirrors, clocks – decorates corridors and the cozy bedrooms. There are no TVs or minibars, and to maintain a tranquil atmosphere children under 12 are not welcomed.

🚇 201 D2 ✉ Keizersgracht 148, 1015 CX ☎ 020 622 5182; fax: 020 624 1317

Estheréa

A comfortable, central canalfront hotel with some character at reasonable rates. Occupying several 17th-century red-brick houses, it has been in the Esselaar family for three generations. Downstairs is a dark but cozy bar and breakfast room. "De luxe" bedrooms are worth the extra cost: they have canal views, often through a whole row of windows.

➕ 203 D4 ✉ Singel 303–9, 1012 WJ
☎ 020 624 5146; fax: 020 623 9001

Jan Luyken

The van Schaik family's mid-sized hotel takes up three adjoining 19th-century houses on a chic, quiet street in the Museum Quarter just one block from the Van Gogh Museum. Public rooms, such as the pillared bar that opens on to a secluded patio, are rather stylish. Bedrooms have less character, but are well equipped; it's worth paying extra for one of the larger ones.

➕ 202 B1 ✉ Jan Luykenstraat 58, 1071 CS ☎ 020 573 0730; fax: 020 676 3841

Vondel

Occupying four houses on a quiet, early 20th-century street a short walk from Leidseplein and the big museums, the Vondel has been given a slick, minimalist revamping. Bedroom walls, bedspreads, curtains, sofas and armchairs are all white or cream. The bar and lobby, with big bold sofas and stripped floorboards, look equally stylish, and radical modern art appears throughout the hotel.

➕ 202 B2 ✉ Vondelstraat 28–30, 1054 GE ☎ 020 612 0120; fax: 020 685 4321

Inexpensive

Agora

One of Amsterdam's best few-frills canal house B&Bs, the Agora could not be more central – the Flower Market is only yards away. Though the house dates from the early 18th century, its plain facade looks more modern. Bedrooms are not fancy, but have the odd antique or two and nice new shower rooms. Unless you are a heavy sleeper, you may want to forgo a view of the Amstel as there is a nightclub right next door. Ask for a room at the rear instead. A big plus

is the hotel's homey breakfast-cum-sitting-room, which opens on to a well-tended garden.

➕ 203 E4 ✉ Singel 462, 1017 AW
☎ 020 627 2200; fax: 020 627 2202

Amsterdam Weichmann

This good value B&B, spread through three canal houses on the edge of the Jordaan, has been run by a gentle Dutch-American couple for more than four decades. Public rooms, full of antiques and fresh flowers, have loads of character – particularly the blue-tiled breakfast room, which was once a café and has picture windows looking over a junction of canals.

➕ 202 C5 ✉ Prinsengracht 328–32, 1016 HX ☎ 020 626 3321; fax 020 626 8962

De Filosoof

Professional philospher Ida Jongsma's friendly little hotel is decorated to reflect her occupation. Murals of Plato and Aristotle line the entrance of the 19th-century house and text from famous philosophical works cover placemats in the breakfast room. Bedrooms are themed after thinkers, and instead of the usual Bible, each comes with philosophical works. The hotel is a 15-minute walk or short tram ride to Leidseplein, but the Vondelpark is on the doorstep.

➕ 206 C3 ✉ Anna van den Vondelstraat 6, 1054 GZ ☎ 020 683 3013; fax: 020 685 3750

Prinsenhof

A simple hotel in an excellent location. This old canal house overlooks a pretty and peaceful stretch of canal, yet lies just off lively Utrechtsestraat and its many restaurants. The bars of Rembrandtplein are just a five-minute walk away. Stairs are so steep that luggage is winched up to the bedrooms. Only two out of 10 have their own bathrooms, but they all have decent quality furniture.

➕ 203 F2 ✉ Prinsengracht 810, 1017 JL ☎ 020 623 1772; fax: 020 638 3368

Rho

You stand a far better chance of securing a place at the 165-room Rho than in most other decent inexpensive hotels. Its location, just 50 yards from Dam square down a quiet side street, could not be more central. Though bedrooms are plain and modern, the lobby, once a theater, is a vast, vaulted, art nouveau wonder.

🏠 201 E1 ✉ Nes 5–23, 1012 KC
☎ 020 620 7371; fax: 020 620 7826

Seven Bridges

In an old house along the city's prettiest canal, this is everyone's favorite B&B. Its owners, who have been here for a quarter of a century, have furnished the 10 bedrooms with eclectic pieces such as Biedermeier cabinets, Louis XVI cupboards and art deco lamps. Breakfast is served in the bedrooms, so you may want to pay extra for one of the bigger rooms.

🏠 203 E3 ✉ Reguliersgracht 31,
1017 LK ☎ 020 623 1329

Winston

A funky option bordering the Red Light District that makes a good choice for party-goers. Works of modern art are hung in public areas and half of the 67 bedrooms. Others are plain and simple, the least expensive with their own shower but sharing a toilet. The popular Winston Kingdom bar stays open very late and has live music most nights.

🏠 203 E1 ✉ Warmoesstraat 123–9,
1012 JA ☎ 020 623 1380; fax: 020 639 2308

Food and Drink

Dining in Amsterdam has improved markedly in recent years. Until then, the choice was between expensive French restaurants, lower priced ethnic establishments and cafés serving Dutch food. Though these options still apply, there is now a much more diverse choice at all price levels, and "fusion" cooking, mixing-and-matching nations' cuisines, is all the rage.

Ethnic Cuisine

Amsterdam's multicultural population is reflected in its restaurants: there are said to be 40 types of cuisine available. Most diners eat ethnic instead of traditional domestic fare.

- The most common ethnic restaurants are **Indonesian and Chinese,** but you'll also come across Surinamese cafés (especially in De Pijp district), Spanish *tapas* bars, Argentinian steak houses and an increasing number of Thai and Japanese establishments.
- **The Dutch consider Indonesian food,** introduced to the Netherlands by the Dutch East India Company in the 17th century, to be virtually part of their own culinary culture. Indonesian restaurants offer *rijsttafels* – literally "rice tables," from the Dutch *rijst* (rice) and *tafel* (table). The table is laden with a large bowl of rice, and anything from 15 to 30 dishes to share with your dining companions. Some sauces, such as *sambal*, are hot enough to blow your head off. Note that you don't have to order such a blow-out; the Dutch often go *à la carte* instead.

Going Dutch

Though there is a trend toward "New Dutch" cooking, with lighter dishes and sauces, a number of atmospheric, old-fashioned restaurants still specialize in traditional Dutch food. Depending on your point of view, it's either simple and nourishing or bland and rather stodgy, with an emphasis on quantity as much as quality.

- **You might want to start** with *erwtensoep*, a warming pea soup containing chunks of ham and vegetables, thick enough to stand your spoon up in.
- **The classic main course** is a stew called *hutspot* (hodgepodge), while meat is often served with *stamppot* – mashed potato with flecks of vegetable and more meat stirred in.

Snacks

- Arguably, Dutch food is better for snacking. Street stalls offer raw herring (► 32–33), and, less of an acquired taste, fries, which the Dutch traditionally eat with a glob of mayonnaise. **Vleminckx**, at Voetboogstraat 33, serves the best fries in the city (crispy on the outside, fluffy on the inside). Other stalls sell Belgian waffles and pancakes; several cafés, such as the **Pancake Bakery** (► 104), serve pancakes and little else.
- If you're feeling brave or desperate, you might want to try a meat or cheese-filled patties deep fried in breadcrumbs from **Febo's coin-operated hatches**: there are outlets all over town.
- **At lunchtime,** most Amsterdammers make do with a *broodje* (sandwich), either in a café or from one of the many take-out sandwich shops. Cafés also traditionally serve *bitterballen* (like round patties), *uitsmijter* (fried eggs on ham and cheese and bread), and often homemade *appelgebak* (apple pie), served with a dollop of *slagroom* (whipped cream). The pie at the **Winkel** (Noordermarkt 43), heavily flavored with cinnamon and with the flakiest of crusts, may be the culinary highlight of your stay.

What to Drink

- Apart from beer (► 34), **the favorite Dutch tipple** is *jenever* (Dutch gin), made from molasses and flavored with juniper berries. Whether *oud* (old – and mellow and a little yellow), or *jong* (young – and sharp and transparent), *jenever* has a stronger taste than English gin but is less potent. *Jenever* is drunk neat, though it can be flavored with black currant or lemon, and served in tulip-shaped glasses filled to the brim. You're expected to leave the glass on the bar and bend down for the first sip. Serious drinkers order a *kopstoot* (a knock on the head) – a beer with a *jenever* chaser.
- **Tasting houses** (► 27) also specialize in fruity liqueurs with delightful names such as Naked Belly Button, which should apparently be served when a mother-to-be shows her tummy to friends and family.
- The Dutch are very partial to coffee. **It is traditionally served black,** always with a cookie, sometimes with a mini carton of evaporated milk. If you want a coffee with milk, ask for a *koffie verkeerd* (literally "coffee wrong").

Practicalities

- Most restaurants open only in the evening. The Dutch tend to **eat dinner relatively early,** so they are busiest between 7 and 8 p.m., and few take orders much after 10 p.m.
- **Cafés usually open** some time in the morning (but drinking-oriented ones often late afternoon), and close at 1 a.m. Sunday through Thursday, 2 a.m. Friday and Saturday, but stop serving food between 10 and 11 p.m.
- More often than not, **a menu is available in English,** and you can invariably rely on the staff to speak English.
- At upscale restaurants, especially at weekends, **make reservations.**
- Only the most formal restaurants in luxury hotels **have a dress code.**
- Service is normally cheerful but notoriously inattentive and offhand. A **15 percent service charge** is automatically included in the bill, but it's common practice to add a couple of guilders or round it up to the nearest guilder for larger amounts.

Shopping

As befits a city founded on trade, Amsterdam offers a lot of pleasures for the shopaholic. It may not have a range of shops to match cities such as London, Paris and New York, but it excels in its dozens of little specialty shops, some dedicated to selling just one item such as old spectacles, toothbrushes or olive oil. Shopping in Amsterdam is all about browsing, and unlike many American cities, an outdoor experience: the city is refreshingly free of shopping malls, and is famous for its many and varied markets.

Best Shopping Areas and Streets

- In the city center, pedestrianized **Kalverstraat** (► 75) has the greatest concentration of mainstream chain stores and department stores. The city's top department store is **De Bijenkorf** (► 76), nearby on Dam square.
- The **9 Straatjes** (► 105), the Nine Streets on the western canal ring, are packed full of tiny, often offbeat stores, and trendy clothes shops and galleries. The nearby back streets of the **Jordaan** offer more of the same, while **Prinsengracht,** which divides the two areas, has a string of alluring antiques shops.
- The **Spiegelkwartier** (► 158–159) is synonymous with expensive art and refined antiques, on display in 70 galleries and shops along one of the city's prettiest thoroughfares.
- **PC Hooftstraat** (► 133), in the Museum Quarter, is for label victims: the designer stores feature what amounts to a roll-call of famous names in the world of international fashion.

Best Markets

- **Noordermarkt** (► 106): the city's most picturesque market – a flea-market one day, farmers' market another.
- **Waterlooplein** (► 77): the city's biggest flea-market.
- **Albert Cuypmarkt** (► 159): the biggest general street market – everything from eels to second-hand clothes.
- **Bloemenmarkt** (► 159): the Flower Market, set up on permanently moored barges, is touristy and crowded but always colorful.

What to Buy

- Art and antiques: in the **Spiegelkwartier** (► 158–159), **De Looier** indoor market (► 107) and along **Prinsengracht** (► 106), you can pick up anything from old Delftware tiles to city prints, toys, clocks and medical instruments.
- Bulbs: tulips, narcissi and hyacinths are on sale at the **Flower Market** (► 159). There are no restrictions for exports to the U.K., but U.S. buyers should ask vendors about certification before buying.
- Chocolates: best from places such as **Pompadour** (► 105) and Holtkamp (► 159), which make their own.
- Cheeses: *jonge* (young) and *oude* (old), and factory-produced or farm-produced, the latter unpasteurised and stamped *boerenkaas*. Specialty cheese shops such as **De Kaaskamer** (► 105) let you taste before buying and vacuum-pack your purchase.
- Delftware: tin-glazed, Dutch earthenware – called porcelain – dates back to the 17th century. Tiles, tulip vases, dishes and knick-knacks are all tradi-tionally decorated in blue and white with Chinese-styled ornamentation. Much of the Delftware on sale is mass-produced imitation, but the genuine article, only made by De Porceleyne Fles, is sold in shops such as

Rinascimento Galleria d'Arte (➤ 106) and **Focke & Meltzer** (➤ 133).
■ Diamonds: diamond-cutting has been big business in the city for centuries. Factories such as **Coster Diamonds** (➤ 128) provide free tours to attract customers into their sale rooms.
■ Reproductions: you, too, can have a Dutch master on your wall, for just a few guilders. Choose from the wide choice of posters in the **Rijksmuseum** (➤ 114–117) or **Van Gogh Museum** (➤ 124–127). For the best selection of postcards, head for **Art Unlimited** (➤ 106).

Opening Hours
■ Though **opening hours are gradually being liberalized,** they are still restricted compared to many big cities. On the main shopping streets in the city center, stores typically open Mondays 11–6, Tuesdays, Wednesdays and Fridays 9–6, Thursdays 9–9, Saturdays 9–5 and Sundays noon–5. Specialty stores, however, generally do not open on Sundays, and on Mondays some do not open until as late as 2 p.m. or remain shut all day.

Taxes
■ **Tax is included in advertised prices.** If you live outside the European Union, you are entitled to a refund on the value-added tax (17.5 percent on most goods) minus a commission at shops displaying a "Tax Free Shopping" sign, as long as you spend 300 guilders or more in the shop in a single day.

Airport Shopping
■ If all you want is a typical Dutch souvenir, you could leave your shopping until just before you leave the country. The **shops after passport control** at Schiphol airport sell chocolates, Gouda, Edam, smoked herring and smoked eel, as well as bulbs, clogs, *jenever* and diamonds. Note that for trips within the European Union, there are no longer any tax benefits on purchases made at the airport.

Entertainment

For after-dark entertainment, it's hard to improve on the simple pleasures of a stroll along the canals and a beer or two in one of the many atmospheric cafés.

■ The liveliest areas at night – worth either seeking out or avoiding, depending on what you're looking for – are the **Red Light District** (➤ 63–65), **Spuikwartier** (➤ 76), **Leidseplein** (➤ 107) and **Rembrandtplein** (➤ 160). Cafés stay open late: last call is around 1 a.m., or 2 a.m. on Fridays and Saturdays.

Information Sources
■ **For such a multilingual city,** there are few events listings in English – effectively just the VVV's bland monthly magazine, *Day by Day What's On in Amsterdam.*
■ The monthly *Uitkrant* listings magazine **is more comprehensive** and, unlike the tourist office's publication, free from cafés and bars, but in Dutch.

Ticket Reservations
■ VVV offices can reserve tickets at major venues, but you're better off going to the **AUB (Amsterdams Uit Buro) Ticketshop,** on Leidseplein at the corner of

Marxinstraat (open daily 10–6, Thursday to 9 p.m.; tel: 020 621 1211). It stocks every possible cultural leaflet. Staff members are helpful and knowledgeable and can make reservations for shows for a small fee.
- You can also **make reservations through the AUB** by phone, daily 9–9 (tel: 011 31 20 621 1288 from the U.S., 0900 0191 in the Netherlands). Its website is www.aub.nl

Nightclubs
- Most clubs only open Thursday through Sunday and **don't get going until around midnight.**
- **Entry is normally inexpensive** (10–20 guilders), but may be dependent on dressing to impress the bouncers.
- www.amsterdamhotspots.nl has **critical reviews of clubs.**

Gay Amsterdam
Ultra-tolerant Amsterdam has one of the most vibrant gay scenes in Europe.
- Many gay bars and clubs can be found around Rembrandtplein, especially on **Reguliersdwarsstraat** (➤ 160) and on **Warmoesstraat** (➤ 78).
- Several bars and clubs stock **free publications** listing gay-oriented venues and events.
- www.amsterdamhotspots.nl has **reviews of the best-known** gay bars and clubs.

Movie Theaters
- Amsterdam has some highly individual movie theaters such as **Tuschinski Theater** (➤ 160).
- Movie theaters screen the vast majority of films in their **original language with Dutch subtitles,** but check before buying a ticket.

Live Music
- The bastions of high culture are the **Muziektheater** (➤ 78) and the **Concertgebouw** (➤ 130).
- Many churches regularly hold classical concerts, baroque chamber music and organ recitals. The Engelskerk in the **Begijnhof** (➤ 54–55) normally has the fullest program. Other venues include: **Oude Kerk** (➤ 64), carillon concerts usually on Saturdays at 4 p.m.; **Nieuwe Kerk** (➤ 61); **Westerkerk** (➤ 92–93), carillon concerts normally on Tuesdays at noon; **Amstelkerk** (➤ 182); and **Waalse Kerk** (Walenpleintje 157). Listings magazines have more details.
- The **Amsterdam ArenA,** Ajax's futuristic soccer stadium on the southeastern edge of the city, holds large-scale rock concerts.
- The more intimate **Melkweg** and **Paradiso** (➤ 108) host up-and-coming bands as well as megastars such as the Rolling Stones, who would never normally choose to play to such relatively small audiences.

Summer Entertainment
- Most cultural events **take place in summer,** under the promotional banner Amsterdam Arts Adventure. They include the **Holland Festival** (www.holland-festival.nl), a highbrow diet of international opera, dance, theater and music every June, and the **Grachtenfestival** (www.grachtenfestival.nl) in August, which culminates in a concert on a floating stage in front of the Pulitzer Hotel.
- **In late August,** dozens of companies advertize their shows for the forth-coming year by performing excerpts free of charge at the **Uitmarkt** (www.uitmarkt.nl).
- See also ➤ 120 for the **Vondelpark open-air theater.**

Getting Your Bearings

The old heart of Amsterdam feels like two distinct cities. The more obvious of the pair contains the sort of brash tourist trappings that you find in any major European city, in this particular case augmented by the unabashed indulgence of the Red Light District. Yet alongside such excess you can find oases of calm and solitude, plus some excellent places to eat, drink and shop that only the locals seem to know about.

Above: In the Begijnhof

Dam, the main square, is not the most beautiful plaza in Europe, but it serves as a good hub for exploring the rest of the area. Everything in Medieval Amsterdam is a short walk from here, including the main shopping streets and the reju-venated Amsterdams Historisch Museum – a user-friendly introduction to the story of this extraordinary city. Almost next door, the Begijnhof, a cloister for the support and protection of women, maintains its principles and decorum. Even in the middle of the Red Light District (Rosse Buurt), there are strikingly beautiful structures, steeped in history. Whatever you want from a place, Medieval Amsterdam can probably provide it.

Previous page: Dam Square by Lingelbach

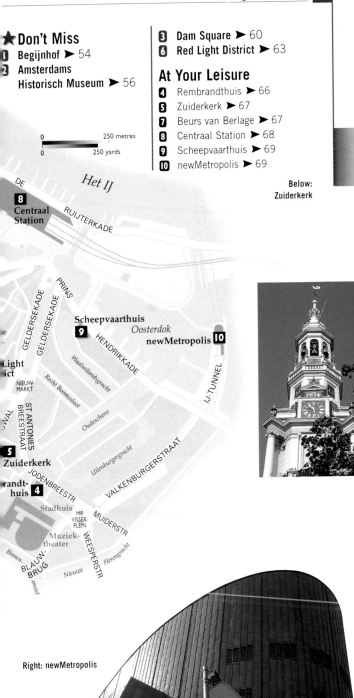

★ Don't Miss

Below: Zuiderkerk

0 — 250 metres
0 — 250 yards

Het IJ

DE RUIJTERKADE

8 Centraal Station

PRINS

GELDERSEKADE
GELDERSEKADE

Scheepvaarthuis
9 HENDRIKKADE

Oosterdok
newMetropolis **10**

IJ-TUNNEL

Light ict

NIEUW-MARKT

Waalseilandsgracht

Recht Boomssloot

Oudeschans

ST ANTONIES BREESTRAAT

Uilenburgergracht

5 Zuiderkerk

randt-huis **4**

JODENBREESTR

VALKENBURGERSTRAAT

Stadhuis

MR VISSER-PLEIN

MUIDERSTR

Muziek-theater

WEESPERSTR

BLAUW-BRUG

Binnen-

Nieuwe

Herengracht

amstel

Right: newMetropolis

Any visit to Amsterdam should begin where the city started – the historic heart that still beats beneath the intriguing layers of gentility and glamour.

Medieval Amsterdam in a Day

10:00 a.m.

This is the earliest you can visit the **Begijnhof** (right, ➤ 54–55), the serene heart of the city; arrive promptly to dodge the worst of the crowds, then have a coffee at the grand Café Luxembourg (➤ 70) on Spui, the square just to the south.

11:30 a.m.

A few minutes' walk north takes you to the **Amsterdams Historisch Museum** (➤ 56–59), the place to brush up on the roots of the medieval city.

1:00 p.m.

Wander east to combine lunch with people-watching at In de Waag (➤ 72), the old weighhouse on Nieuwmarkt, or with shopping at La Place (➤ 72), the cafeteria of the Vroom en Dreesman department store.

3:00 p.m.

Most roads in Medieval Amsterdam lead to **Dam square** (left, ➤ 60–61), where you could wander around the Royal Palace (Koninklijk Paleis), if it's open, or explore some of the more innovative shops hidden away from the main retail drags.

4:00 p.m.

An easy stroll through the university district and past the home of the United East India Company, takes you to Waterlooplein. Here you can search for some end-of-day bargains at the flea market; find out about the worrying water levels at the town hall (► 11–12); visit **Rembrandthuis,** the artist's home (► 66); or enjoy an afternoon break with a new angle at the leaning café, De Sluyswacht (► 72).

5:30 p.m.

Toward Centraal Station you will find some of the oldest parts of the city, such as Oudezijds Voorburgwal, at the time when the day's commerce gives way to the night's activities in the **Red Light District** (right, ► 63–65).

7:00 p.m.

Acquire a taste for *jenever* (Dutch gin) at a tasting house such as De Drie Fleschjes (► 71) or Wynand Fockink (► 72).

8:00 p.m.

Dine out on excellent Thai or Chinese food at giveaway prices on Zeedijk (► 64), or remind yourself that you are in one of the great fishing nations with the superb seafood at Lucius (► 74). To make a drama out of a meal, try the Supper Club (► 74).

10:00 p.m.

Make your way back to where the day began, the area around the Begijnhof. The evening is just beginning at Café Gollem (► 70), though some customers may appear to be well on the way to sampling every beer in the house. Or you could drift across to Spui to help the legendary Hoppe (► 71) maintain its reputation for pumping more beer for its size than any other brown café in the Netherlands.

Begijnhof

A stake in the lawn at the Begijnhof bears the motto: "May peace prevail on earth." Quite remarkably, peace prevails most of the time in a broad, green and pleasant courtyard that is virtually in the center of one of Europe's most energetic cities, yet remains aloof from the indulgence just minutes away.

Lambert le Bègue founded the order of the Begijns in 1180 for women from wealthy Catholic backgrounds who had lost (or never acquired) a husband. The Begijnhof was a more liberal alternative to entering a convent: Begijns lived in comfortable housing while ministering to the poor and elderly – a religious lifestyle, but not one that required strict religious vows.

Below: Houten Huys, the oldest building in the Begijnhof

The Begijnhof was founded in the mid-14th century, but the original wooden houses have been lost. At No. 34 the **Houten Huys** ("wooden house"), built around 1475, is the oldest surviving home in the city. Most of the rest were constructed in the 16th, 17th or 18th centuries, though some are less than 100 years old. The last Begijn died in 1971, but the houses are still occupied by unmarried women. Their prim houses beneath elaborate gables are arranged around well-tended lawns.

Covering most of the southern half of the Begijnhof is the **Engelskerk,** built toward the end of the 15th century and for 100 years

How to Behave
The residents of the Begijnhof tolerate tourism, but ask visitors to follow some common-sense rules to avoid invading their privacy. Photography is permitted, but you should not try to photograph the interiors of individual houses. Voices should be kept down.

Women's refuge: men and married women need not apply for residence

the sisters' place of worship. It was closed after the "Alteration" (➤ 58), and lay idle until 1607 when it was loaned to English-speaking Presbyterians. Some of its worshippers later became the Pilgrim Fathers. The church is now part of the Church of Scotland: among the flags hanging from the north wall is the Royal Standard of Scotland. The pulpit has panels decorated by a young Piet Mondriaan (1872–1944). Besides Sunday services (at 10:30 a.m.), the church is mainly used for lunchtime and evening concerts.

The **Begijnhofkapel**, the Catholic church built in 1671, is just five paces away from the Engelskerk, but not at all obvious. After the "Alteration," Amsterdam's Catholics were obliged to worship clandestinely: the authorities turned a blind eye as long as there was no evidence from the street of a place of worship. Anonymous doors conceal an opulent interior: look for the stained-glass window dedicated to the Dutch national poet, Joost van den Vondel.

Begijnhof
- 203 D4
- Begijnhof
- Visiting hours 10–5; no groups. Begijnhofkapel Sat.–Sun. 9–6, Mon. 1–6:30, Tue.–Fri. 9–6:30
- Café at No. 35, next to the Houten Huys ($$)
- 1, 2, 5
- Free

BEGIJNHOF: INSIDE INFO

Top tips Both entrances are hard to find. The main way in is from **Gedempte Begijnen Sloot,** reached from Kalverstraat along a lane called Begijnensteeg. A second entrance is from the square known as Spui, underneath an arch that looks like an ordinary doorway.

• During the middle of the day, the Begijnhof can become jammed with visitors; plan to be there in **the first or last hour.**

Hidden gem Around the corner from the café/information center at No. 35 is a wall in which **eight of the biblical tablets** taken from demolished houses are embedded.

Amsterdams Historisch Museum

Amsterdam is an extraordinary city, and its strange, exciting history is explained in a masterful manner in the freshly refurbished Amsterdam Historical Museum. The human and economic intrigues that have helped create Amsterdam are laid bare in a venue that is as jumbled as the city itself. A visit will help you to understand and enjoy Amsterdam all the more.

First, though, you have to find it. The museum occupies a substantial chunk of Medieval Amsterdam, but manages to bury itself in a jumble of streets. The most accessible of the three entrances is the doorway at Nieuwezijds Voorburgwal 359, which also puts you in the right place to begin your tour around a hodgepodge of chambers.

The tricky location and strange shape are due to the origins and use of the structure. It was originally established in 1414 as a convent, but after the "Alteration" to Protestantism, it became the city's orphanage. The girls' and boys' halves were separated by a deep (and unsavory) trench, which traced the line of the walkway that now slices through the museum.

Above: A 17th-century market scene

A 19th-century pharmacy sign

One of the
museum's
hard-to-find
entrances

Right: Art and
commerce rub
shoulders at
the Amsterdam
Historical
Museum

Young City

The rooms give a strictly chronological account of the growth
of the city, from the first settlements formed on small, raised
mounds of solid clay. Gradually the mounds grew together,
and Amsterdam acquired the critical mass necessary for its
inhabitants to transcend subsistence lifestyles.

The first dam was built on the Amstel in 1270, something
of a turning point for the infant city. Its immediate effect was
to impede trade – the barrier meant that cargo vessels were
obliged to unload – and the goods moved onward, creating
employment in Amsterdam.

Pragmatism and innovation marked the next few centuries.
The earliest known "map" of the city is on show in **Room 4:**
Cornelius Anthonisz's 1538 bird's-eye view. Other paintings in
the museum include a 1593 work, in the same room, showing
a lottery being conducted to benefit a lunatic asylum.

Mighty City

Amsterdam was central to rapid economic growth in the 14th and 15th centuries as enhanced maritime technology brought more trade. **Room 5** shows how trading with Asia commenced in earnest in 1595 by several competing companies. They merged in 1602 and became a much more potent force – the East India Company (VOC – ► 16–17), the most powerful trading association in the world. Over the next two centuries, nearly a million people sailed from Holland, and some estimates suggest only one in three returned. The eastbound adventures were much more effective than those to the west. On the North American mainland, Nieuw Amsterdam was found, then lost: what is now New York was swapped for Surinam, a small and swampy strip of territory in South America, to save face for the Dutch.

Amsterdam managed to turn the religious turmoil that swept across Europe in the 16th century to its advantage. Skilled Jewish people and Protestants, expelled from other European countries, were given a (guarded) welcome. The city was not immune to the strife, and its version of the Reformation – known as the "Alteration" – took place after considerable bloodshed in the second half of the 16th century. **Room 10** gives an insight into the struggles, and also features a replica of the carillon from the Munt Tower, which you are at liberty to try out.

Modern City

Amsterdam's mercantile and artistic glory dwindled in the 19th century, but the city continued to find innovative solutions to the special problems it faced. One of the funniest described in the museum is J. C. Sinck's hoist, used to rescue the many horses that tumbled into the canal. This Rube Goldberg affair was a wagon with a crane

Above: The museum shows how the Dutch ruled the 17th-century waves

Below: Present-day Amsterdam owes its looks, and its layout, to maritime trade

attachment, from which dangled a harness that was looped around the unfortunate animal. Up to 40 guilders was charged for a rescue – a small price for saving a valuable horse.

The 20th-century section is particularly interesting, focusing on immigration, social welfare and, of course, World War II. During the "Hunger Winter" of 1944–45, more than 2,000 Amsterdammers died.

As the docks wound down during the 1970s and early 1980s, the city went into decline, with 40,000 people leaving each year. Social upheavals since the 1960s are described with a dose of humor: amid the sober graphs of population growth is a diagram of the rise of coffee shops between 1980 and 1999, using the marijuana plant as the symbol of magnitude.

The museum brings you up to date with the contemporary community. Fewer than one in three Amsterdammers have always lived in the city, and the rate of "residential turnover" is high. To remind you of its role as transportation hub for the 21st century, there is even a real-time display of the arrivals and departures screens at Schiphol airport.

A flamboyant 18th-century coat-of-arms, typical of the merchants who made fortunes from the sea

TAKING A BREAK

Besides the museum's own café, there are plenty of options close by, such as the stylish **Esprit Caffè** on Spui.

Amsterdams Historisch Museum
🔢 203 D4
✉️ Nieuwezijds Voorburgwal 357, Kalverstraat 92 and Sint Luciensteeg 27
☎️ 020 523 1822; www.ahm.nl
🕐 Mon.–Fri. 10–5, Sat., Sun., holidays 11–5. Closed Jan. 1, Apr. 30, Dec. 25
🍴 David en Goliath café restaurant, ground floor ($$)
🚋 1, 2, 4, 5, 9, 11, 14, 16, 29, 24, 25
💰 Moderate; free admission to Museum Year Card holders

AMSTERDAMS HISTORISCH MUSEUM: INSIDE INFO

Top tips Pick up the **free plan at the entrance**; despite some reasonable sign-posting, you could get hopelessly lost without one.
• The shop has a great range of **appealing small gifts** – a good place to do your souvenir shopping.

Dam Square

Almost all visitors to Amsterdam find themselves passing through Dam, as the square at the center of the city is concisely known. This was the point at which the Amstel River was first dammed in the 13th century. Since then, the river has been diverted to the east. The square is central to the city and the country, containing both the Royal Palace and the Nationaal Monument. Initially, the unruly architecture and untidy occupants may be disappointing, as well as the fact that the whole place is crisscrossed with over-head power cables for trams. But if you focus on individual elements, the experience is enjoyable and rewarding.

Koninklijk Paleis

The Dutch monarchy is distinct from most royal families. It was established, by common consent less than two centuries ago. The Royal Palace is also rather different from the norm. From its imposing bulk and location on Amsterdam's main square, you could be forgiven for taking it for a city hall; that was, indeed, its intended purpose. Trams pass within about 6 feet of the south wall and from the front door Her Majesty has an excellent view of many of the quaint

The statue of peace atop the palace guards Dam square

excesses of life in Amsterdam, such as people idling around the Nationaal Monument while smoking marijuana.

The palace was built in the mid-17th century, when Amsterdam was the greatest trading city in the world. At the time, the poet Constantijn Huygens (1596–1687) called it "the eighth wonder of the world." When Louis Napoleon took control of the Netherlands, he first resided in Utrecht but soon moved to Amsterdam. The only building grand enough to house him, he decreed, was the city hall. At the top of the pediment is an allegory of war and peace: figures with a club and an olive branch, together with a gilded sailing ship acting as a weather vane above the dome.

It's worth walking all the way around the palace to get an

The controver-
sial Nationaal
Monument adds
to the jumble
of styles on
Dam square

idea of the sheer scale of the place and to see the sculpture of
Atlas supporting a giant copper globe at the rear. Just beware
of the trams that encircle it. Even the row of four lamp posts at
the front of the palace is decorative, each protected by lions
and topped by a crown.

The Royal Palace is open only erratically: it is not open in
winter or when important dignitaries are in town, and remains
closed for no immediately obvious reason on many other days.
Even when it is open, some visitors find the interior unreward-
ing. The tour is confined to certain rooms on the second floor,
most notably the Citizens' Hall, where the floor is inlaid with
superb maps of the eastern and western hemispheres, and
there's a fine collection of sculptures – originals, unlike the
chandeliers, that were added by Louis Napoleon.

Nationaal Monument

The Nationaal Monument marks the suffering during the Nazi
occupation in World War II, a traumatic time for the city and
the country. The white column was designed by John Rädecker
and unveiled to considerable public outcry on May 4, 1956, 16
years after the German invasion. Critics say the design is nothing more than a giant version of the traffic bollards that are
found everywhere in Amsterdam, and you can see their point.
Look more closely at the overgrown salt cellar and you'll see
representations of motherhood and repression, while a flock of
doves flutters down the back of the monument. Urns arrayed
around it contain soil from the states of the Netherlands and
the greatest former Dutch colony, Indonesia.

Nieuwe Kerk

Nieuwe Kerk is the church used for the investiture of Dutch
monarchs and, despite its name, is very old. It's at its loveliest
on a sunny morning when the gold figures on the sundial
above the deep window on the south side glitter like a neck-
lace. Until the coming of "railway time" at the end of the 19th
century, all the city's clocks were synchronized to this sundial.

The elaborate tomb of 17th-century Admiral Michiel de Ruyter

The original "New Church" was founded in 1408, but fire destroyed the first two versions. Its present shape dates from the early 16th century. In 1578, the Dutch Reformed Church took it over and cleared it of statues, altars and murals. A fire started in 1645 by plumbers melting lead to repair the roof destroyed everything except the walls and the pillars. This allowed the interior to be reconstructed with the best that the Golden Age could provide.

On the right of the entrance as you go in is a monument to Joost van den Vondel (1587–1679), the national poet and a contemporary of Rembrandt, whose remains are contained in an urn in the church. Many naval heroes – commonly regarded in the 18th and 19th centuries as the closest thing to royalty – are buried here. Most notable is Michiel de Ruyter (1606–76), an admiral in the Dutch fleet that fought in the Second and Third Anglo-Dutch Wars. In the course of the former, he sailed up the Thames Estuary almost as far as London; during the latter, he died, and the battle in which he lost his life is depicted on his tomb.

TAKING A BREAK

Looking north along Nieuwendijk from Dam, a succession of fast-food outlets stretches into the distance. There are various other options, few of them wildly appetizing. On the square itself is the **Nieuwe Kafe,** which sprouts from the Nieuwe Kerk and is an excellent venue for people-watching. For something different, try the **Wynand Fockink** tasting house (► 72) at Pijlsteeg 31, a lane behind the Krasnapolsky Hotel.

Royal Palace
🕂 203 D5
☎ 020 620 4060; www.kon-paleisamsterdam.nl
🕐 12:30–5; no fixed days
🚊 All trams to and from Centraal Station
🎫 Moderate

Nieuwe Kerk
🕂 203 D5
☎ 020 638 6909 recorded info); www.nieuwe-kerk.nl
🕐 Daily 10–5, except during special events
🎫 Free, but inexpensive for events

ROYAL PALACE: INSIDE INFO

Top tips If you are especially eager to see the inside of the palace, **contact the tourist office** before your visit to find out when it is open – or look for the list of opening days posted outside the palace.

• The **audio tour** is a worthwhile optional extra.

Red Light District

Amsterdam's Rosse Buurt (Red Light District) is outrageous. Prostitutes pout in the glare of pink lighting. A sign on the window of a coffee shop reads "Dear Customers, Please roll your joints *inside* the shop, thank you." Every big city has its red light district where the normal rules of society are suspended, but nowhere is it quite like Amsterdam.

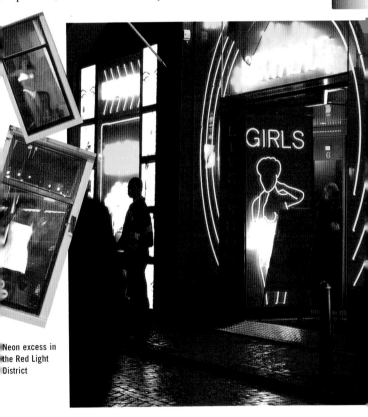

Neon excess in the Red Light District

Some visitors are intrigued by this area; one of Amsterdam's main attractions, it offers a vivid slice of a lifestyle that, in other cities, is largely concealed. Others feel very uncomfortable about venturing into the compact, ragged triangle enclosed by Warmoesstraat, Zeedijk and the street running east from Dam square. Yet it would be a shame to avoid the area completely.

Certainly, the Red Light District contains prodigious quantities of lowlife. Yet the slumping houses and upright churches make it clear that there is plenty of history here, too, and any visitor should explore the maze of streets that is the historic core of Amsterdam. During the day, at least, the area is safe.

Warmoesstraat and its continuation, **Nes**, comprise the oldest street in the city, which grew up as the eastern bank of the Amstel. At the same time, the **Zeedijk** (sea dike) was built as a barrier to high tides and storms on the Zuider Zee. Between the two, the present warren of alleyways began to develop. From Amsterdam's earliest days as a port, the area catered for sailors who came ashore in need of alcohol and female company. Now, as then, between the brothels and bars, there are some notable ecclesiastical attractions.

As early as 1300, a small chapel stood on the present site of

The crimson glow of the Red Light District

the **Oude Kerk** (Old Church). It was dedicated to St. Nicholas, who protected people against the dangers of water. In the 15th century, the basic stone structure was established, making it the oldest existing building in Amsterdam. It has weathered the turbulence of the city remarkably well – though some dignity has been lost with new accoutrements such as the open-air urinals in the square outside. Inside, you are likely to find much of the space used for a temporary exhibition, but the fine stained-glass windows are undiminished and memorials to the illustrious dead are visible everywhere. Rembrandt's first wife, Saskia, is buried beneath one of the 2,500 gravestones.

Amstelkring is a marvelous museum offering two experiences for the price of one. The first three floors give an insight into 17th-century life in Amsterdam, with rooms preserved in

the style created by the owner, Jan Hartman. On the three upper floors, a dazzling Catholic church, dripping in statuary and silver, has been crowbarred into the narrow confines of the house. Its nickname is "Our Lord in the Attic." After the "Alteration," several wealthy Catholics converted part of their houses into churches, but this is the only one to have survived.

Above: The Amstelkring Museum is full of religious treasures

Right: One of these buildings conceals a hidden church

Oude Kerk
- 203 F5
- Oudekerksplein 23
- 020 625 8284; www.oudekerk.nl
- Mon.–Sat. 11–5 (1–5 Dec.–late Mar.), Sun. 1–5
- 4, 9, 16, 20, 24, 25 to Damrak
- Inexpensive; free admission to Museum Year Card holders

Amstelkring
- 204 A4
- Oudezijds Voorburgwal 40
- 020 624 6604
- Mon.–Sat. 10–5, Sun. 1–5. Closed Jan. 1, Apr. 30 and for special functions
- 4, 9, 16, 20, 24, 25 to Damrak
- Inexpensive; free admission to Museum Year Card holders

RED LIGHT DISTRICT: INSIDE INFO

Top tips Bear in mind that the sex industry attracts a number of unsavory characters, both as clients and "management." They do not take kindly to **camera-wielding tourists.**

- Leave your bicycle behind: the streets are **too narrow and crowded.**

At Your Leisure

4 Rembrandthuis (Rembrandt House)

The artist's residence is a delight from bottom to top, which is the official sequence of the visit here. You enter through the building next door, and after the cash desk descend to the **kitchen,** where you can see the first of several "box-beds" – the maid was required to sleep in what was effectively a cupboard with a mattress inside.

The ground level is the grandest, with the **entrance hall** being especially opulent. As a dealer in art, as well as a manufacturer, Rembrandt knew the value of making a good impression. There are plenty of paintings by lesser contemporaries on display. The **anteroom** has an entrance and a fireplace that look like marble but turn out to be wood: the marble effect is achieved by expert painting. Behind the anteroom, there was a printing press where he could reproduce his etchings. The **Salon** (drawing room) doubled as Rembrandt's bedroom.

A narrow spiral staircase leads to a **mezzanine floor,** where you find an extraordinary collection of *objets d'art.* Unlike many of his contempo-

Rembrandt, his family and his pupils dined in this kitchen

raries, Rembrandt had a keen interest in the wider world. The artifacts include a hammock from South America and Chinese porcelain; among the exhibits from the natural world are a dazzling blue butterfly and a giant turtle shell.

The biggest room in the house is the large **studio** on the third floor, the north-facing room where Rembrandt and his pupils worked. Some of his etchings are on sale. Picasso took many ideas from Rembrandt's etchings, saying: "Bad artists copy, good artists steal."

On the **fourth floor,** pause to look down on the rear of the house – and the modern apartment building that backs up to it – before beginning your descent. As you leave the building, be sure to see the fine gateway to the left (west) which shows two sulky figures in relief beneath the triple-cross symbol of Amsterdam.

➕ 204 A3 ✉ Jodenbreestraat 4–6
☎ 020 530 0400 🕐 Mon.–Sat. 10–5, Sun. 1–5 🚇 Waterlooplein 🚊 9, 14, 20 💶 Moderate; free admission to Museum Year Card holders

5 Zuiderkerk

The main purpose of a visit to this hard-to-track-down church is to visit the top of the tower for a different perspective on the city. You can also enjoy a quick glimpse at the interesting stainless steel water sculpture opposite the east door and a slightly longer look inside.

Now deconsecrated, the church is home to the Zuiderkerk Informatiecentrum, a municipal information center with exhibits on the planning of Amsterdam.

🔢 203 F4 ✉ Zandstraat ③ Tower tours: at 2, 3, 4 p.m., Wed.–Sat.; Church: Mon.–Fri. noon–5, late closing at 8 p.m. on Thu. 🚊 Waterlooplein 🎟 Tower: inexpensive; church free

Zuiderkerk, the South Church

7 Beurs van Berlage

One building stands out on Damrak: the superb red-brick former Stock Exchange. Hendrik Petrus Berlage, who designed the Beurs a century ago, was a believer in the "higher life of the organization." He had in mind trades unions, but was nevertheless sufficiently broad-minded to accept the contract for Amsterdam's hive of capitalism.

Berlage was not the judges' first choice: the winner of the competition to build a new home for the Amsterdam Stock Exchange was discovered to have copied the plan of the facade from the town hall at Nantes in France. Berlage set to work in 1898 with rather more enthusiasm than fortune, planting a monument in red brick on unsuitable foundations. Nine million bricks were supported by nearly 5,000 piles, but cracks began to appear within a year or two of its completion in 1903. Repairs succeeded in holding it together, and the place survived a demolition threat in the 1950s. It is now open to visitors as well as serving as offices for media companies and as a venue for concerts.

The best view of the **trading floor** is from the third-floor balcony. The hall is topped with a graceful steel-framed roof rising from brick columns with a feast of decoration, from a terra-cotta relief at the south end – depicting the evolution of man from tribal hunter-gatherer to fully developed trader – to a series of shields at the south end.

The tricky climb up a narrow wooden staircase takes you to a **tower** 130 feet above street level, giving a first-rate view of the city – and, in particular, the present Amsterdam Exchange located immediately east, at Beursplein 5.

🔢 201 F1 ✉ Beursplein 4 ☎ 020 530 4141 ③ Tue.–Sun. 10–4 🚊 Centraal Station 🚋 4, 9, 16, 20, 24, 25 🚇 Centraal Station 🎟 Moderate; free admission to Museum Year Card holders

🎱 Centraal Station

One strange thing about this remarkable building is how few visitors appreciate it. New arrivals exit for the city without a glance back. When they leave, they are too concerned about finding the right platform, catching the train and guarding their luggage to notice the magnificent facade that stretches 400m (.25-mile) along an artificial island that cuts off the river from the city.

The style is Northern Renaissance, and the architect was P. J. H. Cuypers,

Look more closely at the decorations and you will see a series of images celebrating the commercial life of the city: manufacture, trade and export. Inside, the unlovely 1970s refurbishment was improved by renovations in 2000, but the highlight remains on Platform 2. There you will find the elegant old **Wachtkammer 1e Klasse,** the first-class waiting room, now divided into two restaurants. Lions flank the original entrance, together with a portrait of a wistful Dutch girl decorated with

who also designed the Rijksmuseum (▶ 114–117), which has a very similar character. The best place and time to appreciate the overall view of the station is from outside the GVB (transportation operator) kiosk, about 100m (110 yards) back from the station entrance on a fine afternoon when the sun picks out the decoration. The eastern tower supports the rail traveler's essential – an elegant clock – while the corresponding face of the western tower contains a device showing the direction of the wind.

More than just a railway station – and definitely worth a backward glance

roses. Just beyond it, heading east along the platform, is a fine example of the city's coat of arms above a stairway down to the concourse.

🕇 204 A5 ✉ Stationplein 🕐 Open 24 hours; access between midnight and 5 a.m. restricted to passengers with tickets 🍴 Many refreshment facilities in the shopping area beneath the platforms and on Platform 2 🚇 All 🚌 All

𝟗 Scheepvaarthuis

The name of this extraordinary building translates simply as "shipping house," but it is also popularly known as the "house with 1,000 windows." Originally the office building was designed to house maritime companies. Accordingly the whole facade is awash with images celebrating navigation and bold announcements of the great seas from the Middellandse Zee (Mediterranean) to the Indische Oceaan (Indian Ocean).

The architects were disciples of P. J. H. Cuypers and concocted the first example of Amsterdam School design. Some visitors see geometrical elements borrowed from the Scottish designer Charles Rennie Mackintosh, or even imagery from the Mayan civilization of Central America. The building is now the headquarters of the local transportation operator, GVB, and organizes tram departures rather than great sea voyages.

🚩 204 B4 ⊠ Corner of Prins Hendrikkade and Binnenkant 🕐 Closed to visitors, but the exterior can be seen at any time 🚇 Centraal Station 🚌 Any serving Centraal Station 🚊 Centraal Station

𝟙𝟘 newMetropolis Science and Technology Center

Whether it was wise to decorate the Oosterdok with what looks suspiciously like a sinking ship has been a subject of great contention among Amsterdammers. Most, though, have grown fond of the massive copper-faced hull rising from (or sinking into) the entrance to the road tunnel under the IJ. The walk up the rim of the building is fun and rewarded with a superb view.

Many residents doubt whether the contents are worth the steep cost of admission. The exhibits are an uneasy mix of hands-on attractions designed for fun as well as education, and displays for adults that are intended to be thought-provoking. Neither is especially well served; children ages 10–12 are most likely to enjoy it.

🚩 204 C4 ⊠ Oosterdok 2 ☎ 0900 919 1100; www.newmet.nl 🕐 Tue.–Fri. 10–5, Sat.–Sun. 10–6 🍴 Café ($$) 🚇 Centraal Station, then walk 800m (880 yards) east along the north side of the Oosterdok and cross the footbridge 💷 Expensive

Millions of guilders were spent on the newMetropolis

Where to...
Eat and Drink

Prices
Expect to pay per person for a meal, excluding drinks
$ under 35 guilders $$ 35–70 guilders $$$ more than 70 guilders

CAFÉS

Café Gollem $

A tiny, moody and dark split-level brown café down an alley off Spuistraat that offers a huge range of imported beers (150 at the last count). The beers are marked on blackboards and beer mats and posters cover the walls and ceiling. Jazz and blues provide the musical backdrop. The clientele is a mix of locals, expats and tourists.

✚ 203 D4 ⊠ Raamsteeg 4 ☎ 020 626 6645 Ⓣ Sun.–Thu. 4 p.m.–1 a.m., Fri., Sat. till 2 a.m.

Café de Jaren $–$$

One of Amsterdam's first grand cafés and one of its most relaxing, De Jaren is popular both with students (the university is next door) and with an arty set, and gives off trendy vibes, especially in the evening. Formerly a bank, it has a vast and airy interior with a striking two-story-high bar, library-style reading desks with newspapers and magazines, and picture windows and terraces looking directly out on to the River Amstel. The food – sandwiches, soups, salads, cakes and, in the evenings, more substan-

tial fare such as steaks and pasta – is simple and wholesome.

✚ 203 E4 ⊠ Nieuwe Doelenstraat 20–2 ☎ 020 625 5771 Ⓣ Sun.–Thu. 10 a.m.–1 a.m., Fri., Sat. till 2 a.m.

Café Luxembourg $–$$

This quintessential grand café popular with Amsterdam's yuppies and media set has the languorous air of a chic Parisian café, and looks as if it's been around for a hundred years (which it hasn't). Choose between the covered terrace overlooking Spui square, the leather banquettes inside, a pew at the long marble-topped bar and the reading tables stocked with international magazines and newspapers. Come for a drink, breakfast or tea, or for a more substantial meal. The food – anything from soups and salads to steaks, dim sum and indulgent pastries – is excellent. The club sandwiches are renowned

✚ 203 D4 ⊠ Spui 24 ☎ 020 620 6264 Ⓣ Sun.–Thu. 9 a.m.–1 a.m., Fri., Sat. till 2 a.m.

Dantzig $–$$

A grand café that is ideal for a drink before a night at the Stopera or a morning rummaging in the Waterlooplein flea-market. It's right next to both, with a large terrace overlooking the Amstel. The vast, modern interior has theatrical touches such as chandeliers hanging from frescoed skies, as well as a peaceful library-style reading area. Very palatable sandwiches and snacks are served during the day, but for a full meal you can eat better elsewhere.

✚ 203 F4 ⊠ Zwanenburgwal 15 ☎ 020 620 9039 Ⓣ Sun.–Thu. 9 a.m.–1 a.m., Fri., Sat. till 2 a.m.

't Doktertje $

Hidden away down a side street off Kalverstraat, the 200-year-old "Little Doctor," once a doctor's office, now dispenses medicines of a different kind in what is claimed to be Amsterdam's smallest brown café. It's moody and candlelit, even on a bright sunny afternoon, and looks more like a junk shop than a bar. Lamps and old bottles gather dust, musical instruments hanging on the walls rust away, and the telephone is old enough to have bells on it – but, surprisingly, it works.

🔼 203 D4 ◻ Rozenboomsteeg 4 ☎ 020 626 4427 🕐 Tue.–Sat. 4 p.m.–1 a.m.

De Drie Fleschjes $

The fashionable "Three Little Bottles" is the city's best known *proeflokaal* (tasting house). It dates from 1650 and has rows of ancient wooden casks running its length. All the various special liqueurs and *jenevers* are detailed on blackboards that hang from hooks over the bar. On the bar are decanters of flavorings to add to the *jenevers* The *proeflokaal* is tiny with virtually no seating inside, but in summer there are tables outside on the pretty cobbled square.

🔼 203 E5 ◻ Gravenstraat 18 ☎ 020 624 8443 🕐 Mon.–Sat. noon–8:30 p.m., Sun. 3 p.m.–7 p.m.

Esprit Caffe $

The Esprit fashion store backs on to this hip "*lunchcafé*." The minimalist decor, with exposed metal girders and the giant windows overlooking Spui square, ensure maximum attention for the twenty-something clientele and the staff, whose uniform seems specifically designed to expose navels. The uncomplicated food, billed as Californian (consisting mostly of sandwiches with ciabatta and focaccia bread, pastas, salads, burgers, bagels, and Ben & Jerry's ice cream), is surprisingly decent. Outdoor seating covers a large area of the square when it's fine.

🔼 203 D4 ◻ Spui 10 ☎ 020 622 1967 🕐 Mon.–Wed., Fri., Sat. 10–6, Thu. 10–10, Sun. noon–6

't Gasthuys $

Atmosphere oozes from every pore of this down-to-earth cafe that's popular with students. Downstairs is a long narrow bar and beams plastered with banknotes. Steep stairs climb to two tiny rooms up among the rafters. 't Gasthuys bills itself as an *eetcafé* (▶ 28), and its tiny, open kitchen miraculously produces good, inexpensive, nononsense food, which comes in the form of sandwiches as well as more substantial main courses consisting of a variety of meat dishes plus salad and fries.

🔼 203 E4 ◻ Grimburgwal 7 ☎ 020 624 8230 🕐 Daily noon–1 a.m.

Grand Café Restaurant 1e Klas $–$$

This over-the-top neo-gothic room, with its lofty ceiling, pillars painted onto walls and monumental carved bar, used to be (along with the adjacent Burger King) the Centraal Station's first-class waiting room. It's quite a sight and worth a visit even if you're not waiting for a train. You can enjoy the surroundings for the price of a drink, a sandwich or a bowl of lobster bisque, or have a full (Dutch/French) meal: commuters often dine together at reserved tables before heading home.

🔼 204 A5 ◻ Centraal Station, platform 2B ☎ 020 625 0131 🕐 Daily 9:30 a.m.–11 p.m.

Hoppe $

This convivial brown café reputedly dates from 1670 and apparently sells more beer in proportion to its size than any other cafe in the Netherlands. Its standing-only older half is most atmospheric – it has sawdust on the floor and barrels set into partially panelled walls. The relatively modern half (with waiter service) is more comfortable and has a terrace overlooking Spui square. This is a place to come and drink, though there are a few snacks on sale. Hoppe is normally busiest just after work, when crowds of drinkers spill out on to the pavement, and on Monday evenings when there is live jazz.

🔼 203 D4 ◻ Spui 18–20 ☎ 020 420 4420 🕐 Sun.–Thu. 8 a.m.–1 a.m., Fri., Sat. till 2 a.m.

In de Waag $-$$

This café/restaurant is, as it says, in the Waag (▶ 23), the multi-turreted, Disneyesque medieval gatehouse-turned-weigh house that dominates the Nieuwmarkt. Inside it's grand yet intimate, with its bare walls, wooden tables and vaulted ceilings lit by 300 candles. The sandwiches at lunchtime are recommended, but dishes from the more elaborate, eclectic dinner menu have met with mixed reviews. The reading desks have Internet terminals.

🚶 203 F5 ✉ Nieuwmarkt 4 ☎ 020 422 7772 🕐 Daily 10 a.m.–1 a.m.

In de Wildeman $

The immaculately kept "Savage," founded as a liqueur distillery in 1690, now accurately bills itself as a *bierproeflokaal* – a beer-tasting house. There are no fewer than 180 bottled beers to choose from (all listed on a menu), and a further 17 beers on tap. With its beautiful old bar and ancient liqueur barrels, it's

atmospheric enough to entrance even teetotallers, and is a wonderful hideaway in which to hole up on a rainy afternoon. Its no-smoking room may be unique in Amsterdam cafés.

🚶 201 E2 ✉ Kolksteeg 3 ☎ 020 638 2348 🕐 Mon.–Sat. noon–1 a.m., Sun. 2 p.m.–9 p.m.

De Ooievaar $

The Stork is the Netherlands' smallest tasting house: no bigger than a small living room, it feels crowded with just 10 customers. Though it occupies the corner of an ancient, tipsy house and has old tiled and paneled walls and liqueur-lined shelves inside, the bar has in fact been here only since the mid-1990s. Despite its dubious location at the entrance to the Zeedijk (▶ 64), it is a thoroughly civilized bolthole with a high quotient of regulars.

🚶 204 A2 ✉ Sint Olofspoort 1 ☎ 020 420 8004 🕐 Sun.–Thu. 1 p.m.–1 a.m., Fri., Sat. till 2 a.m.

La Place $

The bustling self-service cafeteria of the Vroom en Dreesman department store is ideal for a quick, inexpensive lunch. It offers a vast range of appealingly presented hot and cold food, from pastries and a salad bar to Thai dishes and steak and fries. Or you could buy picnic provisions: the part on the Kalverstraat side is a large and tempting bakery serving every kind of bread, plus sandwiches, pastries, quiches and apple pies.

🚶 203 E4 ✉ Rokin 160 ☎ 020 622 0171 🕐 Mon. 11–7, Tue. Wed., Fri. 9:30–7, Thu. 9:30–9, Sat. 9:30–6, Sun. noon–6

De Sluyswacht $

An alarmingly sloping 17th-century former lock-keeper's house has been turned into a brown café right across the road from the Rembrandthuis. It doesn't quite live up to expectations inside, but is cozy and friendly. You can also sit out on the large terrace and admire the views down the Oude Schans

and of the T-Boat, Amsterdam's only floating coffee shop.

🚶 204 A3 ✉ Jodenbreestraat 1 ☎ 020 625 7611 🕐 Mon.–Thu. noon–1 a.m., Fri., Sat. till 2 a.m., Sun. till 7 p.m.

Villa Zeezicht $

This oddly named daytime café occupies a prime canalfront spot: its picture windows overlook the Torensluis bridge, one of the widest in the city. Inside, the hodgepodge of battered old furniture, the jazz music gently wafting in the background, and the informal young waitresses all help make this a thoroughly laid-back place. Quiche, sandwiches, croissants and famously good apple pie are available.

🚶 201 D1 ✉ Torensteeg 7 ☎ 020 626 7433 🕐 Mon.–Fri. 8–8, Sat. Sun. 9–8

Wynand Fockink $

This enchanting little time capsule of a tasting house, hidden down an alley behind the Grand Hotel

Krasnapolsky, dates from 1679. Bottles of its own liqueurs from the distillery next door line the sagging shelves behind the bar and include obscure concoctions with names like Parrot Soup. Though the bar is standing room only, its quaint café has wooden banquette seats and more tables and chairs in a courtyard garden for those who want coffee, a sandwich or salad.

➕ 203 E5 ⊠ Pijlsteeg 31 ☎ 020 639 2695 🕙 Bar daily 3 p.m.–9 p.m., café daily 10–6

RESTAURANTS

Bird $

Fantastic and amazingly affordable Thai food is served in this cramped, hectic, no-frills snackbar. You can either take it out or eat in at one of the few tables and window seats (the latter ideal for watching the fascinating comings and goings along Amsterdam's most notorious street). The sensational chicken and coconut soup is a meal in itself.

The Bird restaurant across the street serves similar fare in more comfy but less atmospheric surroundings.

➕ 204 A4 ⊠ Zeedijk 77 ☎ 020 420 6289 🕙 Daily 3 p.m.–10 p.m.

Café Roux $$–$$$

The Grand Amsterdam hotel's (▶ 42) upscale but not overly formal art deco-styled brasserie was once the staff canteen for the city hall. Its highly rated French dishes are inspired by the famous French chef Albert Roux. The *à la carte* menu is pricey, but the short daily menu – which includes half a bottle of wine and maybe *foie gras, confit* of duck and blueberry mousse – is a real bargain.

➕ 203 E4 ⊠ Oudezijds Voorburgwal 197 ☎ 020 555 3560 🕙 Daily noon–11

Centra Spaans Restaurant $–$$

What looks like a dive on an innocuous but bustling side street in the Red Light District is in fact a favorite locals' haunt. They continue returning to this Spanish oasis for a *tapas* selection that includes the usual tortilla, chorizo, olives and manchego cheese, and also traditional dishes such as paella and zarzuela. Regulars don't mind sharing the bench-style tables with first-time visitors, and as the night grows long, the conversation becomes livelier. Like the food, the Rioja house wine is reasonably priced. Save room for the flan.

➕ 201 F1 ⊠ Lange Niezel 29 ☎ 020 622 3050 🕙 Daily from 1 p.m.–11 p.m.

Dorrius $$

This is one of the best places in town to sample traditional Dutch dishes such as smoked eel, pea soup and hearty *hutspot* stews. Occupying a pair of tottering canal houses and founded in 1890, the restaurant looks thoroughly traditional, with paneled walls, beams and a black-and-white marble floor. It manages to retain its old-fashioned atmos-

phere despite now being part of the modern Crowne Plaza hotel. Most diners are foreigners. The staff provides first-rate service.

➕ 201 F2 ⊠ Nieuwezijds Voorburgwal 5 ☎ 020 420 2224 🕙 Daily 5 p.m.–11 p.m.

Het Karbeel $–$$

By day, this 16th-century building in the heart of the Red Light District is a busy sandwich shop. After 6 p.m. it is transformed into an intimate bistro specializing in mouth-watering fondues – for example, blue cheese, traditional, mushroom, as well as a *fondue du jour*. There are also soups and salads and a few decadent desserts. Wines are prominently displayed and there are several good ones by the glass. The service is friendly as well as efficient, something of a rarity in Amsterdam.

➕ 201 F1 ⊠ Warmoesstraat 58 ☎ 020 627 4995 🕙 Daily 9:30–6, sandwiches and drinks; 6–10 p.m. dinner

Kantjil & de Tijger $–$$

Unlike most of the city's Indonesian establishments, the "Antelope and the Tiger" is a large, austere and modern-looking restaurant with a busy buzz to it. It serves some of the best Indonesian food in Amsterdam, and there are extensive explanations on English menus of all the various options. As well as three types of full-blown *rijstafel*, you can order an inexpensive mini-*rijstafel*, where all the dishes come on a single plate. Service is quick, if impersonal.

🕂 203 D4 ☒ Spuistraat 291-293
☎ 020 620 0994 ⏰ Daily
4:30 p.m.–11 p.m.

Kinderkookkafe $

In this unique restaurant, children dressed in chefs' hats prepare the food (fully supervised, of course), as well as serve the drinks and wait on tables. The cozy little room's decor takes a particular kind of licorice candy as its theme. Parents drop off their offspring (they must

be over eight for Saturday dinner, over five for Sunday high tea), and return later in the day to eat the food they have cooked – possibly Belgian or Italian dishes, or sausage rolls and meringues – with them. Reservations are essential.

🕂 203 E4 ☒ Oudezijds
Achterburgwal 193 ☎ 020 625 3257
⏰ Sat. cooking from 3:30 p.m.,
dinner at 6 p.m.; Sun. cooking from
2:30 p.m., high tea at 5 p.m.

Lucius $$–$$$

Huge ceiling fans keep this long, narrow and busy Dutch/French seafood bistro from overheating. While waiters bustle amid tiled walls, marble-topped tables and an aquarium, you can peruse black-boards detailing platters of *fruits de mer*, mussels and fries and local oysters. Other specialties include blue shark, smoked eel and herring served with old *jenver*. To keep the cost down, there is a small selection of set meals. The wine list is long, impressive and expensive. Service is

not quite as polished as the tables, but the food arrives prepared to perfection.

🕂 203 D4 ☒ Spuistraat 247 ☎ 020
624 1831 ⏰ 5 p.m.–midnight

Maximiliaan Cafe-Restaurant $–$$

This friendly establishment, not far from the Waag in the rough-and-tumble Zeedijk quarter, makes its excellent beer on the premises. Visitors can sometimes watch the process during the day when the brewer approaches the impressive copper kettle. There are at least four types of the house brew on tap (which change according to the season) as well as many other brands by the bottle. If you get hungry, there are basic sandwiches and snacks in the afternoon and delicious, straightforward meals of fish, chicken and steak in the evening.

🕂 203 F5 ☒ Kloveniersburgwal 6–8
☎ 020 626 6280 ⏰ Tue., Wed., Sun.
3 p.m.–1 a.m.; Thu. noon–1 a.m.; Fri.,
Sat. noon–3 a.m.

Nam Kee $

A local restaurant guide gives this no-frills Chinese restaurant – one of several in the area – first prize for food and value for the money out of 450 places to eat in Amsterdam. In the two plain white-tiled and cramped dining rooms, you may have to share a table – the restaurant is invariably packed with Chinese and non-Chinese alike. The menu offers giant portions of delicious fried noodles, along with lots of sweet and sour and *teppan* dishes. Service is, at best, brusque.

🕂 204 A4 ☒ Zeedijk 111 ☎ 020
624 3470 ⏰ Daily 11:30 a.m.–midnight

Supper Club $$$

In this windowless, stark white warehouse of a room, you eat off your lap reclining on long rows of mattresses arranged along walls like giant bunk beds. You're entertained by mellow music, cinematic images such as rocket launches and naked swimmers projected onto one wall, and maybe live music and dance. You can take a massage between courses. Go for the whole sensual experience, not for the mediocre international food. Everyone eats the same dishes, served by nubile young waiters and waitresses at the same time: set aside four hours.

Vermeer $$$

With its beamed ceilings, brass chandeliers and marble floors, the Vermeer occupies one of the many 17th-century houses incorporated into the otherwise modern Golden Tulip Barbizon Palace Hotel. It's as formal a place to dine as anywhere in Amsterdam. Edwin Kats' modern French cooking is very highly rated. As well as an extensive set menu, there are more affordable set meals that might include such dishes as asparagus flan with a frog's leg and broad bean ragout, and poached pigeon with foie gras-filled crepes. You can opt to have different glasses of wine with each course.

🕂 203 D5 🖂 Jonge Roelensteeg 21
☎ 020 638 0513 🕘 Daily 8 p.m.–1 a.m.

d'Vijff Vlieghen $$$

With nine dining-rooms spread through five 17th-century canal houses, the "Five Flies" is a romantic, Golden Age timewarp. You may be lucky enough to end up sitting next to an original Rembrandt etching or in a chair once occupied by Elvis Presley or John Wayne. Every seat bears a little plaque naming a famous visitor. The modern Dutch cooking – maybe a timbale of smoked eel or saddle of hare with sauerkraut – is imaginative and beautifully presented, and the set seasonal menu is a good value. Service is formal and the clientele mostly well-heeled foreigners.

🕂 204 A5 🖂 Prins Hendrikkade 59
☎ 020 556 48 85 🕘 Mon.–Fri.
noon–3 and 6–10, Sat. 6–10

🕂 203 D4 🖂 Spuistraat 294-302
☎ 020 624 8369 🕘 Daily
5:30 p.m.–11 p.m.

Where to... Shop

For the most part, shopping in the city center isn't as enjoyable as elsewhere in Amsterdam. Kalverstraat and Nieuwendijk, the city's main shopping thoroughfares, are bustling (especially on the weekends) and rather dreary, though they do have Amsterdam's best range of everyday shops. Beyond these streets lie a few pleasant surprises, such as the grandiose Magna Plaza mall and, in among the graphic sex emporia of the Red Light District, some fun and some very old shops.

Kalverstraat and Rokin

Named after a calf market that was held in this area during the 15th century, pedestrianized Kalverstraat is lined with outlets of unremarkable clothing chains. However, you can usually find a jaunty barrel organ somewhere along it, with attendants who rattle their collection tins in time with the music. The southern (Muntplein) end has more style.

Worth a browse are the department stores of **Maison de Bonneterie** (royal appointed and upscale, with chandeliers under its dome and a chic café) and **Vroom & Dreesman** (part of a nationwide mid-price chain, with the excellent La Place café – ▶ 72).

Across the street is the newish **Kalvertoren shopping mall**: its most interesting feature is its glass-towered café, which enjoys wide views over the canals. **Waterstone's** (No. 185) and the **American Book Center** (No. 152) both specialize in English-language publications and have a good selection of books on Amsterdam and all things Dutch.

While at the Muntplein, browse in the **Gallery de Munt** in the old gatetower (▶ 58): dating from

1890, the rather stuffy shop specializes in Delftware and Makkumware. Ask to be shown the antique pieces kept upstairs.

Rokin, which runs parallel to Kalverstraat, is a busy tram thoroughfare not particularly pleasant for a stroll. However, it has a few enjoyable old-fashioned antiques shops such as **Premsela & Hamburger** (No. 120), which has dealt in silverware since 1823. Rokin's one unmissable shop, however – whether or not you are a smoker – is the tobacco shop **PGC Hajenius** (Nos. 92–96). The art deco, marble-walled interior looks much as it did when it was designed in 1915. There are displays of handmade clay pipes, a wall of humidor lockers rented by clients, a bar, a library of books on smoking, and often cigar tastings.

Around Dam

De Bijenkorf (Dam 1), which translates as The Beehive, is the most famous department store in

the country. While not exactly a Harrods or Macy's, it has the requisite cosmetics counters on the ground floor, along with a good café with picture windows onto the Damrak and clubwear and glow-in-the-dark handcuffs in its trendy Chill Out collection on the sixth floor.

Across the square is the **Amsterdam Diamond Center** (Rokin 1–5), where you can watch cutters at work and buy watches as well as diamonds. The shops just around the corner on Damstraat peddle classic Dutch souvenirs such as cheeses, clogs and canal-house fridge magnets.

Just west of the square behind the Royal Palace on Nieuwezijds Voorburgwal is the **Magna Plaza shopping mall**, housed in a splendid neo-Gothic building that used to be the city's main post office. It's devoted mainly to clothes boutiques (look out for **America Today**, where staff slide between floors down a fireman's pole), and

has a large **Virgin Megastore** in the basement. Beer-drinkers should not miss the liquor store **De Bierkoning** (▶ 34) around the corner at Paleisstraat 125, which sells more makes of beer than Amsterdam has cafés.

Nieuwendijk

This major shopping street is a poor relation of Kalverstraat. Few of the cheap-and-not-so-cheerful shops on this scruffy pedestrian street are likely to detain you on your way between Dam and the train station. One exception, however, may be **Oud Amsterdam** (No. 75), a specialty liqueur shop that is worth visiting if only to take a look at its amazing collection of miniatures – 14,852 at the last count, apparently a world record.

Spuikwartier

Better known for its cafés and restaurants, this area also has a concentration of new and second-hand bookshops and a book market

(▶ 77). Also of interest on Spuistraat is **Dom** (No. 283), for unusual items for the home such as inflatable sofas.

For pleasures such as home-made ice-cream and apple turnovers, pop in to **Lanskroon** (Singel 385 just off Spui): the *pâtisserie* has a tiny sit-down area.

Around the Red Light District and Nieuwmarkt

Among the grungy coffee shops on Warmoesstraat are a few considerably more civilized establishments. Royal-appointed and wonderfully aromatic **Wijs & Zonen** (No. 102) looks as if it has been transplanted from a different era – which is borne out by the fact that it has been a purveyor of teas and coffees since 1828, while **Himalaya** (No. 56) specializes in New Age books, wind chimes and trance music, and has a pleasant café at the rear.

Just south of the Nieuwmarkt at Kloveniersburgwal 12 is **Jacob Hooy**. Founded in 1743, this timewarp pharmacy is lined with 19th-century drawers and earthenware jars labeled with dozens of medicinal herbs and spices. It also specializes in aromatherapy remedies and health foods.

Farther down Kloveniersburgwal, at No. 39, is the long-established **Head Shop**, with books on how to roll the perfect joint and all sorts of dope-smoking paraphernalia.

Little Nieuwe Hoogstraat is an unexpected oasis of innocence. It is lined with gift-oriented boutiques. **Knuffels** (No. 11) is a children's toy shop with a delightful collection of mobiles and clogs. **De Hoed Van Tijn** (No. 15) an elegant hat shop, and **Joe's Vliegerwinkel** (No. 19) specializes in kites (custom-made on request) and other flying toys such as frisbees and boomerangs.

Just down the street is the **Rembrandthuis** (▶66), whose shop sells good-quality reproductions of Rembrandt etchings, among other souvenirs.

MARKETS

Nieuwmarkt (May–Sep. Sun. 9–5): antiques. **Oudemanhuispoort** (Mon.–Sat. 10–4): this moody passageway through the university has a few permanent second-hand book stands under its arches.

Spui (Fri. 10–6): second-hand and antiquarian books and prints; (Mar.–Dec., Sun. 10–6): a few stands selling decent modern art.

Waterlooplein (Mon.–Sat. 9–5): the city's best and liveliest flea-market used to be even larger and livelier before the erection of the massive city hall and opera complex in the 1980s on what's now an unlovely modern square. It's good for things such as leather jackets, second-hand records, film posters and bicycle chains. Many visitors just come to rummage through the piles of unwanted clothes or nose around the stands with an obligatory plastic tray of fries and mayonnaise in hand.

Where to...
Be Entertained

A night out in the city center can be as seamy or as sophisticated as you wish. You could take in the repulsive yet compulsive spectacle of the Red Light District or spend an evening at the opera or listening to modern jazz.

The Red Light District and Surrounding Area

At night, purple neon, not red, pervades the streets bounded by Zeedijk, Warmoesstraat and a rough line drawn between Dam and Nieuwmarkt. It lights up the prostitutes posing in the windows flashing come-hither smiles one second, looking thoroughly bored the next. Though there are plenty of men prowling around and sizing up their options, many passersby are simply curious tourists. Like it or not, the Red Light District is one of the city's biggest tourist attractions. Few people are hassled in any way and, thanks to the large numbers who come in the evenings to gawk, and to a conspicuous police presence, the main thoroughfares feel safe. However, the back alleys, particularly those off the southern end of Zeedijk, are best avoided.

Zeedijk, once a virtual no-go area, has been heavily cleaned up over the last decade, though homeless people and junkies do still hang out here. Its more respectable northern end is lined with restaurants and several cafes with character, such as **De Ooievaar** (▶72) and, facing it at No. 1 Zeedijk, **In 't Aepjen**. Translating as "In the

Monkeys," this ancient timber-framed building used to be a flophouse where penniless sailors could pay for a bed with their monkey. Now it's full of art and antiques, including painted wall panels of elegant ladies, salvaged from a music hall.

Nieuwmarkt, ringed with more cafés, is also far more salubrious than it once was. Its most interesting haunt is **In de Waag** (▶ 72). If you're looking for an unpretentious brown café, **'t Loosje** (Nieuwmarkt 32) should fit the bill; **Maximiliaan**, just south at Kloveniersburgwal 6–8, is an excellent microbrewery (▶ 74).

Seedy Warmoesstraat must have more coffee shops than any other street in Amsterdam. Intermingled with them are gay venues such as **Getto** (No. 51), a kitsch cocktail bar with DJs that is one of the street's more welcoming and civilized establishments. Loud live rock music is the attraction most nights at **Winston Kingdom** (No. 123).

Spuikwartier

The area around Spuistraat south of Raadhuisstraat has a concentration of restaurants, cafés and bars to suit every pocket and taste, including some of the city's best brown and grand cafes and trendiest bars. The majority can be found at the southern end of Spuistraat and on Spui. As well as those recommended on pages 70–73, **Café Dante** (Spuistraat 320) is worth a visit: its young clientele can be as good-looking as the art on display upstairs. More hip late-night bars are clustered on Nieuwezijds Voorburgwal just south of Dam, such as the **Seymour Likely Lounge** (No. 250 – the one that helpfully says "it's a bar" over the window). Owned by artists, its decor changes – 1960s flower power was a recent look – though the aquarium seems to be a permanent feature.

Music and Theater Venues

The **Muziektheater** (1–3 Amstel, tel: 020 625 5455), Amsterdam's opera house, forms a single complex with the Stadhuis, or city hall. Its construction in the 1980s alongside Waterlooplein at the heart of the old Jewish neighborhood caused enormous controversy. The campaigners' rallying cry has stuck in the complex's nickname, the Stopera. The imposing marble, brick and glass structure is home to the Netherlands Opera and National Ballet. From September through May, free half-hour concerts take place on Tuesday at 12:30 p.m. in the **Boekmanzaal**, a minor hall, and throughout the year you can take a backstage tour on Saturdays at 3 p.m. (reserve on 020 551 8054). For sold-out performances, try your luck at obtaining an unclaimed ticket by asking for a numbered slip at the ticket office an hour before the show.

Beurs van Berlage (Damrak 213, tel: 020 627 0466; www.orkest.nl), the old Beurs (stock exchange) designed by Hendrik Berlage and completed in 1903, is a prime example of the Amsterdam School of architecture. Exhibitions often occupy the impressive main hall, while the Netherlands Philharmonic and Chamber orchestras perform in two further halls – one of which has, as its "stage," a giant, free-standing glass box.

The Bimhuis (Oudeschans 73–7, tel: 020 623 1361; www.bimhuis.nl), up and running since 1974, is Amsterdam's top venue for jazz. A respectful audience comes to listen to mainly improvizational modern jazz in its large auditorium. Concert nights are usually Thursday through Saturday, with free freestyle workshops on Tuesdays. An appealing bar overlooks the canal.

The **Amsterdam Marionette Theater** (Nieuwe Jonkerstraat 8, tel: 020 620 8027; www.marionettentheater.nl) presents shows with wooden puppets in the classical European mold. Operas are its specialty; the theater itself was once a blacksmith's.

Canal Ring –
West

Getting Your Bearings

The most romantic photographs of Amsterdam are taken in the western part of the city – which is also where the real soul of Amsterdam resides. Beautiful canals and calm courtyards coexist with some of the trendiest, and most wayward, locals. Almost any street you walk along is likely to reveal at least one of the following: a lovely old house embellished with a beautiful tablet or gable; an intriguing shop or café; or a good canal view.

The best way to get an overview of the area is to take a boat trip, then to walk around its fascinating streets.

The hub of Bohemian lifestyles is the Jordaan, the working-class fringe of Amsterdam that has become the most sought-after neighborhood in the city. Some new residents are living in the elegant old *hofjes* (almshouses) that dot the district, most of which tolerate visitors. Between the Jordaan and the city center, the "Nine Streets" area is another up-and-coming place with good cafés and restaurants squeezed into a neat three-by-three grid.

Going farther west, fashionableness now extends to a disused gasworks. Most visitors stick to a fairly narrow strip from the Anne Frank House via the Westerkerk to the entertainment zone around Leidseplein, but it is well worth straying away from the beaten tourist trail to discover the Amsterdam that entrances the locals.

The canals offer the best viewpoints for the city

Previous page: The Jordaan at dusk

★ Don't Miss

At Your Leisure

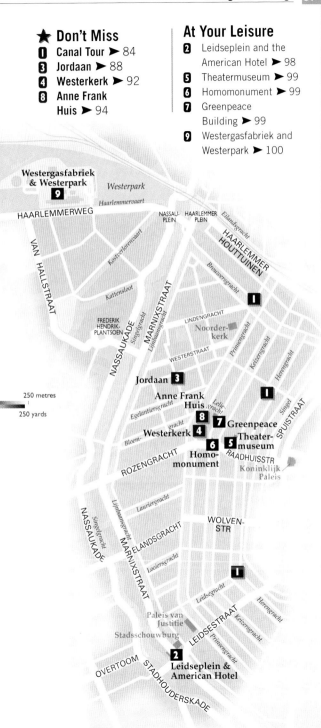

A day spent in this sublimely beautiful area gives glimpses into both the Golden Age and the 21st century, with places of interest ranging from the humorous to the heartrending.

Canal Ring – West in a Day

9:00 a.m.

Beat the crowds – and the canal-jams – with the first boat of the day around the **canals** (▶ 84–87). You will circumnavigate the whole city, but the prettiest and most interesting parts are around the western canal ring.

10:00 a.m.

Wander over to **Leidseplein** (▶ 98) before it gets too overrun with beer-drinking dope-smoking tourists. Enjoy a coffee at an outdoor terrace – or, on a cool or damp day – warm up instead in the opulent Café Américain at the **American Hotel** (▶ 98).

11:00 a.m.

Walk north and work up an appetite for lunch with a long stroll around **Jordaan** (▶ 88–91), admiring some superb views and visiting one or two of the *hofjes* (courtyards) that offer sanctuary from the city.

1:00 p.m.

From anywhere in the Jordaan, you are not far from lunch at a café in the chic and cheerful 9 Straatjes, or "Nine Streets" (▶ 105). Then perhaps go window shopping; this is the area where you will find some of Amsterdam's most imaginative stores.

2:30 p.m.

At the northwest corner of Nine Streets you will find the **Westerkerk**
(► 92–93), the location for royal marriages and the (now lost) tomb of
Rembrandt. On the hour, climb the stairs to the top of the tower, or explore
the beautiful canal house that is home to the **Theatermuseum** (► 99)
across on Herengracht. Afterward, admire the **Homomonument** (► 99) –
a testimony to tolerance, and the handsome headquarters
of **Greenpeace** (► 99).

4:00 p.m.

Have another break for coffee, perhaps at the bizarre Café Chris (► 101) close
by on Bloemstraat or, on a fine day at one of the canalside cafés.

5:30 p.m.

Take advantage of the late
opening hours to visit the
Anne Frank Huis (left,
► 94–97) when it's
quieter than usual, and allow
time to wind down afterward.

7:30 p.m.

You have your choice of brown
cafés for an aperitif.
Alternately, you can head for
Leidseplein for some pils and
people-watching.

8:00 p.m.

Dinner, accompanied by jazz
at De Doffer (► 102), or by
theatricality at the budget-
busting Blakes (► 103) is a great way to finish off the evening – unless you are
considering investigating the nightlife.

10:00 p.m.

Blow the rest of your cash – or make a fortune – at the Holland Casino
(► 107). Or check out the music at the Melkweg or Paradiso (► 108), two of
Amsterdam's finest venues.

Canal Tour

Two-and-a-half-million tourists take a tour each year around Amsterdam's canals aboard a combined fleet of nearly 100 sightseeing boats. The city was made to be enjoyed from the water. At a gentle pace you can appreciate the grace of the canal houses, the profusion of greenery and the appeal of canalside living.

Choosing Your Tour

Each operator has a different starting point and itinerary. Intense competition between the rival companies keeps prices low and standards high. Most companies use a pre-recorded commentary played from a laptop computer; one company which still uses a real-life narrator and offers an appealing route through some of the best waterscapes is Amsterdam Canal Cruises, just opposite the Heineken Brewery.

Below left: The Heineken Brewery is a handy land-mark for the Amsterdam Canal Cruises starting point

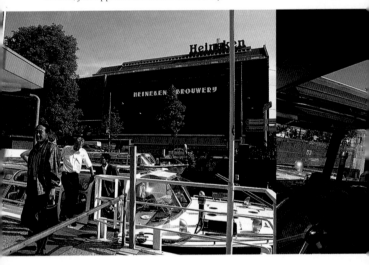

Circuit of the City

This itinerary is based on the Amsterdam Canal Cruises tour (► 87 for details). Like most routes, it goes clockwise around Amsterdam and takes in the Amstel River, the natural waterway that led to the city's foundation. (Some tours go counterclock-wise and avoid the Amstel altogether.)

Notable sights are the **sluice gates**, the grand **Carré Theater** and the **Magere Brug** (► 150–151). Dominating the east bank between Keizersgracht and Herengracht is the handsome **Amstelhof**, one of the city's very first refuges.

The favorite canal on the ring is the **Herengracht**, and the

Above: An open-top boat provides the best panorama

Managing the Water

The level of Amsterdam's water is kept constant thanks to a system of locks. Local people say the 10-foot depth is actually made up of one-third water, another of bicycles and a third of mud. The bicycles are periodically removed, along with old refrigerators, bedframes and anything else that can reliably sink without a trace.

Amsterdam Canal Cruises tour plies its entire length. At the junction with **Reguliersgracht**, the "Seven Bridges Canal," the boat slows to give everyone a view of the identical humped bridges stretching off along the canal.

The standard route enters **Brouwersgracht**, one of the loveliest stretches in Amsterdam, before turning north (an awkward maneuver) into Singel and onward through a succession of bridges into the IJ River. The sense of breaking free from the city can be liberating – though if a big cruise ship is bearing down it can also feel intimidating.

The stretch of open water lasts about half a mile, taking you past the unattractive rear of **Centraal Station** and giving a rare view of **Amsterdam Noord**, including the headquarters of the

Below right: Some of the city's bridges are a tight squeeze for sightseeing boats

Right: The "Seven Bridges Canal" is a must for photographers

Houseboats

The dwellings of all shapes and sizes that are moored to the banks of Amsterdam's canals are a relatively new addition to the city's waterscape. The practice of living aboard houseboats began at the end of World War II, when there was a scarcity of housing in the city. Now, there are around 4,000 – the majority legitimate, with access to electricity and drinking water, and around 1,500 illegal but "tolerated." Many are made from the blackened hulks of old steel freight barges; every few years, these have to be towed to a shipyard for the soundness of their hulls to be checked. Increasingly, though, the design is a concrete box. This requires no maintenance and gives a much greater living area – it is possible to have a floor below the surface of the canal (look for narrow windows just above the waterline for evidence of this). On top of the concrete base, some people have built proper brick houses, sometimes with a garden or patio area. Even for the legal houseboats, there is no sewage system except the canals themselves. This is why the waterways have to be flushed out frequently, a carefully managed process that involves pumping through water from the Amstel River.

To see what life is like aboard, you could visit the **Houseboat Museum** (Woonboot Museum – tel: 020 427 0750, open Tue.–Sun. 10–5, inexpensive), moored on the west bank of Prinsengracht, just south of its intersection with Berenstraat.

huge oil multinational Royal Dutch Shell. The vessel turns south under two swing bridges – one carrying eight railway tracks into the main station – and into **Oosterdok.** This used to be the main harbor of Amsterdam until the railway closed it off from the IJ. Your field of vision is filled by the vast copper "hull" of the **newMetropolis Science and Technology Center** (► 69). Leaving this to the right, you approach a highlight of the tour: the chance to see the replica clipper *De Amsterdam* (► 148) at close quarters. In particular, admire the wonderful figure-head and the stern decorated to resemble a city mansion.

Most vessels turn around here to go back past newMetropolis and home to their moorings; the Amsterdam Canal Cruises trip carries on around **Nieuwe Herengracht**, into the Amstel once more and back to base on Singelgracht.

Life afloat in Amsterdam can be blissful

Canal Tours
✉ Most cruise companies: in and around the Damrak basin opposite Centraal Station. Kooij: outside the Allard Pierson Museum on the Binnen Amstel canal

Amsterdam Canal Cruises
✉ North bank of Singelgracht directly opposite the Heineken Brewery
🕐 First tours generally depart at around 9 a.m., last at 4, 5 or 6 p.m. (earlier in winter, later in summer), with special cruises in the evenings. The scheduled departure of the next vessel is usually shown on a clock face at the company terminal, but these times should be taken with a grain of salt

he city's
anals are full
f activity

CANAL TOURS: INSIDE INFO

Top tips Such is the extent of competition that **buying a ticket in advance** can undercut the "turn-up-and-go" price – budget hotels and backpacker hostels sometimes advertize discounts of one-third or more.
• Don't board with a thirst or an empty stomach: **few of the vessels have any kind of refreshment facilities,** except for the evening dinner cruises.
• **Canal Bike** (tel: 020 626 5574, open 10–6 approximately) offers a "rent it here, leave it there" service of two-person pedal-boats for do-it-yourself tours between any of four locations at key tourist sites. You can pick up and/or drop off a Canal Bike at three points in the western canal ring – the north side of Leidseplein, Keizersgracht where Leidsestraat crosses it, and outside the Anne Frank Huis. The fourth option is the company's main base, on Weteringschans, close to the Rijksmuseum entrance.

How to avoid the crowds In summer, 80 or more canal boats can be on the water during the day, along with numerous smaller craft and dozens of erratically steered Canal Bikes. Congestion can be severe, adding a lot of time to the average trip. Some departures may be fully booked with tour groups. **Try to be aboard one of the first departures of the day,** at around 9 a.m.; beginning at 10 a.m., the "rush-hour" begins and lasts until 5 or 6 p.m.

Jordaan

Nowhere in Amsterdam is better preserved than this former working-class area, and anywhere you wander within the tight web of streets and canals is likely to reward you with a rich mix of impressive architecture, intriguing shops, dreamy views and a village ambience. These pages provide a walk that can be used as a basis for exploring the area, from which you can (and should) deviate at will, maybe with a glimpse into one or more of the hidden courtyards that make the Jordaan so special.

The Golden Age of the 17th century was accompanied by a population explosion as Amsterdam enticed craftspeople and drew fortune-seekers from all over Europe. As the wealthy staked their claims around the new canal ring, an area of high-density housing was created beyond it in what had been green fields. The name "Jordaan" derives from the French word *jardin*, though with tens of thousands of people packed into the area, there was little resemblance to a garden. The area forms a finger of land curling around the west of the canal ring, flanked by Prinsengracht to the east and Lijnbaansgracht to the west. The northern boundary is Brouwersgracht, with Looiersgracht marking the southern edge – and the start of this stroll.

Jordaan is home to plenty of quirky shops

The quirky quality of the Jordaan is immediately apparent at the **Rommelmarkt** at No. 38 (► 107). At first this indoor market may appear to be an (only slightly) upscale version of the flea-market at Waterlooplein, and you will not be surprized to learn that *rommel* translates as "rummage." But there are some genuine antiques to be discovered beneath the piles of 1970s vinyl discs and stone-age electronic equipment.

Northeast along **Looiersgracht** is one of many superb viewpoints: climb to the middle of the bridge for fine vistas along each side of the canal. Then amble through the fancy shops along **Looiersdwarsstraat** and its continuation, **Hazenstraat,** to find just the grade of olive oil you need (► 106). Your reverie may be rudely interrupted by the only big street in the Jordaan: **Rozengracht.** With four tram routes and lots of traffic cutting through a rather down-at-heel string of shops, it seems disconnected from the rest of the neighborhood.

Once safely across, you hit **Bloemstraat** – but don't expect too many blooms along this street, nor many others in the Jordaan. Walk toward the unmistakable tower of the

Westerkerk (▶ 92–93), which serves as an instant beacon for the befuddled tourist (or local). Before you reach it, turn left along **2e Leliedwarsstraat;** this will take you to the area where several *hofjes* (▶ 90) are concentrated. Zigzag toward **Westerstraat**, making sure you take the **1e Leliedwarsstraat** bridge over **Egelantiersgracht** for perhaps the finest canal perspective in Amsterdam.

Westerstraat is the *de facto* Main Street for the Jordaan, but its appeal is muted because of all the parked cars. Take the street heading north from the center of **Lindengracht,** and within five minutes you will emerge at the northernmost point of the Jordaan.

From here, you can embark on Walk 1 (▶ 174–177) or Walk 3 (▶ 181–183), venture westward to **Westergasfabriek** and **Westerpark** (▶ 100), or just wander back a different way to see more facets of this multi-dimensional district.

Egelantiers-
gracht, one of
the most photo-
genic canals in
Amsterdam

The *Hofjes* of Jordaan

The Jordaan hides its secrets well. Behind a succession of innocuous doorways are hidden courtyards, most built by the high and mighty for the benefit of the poor and lowly. They tended to shelter the elderly of a particular religious denomination, and some of them still adhere to the original faith. These *hofjes* range in style from collections of houses spilling onto a workaday yard, to prim cottages precisely arranged around well-kept gardens. These can be found in other parts of Amsterdam, too, but the highest concentration is to be found in the Jordaan.

If you have time to visit only one Jordaan *hofje*, make it **Karthuizerhof.** Grander and lovelier than all the others, the Huyz-Zitten Weduwen Hofje (the names of the founders) consists of a large courtyard whose central point of interest is a pair of ornate water pumps. All the dwellings are arranged strictly symmetrically, as was the style in the mid-17th century, when it was built. Note how, on the upper level, a space has been left where a window should be, helping to reveal the extent of the *hofje*.

Claes Claesz Hofje, Egelantiersstraat 34–54, is one of the most accessible *hofjes* (open 24 hours). It is buried in a tightly packed area of the Jordaan and merges with the houses on Egelantiersstraat, the parallel Tuinstraat and Eerste Egelantiersdwarstraat, where the main entrance is located. Claes Claesz was a Mennonite textile merchant who founded the *hofje* in 1626. It consists of three linked courtyards in which the greenery runs wild and is nowadays a residence hall for music students. On wet days it is sometimes also used as a refuge by dope-smokers. There is a second entrance around the corner, just next to a tavern that intrudes into one of the courtyards. If you exit through this doorway and look above the entrance to the tavern, you can see a particularly

Lively markets are a feature of Jordaan

**Right:
Karthuizerhof,
the grandest
hofje in Jordaan**

**Every archway
in Jordaan
reveals some
secret**

splendid tablet showing the coat of arms of Anslo, at
one time the Dutch name for the Norwegian capital of
Oslo.

St. Andrieshofje, Egelantiersstraat 107–114, toward
the far end of the street, is a complete contrast to the
Claes Claesz Hofje – a model of calm and order, with
well-tended gardens and demure cottages. Visitors are
allowed between 9 a.m. and 6 p.m., but outside these
hours the residents guard their privacy jealously.

You will be fortunate to find **Zevenkeurvorsten-
hofje,** Tuinstraat 187–221, open even during the day.
If you do, the reward is a concise courtyard that manages to shut out the city entirely. It now belongs to a
housing association; the waiting list for residence is
lengthy.

The most attractive feature of **Bosschehofje,**
Palmgracht 20–26, is the main entrance as seen from
the street. High above the gate is a big, extravagant tablet;
beneath that, a porthole and a keystone above a stout brick
archway. Inside, it is like any ordinary communal living space,
with children scuttling and laundry drying, though there are
good views over the back wall to the rear of some handsome
houses.

Jordaan
✉ 202 B2

JORDAAN: INSIDE INFO

Top tips The alignment of the streets and canals in Jordaan mean that the **best
light for photography** is usually in the late afternoon.
• If you find yourself in Amsterdam for **Queen's Day on April 30,** the Jordaan is a
good place to celebrate.

Hidden gem To experience life on an Amsterdam houseboat, **check out the
Houseboat Museum** (▶ 86) moored on Prinsengracht at Johnny Jordaan Plein.

Westerkerk

Of all the handsome churches in Amsterdam, this is the most central to the life of the city – and, indeed, to the country. The tower – a miracle of construction, given the soupy geology – dominates western Amsterdam and Amsterdammers consider it a blessing to have been born within the sound of the Westerkerk's carillon, a mark that identifies them with the densely populated and dearly loved neighborhood west of the city center.

The Westerkerk, one of the city's first Prostestant churches, was built by Hendrick de Keyser (1565–1621) and opened on Whit Sunday 1631. The tower, which was completed seven years later, is nearly 280 feet high, and contains the city's heaviest bell.

The church is assertively plain, in deliberate contrast to the Catholic tradition. The box pews are the most elaborate furnishings: wealthy families would buy up a separate section to keep them apart from the proletariat. The large, ornate organ above the west door was added more than 50 years after the church was completed; before that, there had been heated debates about whether musical accompaniment was appropri-

A view of Westerkerk from Keizersgracht

ate. Supported on marble columns with the assistance of a cherub or two, it provides the one touch of extravagance in the whole church. The decoration is most effusive on the shutters depicting Old Testament scenes.

The most notable person to be buried in the Westerkerk is so well hidden that no-one knows where he is. Rembrandt was buried in a rented grave, but after 20 years or so his remains were moved to make room for more burials. An optimistic memorial on the north side of the church claims that "Here lies buried R. Harmensz Van Ryn, Born 15 July 1606, Died 4 October 1669."

A climb to the top of the tower is rewarded with a fine panorama; it bills itself as the "Best View of the City." In the 17th century, as well as glorifying God (and the city), the tower also served as an early-warning station with a permanent look-out alert for fires or dambursts. The base of the tower is made

The climb to the tower reveals a new panorama of Amsterdam

of brick, but beyond the first gallery the structure is wooden with a facing of sandstone or lead, thus reducing the tower's weight. The circle at the center of the floor on the first gallery, now filled in, was used to haul up materials and bells. At the fourth gallery you can see the beams that were added to absorb the vibrations from the 8-ton hour bell; without them, the tower could shake itself apart.

TAKING A BREAK

There are plenty of possibilities around the Westerkerk. **Van Puffelen** (➤ 104) is just south, though it is open for lunch only on weekends. Going north along Prinsengracht, the **Pancake Bakery** (➤ 104) is a reliable standby.

Westerkerk
➕ 202 C5
✉ Prinsengracht 281
☎ 020 624 7766
⏰ Note that opening is erratic; official hours: church Apr. 10–Sep. 15, Mon.–Fri. 11–3; Jun.–Aug., Sat. 11–3. Sunday services are in Dutch and take about 1½ hours; tower tours Apr.–Sep., daily 10–5, on the hour
🚋 13, 14, 17, 20
💶 Church: free; tower: inexpensive

WESTERKERK: INSIDE INFO

Top tip The tower climb is not too difficult for able-bodied people, though **the steeper sections toward the top require special care.** Those who suffer from vertigo can be reassured that the barrier around the platform at the top is both high and solid.

Anne Frank Huis

A prettier place is hard to imagine: in the benevolent shadow of the Westerkerk, on one of Amsterdam's loveliest canals, stands a well-proportioned merchant's house built in 1635. Yet behind its handsome exterior lay a sanctuary, a prison and, ultimately, a place of betrayal. It is now a shrine to the victims of World War II, and in particular to a teenager whose eloquence has endured into the 21st century.

Below: Anne's diary was found lying on the floor after the family was arrested

Left: Anne Frank – a life cut tragically short

For 25 months, the Frank family and the Van Pels family lived in fear in the annex at Prinsengracht 263. As the war drew to a close they were discovered and deported. Only Otto Frank, the father of Anne and Margot, survived; the others perished in Nazi death camps. When Otto returned to the house, one of the people who had helped them hide returned Anne's diaries, which were published to wide acclaim.

Above:
Prinsengracht
263 in 1940

Top: The house
today, now a
museum

The house where they had hidden remained empty for years. In the late 1950s a plan was put forward to demolish it, which led a number of prominent citizens to establish the Anne Frank Foundation. Its primary goal is the preservation of the annex, but increasingly the foundation is concerned with education about the dangers of racism.

Anne Frank's story unfolds as you pass through a series of rooms on the prescribed tour. There are no guides: you proceed at your own pace. Having entered through the modern building at Prinsengracht 267, you pass some introductory exhibits in No. 265. You then enter the house on the ground floor at what was the warehouse and spice-grinding room.

Otto Frank had moved his family from the German city of Frankfurt in 1933, when Adolf Hitler came to power. In Amsterdam he set up two businesses: Opekta, making pectin as a gelling agent for jam, and a spice company called Gies & Co. The herbs and spices would provide an ideal excuse for blacking out the windows in the annex at the back of the house: they needed to be kept in the dark.

The Nazis invaded the Netherlands in May 1940 and gradually stripped the Jewish community of rights. Otto Frank, his wife Edith and their daughters Anne and Margot went into hiding on July 6, 1942 after Margot was called up for a "workforce project" in Germany, a euphemism for enforced deportation to the concentration camps. In a video on the **second floor,** Miep Gies – one of the family's helpers – explains how the family hid at the back of the residence that housed Otto's business. They were joined by one of Otto's business associates, Hermann van Pels, his wife Auguste and son Peter. In November, an eighth person arrived: Fritz Pfeffer, who had fled from Germany to Holland with his non-Jewish fiancée.

One of the key figures in the concealment was Victor Kugler, a manager for the company. You will pass through his office on the second floor. Sometimes at night, the hideaways would slip down to the office and listen to broadcasts from Britain. Otto

Frank even continued his involvement in the business, with Kugler's help.

On the **third floor** is the office shared by three other helpers: Johannes Kleiman, Miep Gies and Bep Voskuijl. On Saturday afternoons, the front office on the third floor acted as the bathroom for the Frank sisters. "We scrub ourselves in the dark," wrote Anne, "While the one who isn't in the bath looks out the window through a chink in the curtains." In the storeroom, exhibits show how persecution of Jews gradually increased during the German occupation. You then move in to the **annex.** Here, eight people were crammed into two floors, where they had to live in near silence to avoid being overheard by employees. The door was concealed by a bookcase containing a few dusty files. Beyond this, a narrow stairway leads up to the annex.

Above: Anne's room

Top: The bookcase that concealed the entrance to the hiding place

Each week, Victor Kugler brought Anne a copy of the magazine *Cinema and Theatre*; she cut out the pictures of idols and pinned them to the walls. She had kept her diary since her 13th birthday on June 12, 1942, a few weeks before they went into hiding: "I hope I will be able to confide everything to you," read her first entry. The last was on August 1, 1944, in which she wrote "A voice within me is sobbing."

You move from the annex into a bare, modern **exhibition room,** where the fate of the eight is explained. On August 4, 1944, German police were led here by Dutch collaborators. The eight were taken to a police station, then sent to Westerbork transit camp. Johannes Kleiman and Victor Kugler were also arrested, but eventually released. The prisoners were among the last to be despatched to Auschwitz from Westerbork. Hermann van Pels was gassed shortly after arrival. His wife and son were moved from camp to camp, and six months later died within a few days of each other from illness and hunger. Fritz Pfeffer perished from the same causes. Otto and Edith escaped the gas chamber, but Edith died from disease and malnutrition in January 1945. Anne and Margot ended up at Bergen-Belsen concentration camp, where they died in March from a typhus epidemic that spread through the camp.

After the war Otto Frank decided to fulfill Anne's wish that her diary be published, and the book first appeared in Dutch in 1947. Foreign translations followed quickly and it has been published in more than 60 languages.

TAKING A BREAK
The venue has a bright and pleasant café on the south side looking across to the Westerkerk.

Below: The attic where Anne and her family spent more than two years in hiding

Anne Frank Huis
- 200 C1
- Prinsengracht 263 (entrance at 267)
- 020 556 7100; www.annefrank.nl
- Sep.–Mar. 9–7, Apr.–Aug. 9–9, daily except Yom Kippur
- 13, 14, 17, 28
- Moderate

ANNE FRANK HUIS: INSIDE INFO

Top tips At the end of the tour, a series of **interactive video positions** allow you to research particular topics. These are slow and often crowded: go to the café/library, instead, where you can browse through a multilingual library of books about Anne Frank.

• Most visitors **find the experience very moving;** some are visibly distressed. Build in time to come to terms with what you have seen and heard before going on to your next destination.

At Your Leisure

2 Leidseplein and the American Hotel

Leidseplein comes to life at night

As with so many so things in Amsterdam, a sense of timing is important when visiting the hub of the city's many tourist trails. Mornings see the square spruced up after the previous night's excesses and the eastern light illuminating the American Hotel to good effect. The hotel (► 101) is Leidseplein's main attraction – a crazed art nouveau interpretation of a Scottish baronial castle. The exterior rewards a good, close inspection and the interior is also well worth investigating.

Start on the northeast corner where, beneath an arching window, there are decorations of storks on one face and squirrels on the other. The gable is enlivened by a stylized sunbeam. The main facade of the hotel, to the southeast, has a fishy fountain at the front. What may be of more interest, however, is to the left of the café entrance above the Nightwatch Bar: a relief showing the hotel itself. On the southern corner, a Venus figure appears on tiles, guarded by a pair of owls, a couple of serpents and a menacing-looking bat. The words "American Hotel" are picked out in a mosaic that has the look of embroidery. The rest of the awkwardly shaped square is not without

ppeal. The imposing Hirsch & Cie
eo-classical lump on the southern
dge is, like so many buildings in
msterdam these days, a bank. Along
Marnixstraat, which marks the
ortheast edge of the American Hotel,
ere is an attractive curve of houses –
ost of which have been converted to
otels. At the **AUB Ticketshop**
(➤ 47), built into the
tadsschouwberg, you can pick up
argains for shows the same day.

Most of the people who congregate
n Leidseplein have rather more
rosaic concerns, as symbolized by
he entertaining sight atop the grand
afé opposite: two clinking, foaming
5-foot-high glasses of Heineken.

he fascinating Theatermuseum

] Theatermuseum

Even if you have no interest in drama,
ou are likely to be enthralled by the
Theatermuseum. It is located in one
of the most beautiful 17th-century
mansions in Amsterdam. Built in
1638 on the site of a former bakery, it
has been well looked after ever since,
with new touches such as the fine
marble corridor added over the years.
The entrance to the museum is next
door to the **Bartolotti House,** an even
more lavish 17th-century creation.

This is far from a dry collection of
exhibits associated with theater: a
visit is more like attending a
performance. You may be equipped
with a radio receiver and a pair of
headphones and be dispatched on a
labyrinthine tour through the
beautiful old canal house; this was the
arrangement for the first nine months
of 2001.

The garden outside is one of the
hidden gems of Amsterdam, trans-
porting you from the busy streets to a
study in tranquillity. Birdsong fills the
void between the canal houses that
face on to Keizersgracht, while across
the fence the garden of the Bartolotti
House next door is populated by
elegant statues.

➕ 201 D1 ✉ Herengracht 168 ☎ 020
551 3300 🕙 Tue.–Fri. 11–5, Sat.–Sun.
1–5 🍴 Café with outdoor terrace ($)
🚋 13, 14, 17, 20 🎟 Moderate; free
admission to Museum Year Card holders
(except special exhibitions)

6 Homomonument

The city's tolerance is, once again,
evident, in the location – right next to
Westerkerk – of this monument to
men and women persecuted because
of their homosexuality. The triangular
slab of pink granite protruding into
the Keizersgracht is based on the pink
triangle symbol that gay men and
women were obliged to wear during
the German occupation. It is something of a shrine and you may see
people placing flowers there.

➕ 202 C5 ✉ Westermarkt 🕙 Always
accessible 🚋 13, 14, 17, 20

7 Greenpeace Building

Near the Westerkerk and Anne Frank
Huis you will find two contrasting but
complementary 20th-century additions to the area: the Homomonument
(➤ above) and the Greenpeace
Building. The latter, the organization's
international headquarters, occupies a
suitably verdant location on the
corner of Keizersgracht. The structure
is not, unfortunately, open to the
public, but it is well worth admiring
from outside. It began life in 1905 as

an office building for an insurance firm: the name of the Eerste Hollandsche Levensverzekeringsbank still appears on the facade, together with a mosaic showing an angel selling an insurance policy to a mother and child.

➕ 201 D1 ✉ Keizersgracht 174–176
🕐 Not open to the public 🚌 13, 14, 17, 20 stop two blocks south

9 Westergasfabriek and Westerpark

The western reaches of the city, particularly north of Haarlemmerweg, have long been overlooked, which helps explain why the Western Islands are so splendidly preserved. Squeezed between a canal and the main rail line, this triangle of land is occupied by a park and a weird and wonderful former gasworks, now transformed into an *avant-garde* arts venue (▶ 108). The Westergasfabriek is a cluster of buildings on the north side of the Haarlemmervaart canal amid the sort of scruffiness that gives inner cities a bad name. The main "avenue" through them takes you past several handsome structures, some of which are likely to be filled with experimental arts projects. At the eastern end, the Westergasfabriek merges with Westerpark, one of the city's smaller parks. Be alert for a

Winding down in Westerpark

series of sculptures, the most striking of which is a primary-colored column at the east entrance to the park.

➕ 200 A4 🚌 10 terminates on Van Hallstraat. From here it is a short walk north to Haarlemmerweg and across the canal to the Westergasfabriek (gate open 8 a.m.–11:30 p.m.). Tram 3 serves Haarlemmerplein, at the east end of Westerpark 🎟 Free

Where to...
Eat and Drink

Prices

Expect to pay per person for a meal, excluding drinks

$ under 35 guilders $$ 35–70 guilders $$$ more than 70 guilders

CAFÉS

De Admiraal $–$$

This *proeflokaal* (▶ 27), in an old canal warehouse, has 20 types of jenevers and 60 liqueurs (some with fun names such as Perfect Happiness and Lift up your Shirt), produced by its own long-established distillery. Old oak barrels, giant stone liqueur bottles and copper distillery kettles decorate the large, chic bar. Unlike most other tasting houses, it offers interesting snacks such as herring and smoked eel, full meals and comfy seating. Its only drawback is that it can be swamped by groups of tourists at times.

🚹 203 E3 ⊠ Herengracht 319 ☎ 020 625 4334 🕑 Mon.–Sat. 5 p.m.–midnight

Café Américain $–$$$

This ultra-civilized landmark grand café – part of the American Hotel (▶ 98) – has an art nouveau interior so fabulous that it has been declared a listed monument. There are beautiful stained-glass motifs above stone arches and weird and wonderful chandeliers, but your eye may equally be drawn to the ever-changing scene on Leidseplein through the café's giant windows. Snacks, full-blown meals covering every culinary persuasion and indulgent teas with cakes and sandwiches are available, but you can also lap up the atmosphere for the price of a coffee or a beer. Jazz accompanies Sunday brunch.

🚹 202 B3 ⊠ Leidsekade 97 ☎ 020 624 5322 🕑 Daily 7 a.m.–1 a.m.

Café Chris $

A good choice if you're looking for a traditional brown café in the Jordaan that receives few tourists (it's not on a canal). It makes a fair claim to be Amsterdam's oldest café. It started life in 1624, when the builders of the nearby Westerkerk would receive (and presumably spend) their wages here. Quirky features include a bike hanging from a winch, a toilet that you have to flush from inside the bar, and opera on Sundays.

🚹 202 B5 ⊠ Bloemstraat 42 ☎ 020 624 5942 🕑 Sun.–Thu. noon–1 a.m., Fri., Sat. till 2 a.m.

Café Dulac $–$$

This café, housed in a former 1920s bank, is a strong contender for the most outrageously furnished grand café in Amsterdam. Post-modern kitsch rules in the form of trumpets and model boats hanging from the ceiling and gargoyles and naked women erupting out of the walls. In one corner is a tree with metal branches, in another a pulpit flanked by angels. It's a trendy young person's haunt with a DJ performing on Friday and Saturday nights. Decent food comes in the form of salads, steaks, pasta and tarts.

🚹 201 E3 ⊠ Haarlemmerstraat 118 ☎ 020 624 4265 🕑 Sun.–Thu. 4 p.m.–1 a.m., Fri., Sat. till 2 a.m.

Café Papeneiland $

The diminutive "Popes' Island" is one of Amsterdam's oldest brown cafés. In the early 17th century, its landlord sold ale as a sideline; his main source of income was making coffins. With wood paneling and old

Delft tiles adorning the walls, tankards hanging from beams, a large old stove and, in traditional fashion, boiled eggs and apple pie displayed on the bar, the café oozes character from every pore. Despite its prime location – it's just up from the Noordermarkt at the junction with Brouwersgracht – its clientele is mainly local.

➕ 201 D3 ✉ Prinsengracht 2
☎ 020 624 1989 🕐 Mon.–Thu. 10 a.m.–1 a.m., Fri., Sat. 10 a.m.–2 a.m., Sun. noon–1 a.m.

Café de Prins $-$$

A brown *eetcafé* (note the typical old bar, bare wooden tables and partially paneled walls) that is always busy with both diners and a young, boisterous crowd of drinkers. Its main selling points are its canalside location (with outdoor seating, weather permitting) close to the Anne Frank Huis, and its good, inexpensive Dutch/French food. Try the cheese fondue, the light quiches crammed with the vegetable

filling of the day, or at lunchtime the excellent *uitsmijter* (fried eggs on bread).

➕ 200 C2 ✉ Prinsengracht 124
☎ 020 624 9382 🕐 Sun.–Thu. 10 a.m.–1 a.m., Fri., Sat. till 2 a.m.

Café 't Smalle $

Brown cafés don't come any quainter than this tiny, split-level corner building. Candles line the bar, wood paneling covers the walls and the stained glass dates back to the late 18th century. The café is usually packed, but retains a civilized air. Rare *jenevers* and a good range of snacks are on the menu, including slices of apple pie. The canalside location is simply idyllic, and there is a terrace right by the water.

➕ 200 C2 ✉ Egelantiersgracht 12
☎ 020 623 9617 🕐 Sun.–Thu. 10 a.m.–1 a.m., Fri., Sat. till 2 a.m.

De Doffer $-$$

A roomy, brown *eetcafé*, with a second bar next door that hits all the right notes (and that's not just

the jazz music that might be playing in the background). The requisite boarded floors, paneled walls and candlelit tables are all here, and the food – the menu may feature wild mushroom soup and smoked pigeon breast salad – is a cut above average. The café is slightly more upscale than many of its counterparts, which is reflected in the clientele.

➕ 202 C4 ✉ Runstraat 12-14
☎ 020 622 6666 🕐 Sun.–Thu. 11 a.m.–2 a.m., Fri., Sat. till 3 a.m.

Land van Walem $-$$

One of the first of the new breed of so-called "designer bars" – hence the waitresses dressed in black, the blown-up photos of models on the walls and the bold plant displays – Walem is none the less refreshingly attitude-free. The main reason for its popularity is the excellent food produced by its open-plan kitchen. For lunch you many have a simple *croque madame* (a toasted sandwich with a fried egg on top); for dinner, braised rabbit with sauerkraut

cooked in Riesling. When it's fine, you can sit out by the canal or in the garden at the rear.

➕ 202 C3 ✉ Keizersgracht 449
☎ 020 625 3544 🕐 Sun.–Thu. 10 a.m.–1 a.m. Fri., Sat. till 3 a.m.

Metz & Co $

On the seventh floor of the chic, department store of the same name (▲ 106), this light and airy café is worth a visit for the excellent views it affords in all directions across the city's steeply pitched roofs. The service and the food – soups, various egg dishes, sandwiches, English "high tea" – receive fewer plaudits.

➕ 202 C3 ✉ Keizersgracht 455
☎ 020 520 7020 🕐 Mon. 11–6, Tue., Wed. Fri., Sat. 10–6, Thu. 10–9, Sun. noon–5

Spanjer & Van Twist $-$$

This modern, canalside *eetcafé* serves some of the best café food in Amsterdam. Lunches include delicious omelettes baked in earthenware pots and interesting open sandwiches such as salmon, mozzarella and pesto. More substantial dinners run to fish stew and jugged hare with turnip mash. The café is an intimate, split-level space with an eye-catching bar backed by Mondrian-style glass.

201 D1 Leliegracht 60 020 639 0109 Daily 10 a.m.–midnight

De Tuin $

"The Garden" is one of the Jordaan's classic little brown cafés. There is nothing particularly remarkable about it, but it has all the necessary features to make it ever so cozy: a lovely old worn bar, candles on bare wood tables, walls covered in yellowing paneling and old posters advertising Dutch beer. It's popular with the neighborhood's young liberal set (well-pitched pop music plays most of the time), but outsiders are made to feel welcome.

200 C2 2e Tuindwarsstraat 13 020 624 4559 Mon.–Thu. 10 a.m.–1 a.m., Fri., Sat. 10 a.m.–2 a.m., Sun. 11 a.m.–1 a.m.

RESTAURANTS

De Belhamel $$

An intimate, romantic restaurant that looks across the lovely Brouwersgracht and right down Herengracht. Try to bag a window seat when you make your reservation. Both the dining room and grotto-like bar are decked out in authentic art nouveau décor. The French food is reliably good: a dinner might start with shrimp mousse, be followed by poached calf's tongue and end with a pear tarte tatin.

201 E3 Brouwersgracht 60 020 622 1095 Mon.–Fri. noon–3, 6–10, Sat., Sun. 6–10

Blakes $$$

Set in the vaulted, brick-lined old bakery of the exclusive Blakes hotel (▲ 41), Blakes the restaurant serves some of the most creative (and expensive) food in Amsterdam. The cuisine swings from Japanese/Thai, in sensational dishes such as tuna sushi topped with flying fish eggs and flavored with shavings of pickled ginger, to French/Italian in tortellini stuffed with foie gras. Presentation – for example, coffee comes with a bowl of steaming dry ice – is as theatrical as everything else in the hotel. A sybaritic adventure.

202 C4 Keizersgracht 384 020 530 2010 Mon.–Fri. noon–2, 6:30–10:30, Sat. 6:30–10:30, Sun. noon–3

De Blauwe Hollander $

Robust home Dutch cooking is the order of the day at this tiny, no-frills restaurant just off Leidseplein. There are just half a dozen wooden tables, which you have to share with strangers. The portions are vast: a main course of meatballs or liver and bacon or stamppot (mashed vegetables) with smoked sausage, may be enough for a full meal. However, the pea soup is very good and you may want to try a Dutch dessert such as vlaflip (custard and orange syrup).

202 C2 Leidsekruisstraat 28 020 623 3014 Daily 5 p.m.–10 p.m.

Bordewijk $$$

This is one of the city's most fashionable restaurants (reservations are necessary any night of the week). The spare, modern dining room with bold splashes of color on the walls looks through large windows onto the lovely Noordermarkt. The exciting menu swings between Italy and France – from dishes such as roasted foie gras to ravioli made with artichokes, Dutch shrimp and spring onions. The daily menus are an excellent value and the atmosphere is more relaxed than at some of the city's other top restaurants.

201 D3 Noordermarkt 7 020 624 3899 Tue.–Sun. 6:30 p.m.–10:30 p.m.

Café-Restaurant Amsterdam $$

It's worth taking the 10-minute tram ride from the city center (on tram 10 to its last stop) just to ogle the scale of this restaurant. Occupying the gleaming hall of a former 19th-century pumping station, it could fit a dozen canal houses into the space. The largely French, brasserie-style food – snails, *boudin noir*, steak and fries served Dutch-style with mayonnaise – all simply prepared and well priced, is worth coming for, too. Amsterdammers of all ages love this place: it is advisable to make a reservation or you may have to wait a while for a table in the café area.

Christophe $$$

This elegant, sophisticated restaurant, boasts striking flower displays and modern art. The creative cuisine focuses primarily on the southwestern region France, where chef/owner Jean Christophe Royer, who often appears at tables during the course of the evening, grew up. However, the food also shows North African influences in the langoustine tagine, while other dishes such as a risotto of quail with artichokes and shitaki mushrooms could be called "fusion" cooking. As well as an *à la carte* menu, there are more affordable no-choice menus.

➕ 200 off A4 ⊠ Watertorenplein 6 ☎ 020 682 2666 ⊙ Sun.–Thu. 11 a.m.–midnight, Fri., Sat. till 1 a.m.

Grekas Griekse Traiterie $

This excellent Greek take-away has evolved in the last few years into a canalside taverna that makes you feel you are really in Greece. The lighting is too bright and the tables too close together, but the music is as authentic as Nico's cooking. Instead of walking into the kitchen to choose, just check out the refrigerated display case. *Mezedakia* starters such as *kolokithakia* (zucchini croquettes) and *melanzosdlata* (eggplant salad) make a meal in themselves, although the delicious chicken with lemon sauce or vegetarian moussaka are also hard to pass up.

➕ 201 D1 ⊠ Leliegracht 46 ☎ 020 625 0807 ⊙ Tue.–Sat. 6:30 p.m.–10:30 p.m.

The Pancake Bakery $

A sure-fire winner with children: more than 50 pancakes, and little else, are served here amid the flagstone floors and exposed brick walls of the basement of an old canal house. Fillings range from lamb and paprika to cherries and whipped cream; you add jam, butterscotch syrup and icing sugar (powdered sugar) from pots on each table. The pancakes, though pricier than you might expect, are enormous.

➕ 203 D4 ⊠ Singel 311 ☎ 020 3590 ⊙ Tue.–Sun. 4 p.m.–10 p.m.

D'Theeboom $$$

This elegant bistro is situated along the Singel canal in a refurbished cheese warehouse (called D'Theeboom, or the tea tree). Although proprietor Georges Thubert hails from the Luberon in France, he has created more of a Greek or Portuguese ambience, with walls decorated with distinctive ceramic trees and warm hues of green and black. The menu reflects his love for fresh ingredients simply prepared. Although the young waitresses sometimes seem overwhelmed when things get busy, the coquilles St. Jacques, monkfish and fillet of sole are worth the wait. The wine list is exclusively French. In warm weather, you can dine on the terrace.

➕ 203 D5 ⊠ Singel 210 ☎ 020 623 8420 ⊙ Mon. 6 p.m.–10 p.m., Tue.–Fri. noon–2, 6–10, Sat. 6 p.m.–10 p.m.

Van Puffelen $$

This friendly canalside establishment is unusual for being both a classic brown café and a full-fledged restaurant. Heavy velvet drapes lead from the café through to a spacious, beautiful paneled and boarded dining room that manages to be both convivial and romantic. The hearty food is chiefly French, but includes multi-ethnic forays in such dishes as fillet of ostrich in a goat-cheese sauce.

⊞ 202 C5 ⊠ Prinsengracht 375–7 ☎ 020 624 6270 ⓒ Café Mon.–Thu. 3 p.m.–1 a.m., Fri. 3 p.m.–2 a.m., Sat. noon–2 a.m., Sun. noon–1 a.m.; restaurant daily from 6 p.m.

Zest! $$$

This modern-looking restaurant with its stark furniture is owned by the same two women who operate Zabars (➤ 133) and Le Zinc...et les Dames (➤ 158). Unlike most dining establishments in casual Amsterdam, its clientele is fairly dressy. The world cuisine offers many unusual combinations of ingredients: wild salmon steaks with a soy and lime marinade, fried oysters Japanese style with Dutch potatoes and turnips, and black pudding with roasted apples. The attentive staff is a plus.

⊞ 201 D2 ⊠ Prinsenstraat 10 ☎ 020 428 2455 ⓒ Mon.–Sat. 6 p.m.–11:30 p.m.

Where to... Shop

The western canal ring and the Jordaan district encapsulate all that is best about shopping in Amsterdam. You'll find dozens of endearing, one-of-a-kind shops overlooking the canals and in the tiny back streets between them, along with art galleries, and antiques and flower shops. Individualism rules to the exclusion of corporate commercialism. Rather than making a beeline for any particular shop or street, it's best to go on a window-shopping stroll that ties in a visit to the Jordaan's covered markets. Note that many shops hereabouts don't bother to open on Monday.

9 Straatjes

The Nine Streets are the virtually car-free radial lanes crossing the canals between the Singel and Prinsengracht, and Leidsegracht and Raadhuisstraat. Their modest houses, once occupied by the servants who worked in the far grander canalfront homes, are now a treasure trove of whimsical, sometimes slightly eccentric shops.

Working north to south, at No. 7 Gasthuismolensteeg you'll find **Brillenwinkel**. Downstairs you can buy antique opera glasses and flamboyant specs, while the upper floors are devoted to the **Brilmuseum** – where you can admire pince-nez, 19th-century safety goggles and glasses shaped like TV sets. Shop and museum are only open Wed.–Fri. noon–5:30, Sat. noon–5. Across the street at No. 12, **Antonia by Yvette** specializes in funky shoes. On Hartenstraat, check out **BLGK** at No. 28: the jewelry here is much more fun and creative than anything you're likely to come across in the city's diamond factories.

On Wolvenstraat, **Knopen Winkel** (No. 14), the "Button Shop," has a button even as a door handle, while **Laura Dols** (No. 7) is the place to go for clothing from the 1940s and 1950s. On Berenstraat, **De Beeldenwinkel** (No. 35) displays exquisite modern sculpture by local artists.

Time for a break? Head for **Pompadour**, at No. 12 Huidenstraat. You can eat its delicious, incredibly rich chocolates and cakes on the premises in its tiny Louis XVI-style salon de thé. Also on Huidenstraat is **Fifties-Sixties** (No. 13), stuffed full of goods from the 1950s and 1960s, such as toasters and vacuum cleaners.

Runstraat has one of Amsterdam's most appealing shops in **De Witte Tandenwinkel** (No. 5). "The White Teeth Shop" has been selling toothbrushes and other dental accoutrements for 20 years; note, in the window, passengers created out of toothbrushes riding a ferris wheel. Next door is **De Kaaskamer** (No. 7), "The Cheese Room", with more than 200 kinds of cheese for sale.

Jordaan

The diminutive cross-streets in the Jordaan south of Westerstraat, which take as long to pronounce as to walk, have lots of quirky little shops worth snooping around for things such as second-hand records, miniature violins, film posters and interesting clothes.

Rozengracht is the area's least charming street, but on it you'll find **Wegewijs** (No. 32), another of the city's best cheese shops, founded in 1884, and **1001 Kralen** (No. 54), which sells beads arranged by color in jars.

South on Hazenstraat, **Olivaria** (No. 2a) sells olive oil products and nothing else: bottles of olive oil are racked by country; as in a liquor store, and tastings are possible. Just along at No. 26 is **Cats & Things**, which concentrates on feline-themed goods such as tea cozies, playing cards and cute, cuddly toy cats (easily confused with a resident live cat that is definitely not for sale).

Prinsengracht and Haarlemmerstraat

The stores along the lovely stretch of Prinsengracht that borders the Jordaan range from elegant antiques emporia to appealing gift shops devoted to the likes of comics and candles. Heading south from Noordermarkt on the western side of the canal, you might want to stop off at **Rinascimento Gallerie d'Arte** (No. 170) which is piled high with an excellent range of old and new Delftware. Farther along, **Simon Levelt** (No. 180) has been selling tea and coffee since 1839; you can also buy chocolates in the shape of Amsterdam's landmark bollards. **Nieuws** (No. 297) is a fun novelty gift shop: how about a clock that runs backward? A couple of notches up in sophistication, **Van Hier tot Tokio** (No. 262) specializes in highly desirable Japanese antiques such as beautiful crafted cabinets from the 1920s and 1930s. **Steensma & Van der Plas** (No. 272) deals in

globes and big old clocks, the latter salvaged from offices and railway stations.

With time to spare, you might also want to venture north of Brouwersgracht to up-and-coming Haarlemmerstraat, which has several good delicatessens and intriguing art galleries among its less salubrious coffee shops.

Leidsestraat and vicinity

The constant stream of trams and cyclists takes the edge off window-shopping in Leidsestraat's mid-range mainstream boutiques and its tacky gift shops. However, **Metz & Co** (▶ 102), at Keizersgracht, is worth a browse or cup of tea. This small and exclusive department store stocks designer clothes and kitchen-ware in what was the city's tallest building when it was built in 1891. Finding tasteful or cliché-free postcards in Amsterdam can be a challenge. **Art Unlimited**, across the street at 510 Keizersgracht, has an amazing collection filed by artist,

photographer and subject matter. **Heinen**, a lovely canal house, just off Leidsestraat at Prinsengracht 440, sells modern Delftware and high-quality pottery painted in Delft style on the premises.

MARKETS

Noordermarkt (Mon. 8–1): a flea-market selling lots of clothes, records and books along with more arcane stuff ranging from flags and rusting tools to classical statuary. Though not as large or diverse as Waterlooplein's (▶ 77), it's more picturesque, with gabled houses and Prinsengracht as its backdrop.

On Saturday from 9–4, the square is taken over by the **Boerenmarkt**, which specializes in organic food, including enticing displays of wild mushrooms, cheeses, interesting breads and organic produce such as vegetarian pâté. Part of the tradition of visiting either market is to pop in to Café Winkel, on the corner of the square at Noordermarkt 43, for a slice of justly famous cinnamon-flavored apple pie.

Lapjesmarkt (Mon. 8–1): from the Noordermarkt right along Westerstraat, a large, bustling locals' market devoted to fabrics and inexpensive clothes.

De Looier Kunst en Antiekcentrum (Elandsgracht 109, Sat.–Thu. 11–5): a civilized, labyrinthine indoor antiques-and-curios center occupied by more than 80 stands and many showcases displaying such items as china, glassware, telescopes, military memorabilia and toy cars. It's worth searching out the "table market," where anyone can rent a table to sell their own things.

Rommelmarkt (Looiersgracht 38, daily 11–5): you may decide that it's not worth doing that much rummaging in the "Rummage Market": the large, permanent indoor flea-market tries to offload castaways of everything from electric toasters and typewriters to religious trinkets.

Where to...
Be Entertained

With dozens of restaurants and cafés, nightclubs, movie theaters and theaters, the Leidseplein and its surrounding streets form the epicenter for most kinds of nighttime entertainment. For a more tranquil, romantic evening, take a stroll through the Jordaan and along Prinsengracht, admiring the bridges and fairy lights outlining the bridges and stopping off at a brown café or two. North of the Jordaan, the Westergasfabriek, Amsterdam's former gasworks, is the city's latest and most intriguing cultural center.

The Leidseplein and vicinity

Leidseplein may be no beauty, and it's certainly not somewhere to come for a quiet drink, but its vivacity can be invigorating. Often noisy cafés filled with tourists watching soccer

on satellite TV ring the square. In summer, their tables and chairs smother half of the square and enthusiastic street musicians entertain the drinkers.

If you want a civilized, ringside, people-watching seat, head for the **Café Americain** (▶ 101). The most traditional café on the square is the brown café **Reynders** (Leidseplein 6). Other interesting drinking haunts nearby are **Schaakcafé Het Hok** (Lange Leidsedwarsstraat 134), a "chess café" that is equally popular with backgammon players, and **Lux** (Marnixstraat 403), a trendy late-night bar decorated with giant photos of naked women and employing a DJ most evenings.

Several atmospheric bars on the backstreets near Leidseplein provide spirited live jazz every night. See

what's playing at **Café Alto** (Korte Leidsedwarsstraat 115) and **Bourbon Street** (Leidsekruisstraat 6): the cover charge at each is small or non-existent.

For human stimulation, consider **Boom Chicago** (Leidseplein 12, tel: 020 423 0101; www.boomchicago.nl), where American expatriates perform quick-witted improvizational comedy feeding off suggestions from the audience. It also has a trendy café downstairs.

Amsterdam's casino, **Holland Casino** (Max Euweplein 62, tel: 020 521 1111; daily 1:30 p.m.–3 a.m.), is a magnificently garish affair. Expect all the usual table games, plus Sic Bo (a Chinese dice game). You must pay a small entrance fee, be over 18 and present your passport, but there is no strict dress code.

Just off Leidseplein are the **Melkweg** (Lijnbaansgracht 234a, tel: 020 531 8181; www.melkweg.nl), to the northwest and **Paradiso** (Weteringschans 6–8, tel: 020 626 4521; www.paradiso.nlto), to the southeast, the former converted from a dairy (and translating as the "Milky Way"), the latter from a church. The multifaceted venues were focal points for love, peace and hashish in Amsterdam's hippie era in the 1960s and '70s.

The Melkweg has evolved over the years into a multi-media cultural center. The emphasis is on giving new, up-and-coming Dutch bands a break and promoting world music at its two cozy concert halls; on weekend nights, they turn into nightclubs. The center also contains a movie theater (old genres such as martial arts and monster films are favored), theater, art gallery, café and chill-out room. A liberal, anything-goes (and that includes dope-smoking) policy still pervades the place.

On weekends, clubbers also head to Paradiso – a wonderful, grand, ecclesiastical space – for techno, funk, disco and soul. Often referred to as "the temple of pop," it also hosts rock bands, jazz groups and classical concerts.

The Odeon (Singel 460, tel: 020 624 9711), a 17th-century canal house on the Singel one block west of the Flower Market, has a very relaxed door policy and, unlike most of the city's clubs, is open every night. The token entrance fee is worth paying just to see the fabulous interior that includes a grand frescoed bar. On weekends, different floors are given over to different styles of music, such as house and R&B.

The Jordaan

As well as its traditional brown cafés (▶ 26–27), there are two Jordaan cafés/bars where singing, as much as drinking, is the focus of activity. At the kitsch and lurid Café Nol (Westerstraat 109), locals sing along to taped folksy Dutch music.

Smaller, seedier Twee Zwaantjes (Prinsengracht 114, located at Egelantiersgracht) is often populated by rather inebriated Amsterdammers accompanying live accordion music. Both bars stay open until the early hours (don't bother turning up until 11 p.m.), and are liveliest on weekends. A fun, if less authentically Dutch, experience is Rum Runners (Prinsengracht 277, next to the Westerkerk), a Caribbean-themed bar/restaurant with palm trees and caged parakeets that offers live Latin music on Sundays.

Westergasfabriek

In the mid-1990s, the city's former gasworks, Westergasfabriek (Haarlemmerweg 8-10, tel: 020 681 3068; www.westergasfabriek.nl), became a venue for illegal rave parties, but now the development of this huge site is being funded by the city. The inspiring Canadian troupe Cirque du Soleil has its European headquarters here.

All sorts of large-scale events – pop concerts, opera, equine ballets, even conferences – are held in the old structures that used to store the gas. Other buildings are used as film and theater studios, a movie theater (the Ketelhuis, which shows mainly Dutch films), a nightclub called Club de Ville, and Café West Pacific (020 597 4458), a funky bar/restaurant that used to be the workers' canteen. Its tables are pushed aside after dinner, when it is transformed into a nightclub: on weekends, it's one of the hottest places in town and you may have to pay a steep annual membership fee to enter. The Café West Pacific is open every evening and the only part of the complex where you might consider turning up on spec; otherwise, check what's going on before trekking out here.

You could tie in a visit with the highly recommended Café-Restaurant Amsterdam (▶ 103).

A taxi from the city center costs around 20 guilders; otherwise, it's a short walk from tram 10's penultimate stop at Van Limburg Stirumplein.

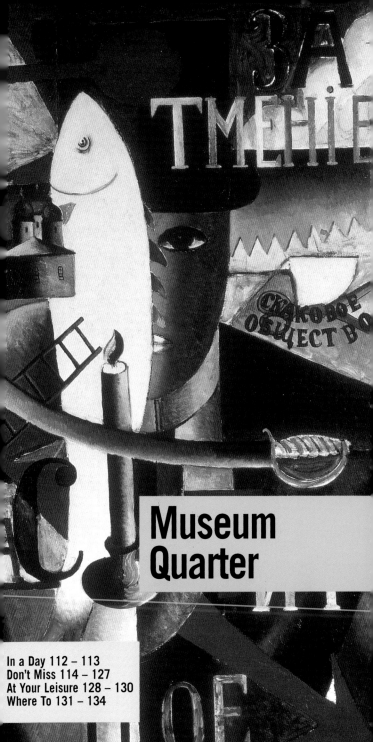

Museum
Quarter

Getting Your Bearings

In other cities, the area beyond the center generally subsides into anonymous suburbia. Amsterdam is different: it reaches its artistic climax in a district set apart from the city's core, to the south of Singelgracht.

Amsterdam has a superb concentration of art. When the Rijksmuseum was built to house the national collection in 1885, its location marked the edge of the city. The museum spent its infancy in splendid isolation. A decade later, the Stedelijk Museum of Modern Art opened, and 83 years after his death in 1890, Vincent Van Gogh was honored by the museum that bears his name. The museums are clustered together in Museumplein. The nearby Vondelpark, central Amsterdam's largest open space, surrounded with handsome housing and scattered with eclectic decoration, provides the perfect breath of fresh air while you contemplate the culture.

In the past few years, the opportunities for good eating and drinking in the Museum Quarter have multiplied; some of the city's best cafés and restaurants can be found here. The area is rapidly acquiring a character of its own, with students and other low-income people squeezed out of the city center, mixing with a variety of ethnic groups.

Previous page: *An Englishman in Moscow* (1913–14) by Kazimir Malevich in the Stedelijk Museum (below)

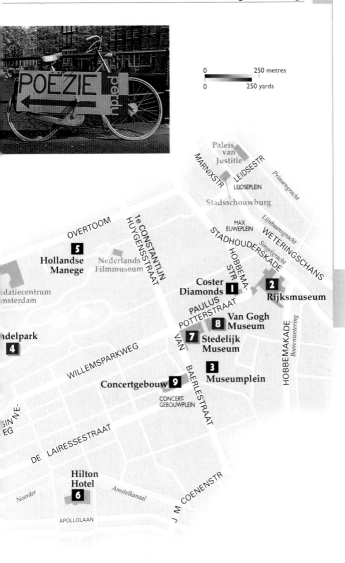

0 ——— 250 metres
0 ——— 250 yards

Paleis van Justitie

MARNIXSTR

LEIDSESTR

LEIDSEPLEIN

Prinsengracht

Stadsschouwburg

MAX EUWEPLEIN

STADHOUDERSKADE

WETERINGSCHANS

Lijnbaansgracht

Singelgracht

OVERTOOM

1e CONSTANTIJN HUYGENSSTRAAT

HOBBEMA- STR

5
Hollandse Manege

Nederlands Filmmuseum

datiecentrum nsterdam

Coster Diamonds **1**

2
Rijksmuseum

PAULUS POTTERSTRAAT

8
Van Gogh Museum

HOBBEMAKADE

Boerenwetering

ndelpark

4

VAN

7 **Stedelijk Museum**

WILLEMSPARKWEG

BAERLESTRAAT

3
Museumplein

HOBBEMAKADE

SIN NE-
EG N.

Concertgebouw **9**

CONCERT- GEBOUWPLEIN

DE LAIRESSESTRAAT

Noorder

Hilton Hotel
6

Amstelkanaal

J M COENENSTR

APOLLOLAAN

★ Don't Miss

At Your Leisure

The art is the main draw, of course, but there are plenty of other attractions to keep you more than busy for at least a day.

The Museum Quarter in a Day

9:00 a.m.

Be first in line at **Coster Diamonds** (➤ 128) before the bus groups arrive and reflect on the dazzling value placed on these tiny stones.

10:00 a.m.

Within a few paces you can sneak through the south entrance of the **Rijksmuseum** (➤ 114–117), the little-used way into a magnificent collection that reflects the Golden Age.

12:30 p.m.

Dispense with the uninspiring museum cafés in favor of the chic Cobra restaurant in the middle of **Museumplein** (➤ 129) – or, on a fine day, take a picnic in the **Vondelpark** (right, ➤ 118–121).

2:00 p.m.

Window-shop among the designer stores lining P. C. Hooftstraat; visit the opulent stables at the **Hollandse Manege** (left, ➤ 129); or stroll down to the **Hilton Hotel** (➤ 130), site of a piece of musical history. All are within easy reach of the main museums.

3:00 p.m.

Back on Museumplein, the **Stedelijk Museum** (➤ 122–123; painting by Picasso, below) will not demand too much of your time. It also has one of the better museum cafés for a mid-afternoon pitstop.

4:00 p.m.

Just along the road, the crowds at the superb **Van Gogh Museum** (left, ➤ 124–127) are beginning to dwindle, which makes this an ideal time to immerse yourself in the light and shade of the 19th-century genius.

6:00 p.m.

Follow the cultural tide to Van Baerlestraat to unwind and reflect over a glass of beer at Welling, or take an early supper in Mediterranean serenity at Zabar's (➤ 133).

8:00 p.m.

Take in a performance at the **Concertgebouw** (➤ 130), or a movie at the Netherlands Film Museum in **Vondelpark**.

Rijksmuseum

The Rijksmuseum is one of the greatest centers of art in
Europe. Fittingly, the building itself is an extraordinary
structure, representing the height of 19th-century Dutch
ambition and providing an extravagant punctuation to the
spread of the city.

The red-brick Rijksmuseum dominates the southwest quarter
of Amsterdam. Even among newer, taller buildings, it maintains a certain sense of majesty. The architect, P. J. H. Cuypers
– who also designed Centraal Station – took a somber and formal Romanesque basic design and enlivened it with Gothic
flourishes (much to the dismay of the Protestant community
at the time, who thought it too "Catholic"). The ensemble is
unmistakably Dutch, though the friezes and reliefs that decorate it could be strays from a German or French cathedral.

Envy was the principal motive for the instigation of the
national collection. A hoard of 200 paintings had been
amassed by Prince William V, who took them to London when
he fled in 1795 from the revolutionary French army. Within a
few years, envoys from the Dutch government had managed to
confiscate the works, and initially housed them at The Hague.
In 1808, Louis Napoleon (the French emperor's brother) was

*Amsterdam's
Rijksmuseum
contains much
more than
paintings.
Below is a
17th-century
dolls' house*

Vermeer's *The Kitchen Maid* (circa 1660)

crowned king of Holland. He grew jealous of his sibling's collection at the Louvre and determined to match it. The collection was moved out of the palace and housed in the city at the Trippenhuis, but this proved too small for a rapidly growing number of paintings, etchings and sculptures.

Road to Art

The Rijksmuseum was deliberately built astride a main road. The museum opened in 1885, coincidentally the year in which the first road vehicle powered by internal combustion was tested. The plan was to create a grand axis to emulate those in Paris and Berlin – a project made awkward by Amsterdam's geography. The course of the straightest line in the jumbled core of the city, Achterburgwal, is taken up by Nieuwe Spiegelstraat, which aims straight for the middle of the Rijksmuseum. After crossing Singelgracht, the axis continues as Museumstraat, ushered under the Rijksmuseum through a large, gloomy tunnel. The tunnel was one of the main entrances to central Amsterdam well into the 20th century, though cars and buses were later diverted around the west side of the Rijksmuseum. Only in the closing years of the century was the grand southwestern prospect of the museum freed by the removal of the highway.

A competition to design a new gallery on the fringe of the city was won by a German, but this was not felt suitable, so a messy compromise was found whereby Cuypers was drafted to create a replacement. His design has proved robust, though the museum was closed for a thorough refurbishment at the end of the 20th century.

Seeing the Rijksmuseum

If you have time, begin with the medieval roots of Dutch art – notably the superb (anonymous) altarpiece of the St. Catherine's Day Flood on the ground floor in the otherwise dull **Dutch History Collection.** Then make your way up the stairs, where you should be able to pick up a floor plan in English and rent an audio tour.

Most visitors head for the **17th-century Dutch paintings,** beginning at Room 207 (on the east side) and ending at 236 (adjacent to the Front Hall on the second floor). This room actually marks one end of the **Gallery of Honor,** which is the location for the finest works in the collection, culminating in *The Night Watch*. Franz

Though darkened by age, Rembrandt's *The Night Watch* still transfixes visitors at the Rijksmuseum

Hals' work is most notably commemorated in Haarlem (► 166), but the Rijksmuseum possesses some classics, including *Wedding Portrait*, which depicts the marriage of an aristocratic couple, and *The Merry Drinker*, with its delicacy and strong sense of character. Jan Steen takes a sterner moral stance in *The Merry Family*, showing the dereliction caused by alcohol. Very few works by Johannes Vermeer survive; the most prominent here is *The Kitchen Maid*, making exquisite use of light and of details such as a cracked window pane.

The world's finest collection of Rembrandts is the Rijksmuseum's strongest suit. Of the 17 paintings, a few deserve extra-special attention. The first is a self-portrait of the artist as a young man; in stark contrast is the self-portrait he made in 1661, at age 55, in which he is cloaked as the Apostle Paul. His genius at conveying emotion is evident in *The Jewish Bride*, which shows the passion between Isaac and Rebecca that gave them away in the biblical story. Rembrandt was principally a painter of commissioned portraits. His picture of the

The
Rijksmuseum; a
majestic study
n red brick

ageing Protestant minister Johannes Wtenbogaert proclaims the wisdom, as well as wrinkles, of age. *The Syndics* was a trickier matter: the customers demanded that they were all depicted on the same level, so to inject energy and a stronger composition he shows one figure half-rising, while the eyes of the ensemble pierce the viewer. His most celebrated work is *The Night Watch*, commissioned by the Kloveniers' Guild. In the 17th century, it was standard practice for the professions to band together for a painting that would immortalize them. The standard portrait was stiff and formal, but Rembrandt broke with tradition to inject a sense of theater, vitality and fun at odds with the serious purpose of the militiamen. Two of the civic guards were lopped off so that the painting would fit its previous location. This is one Rembrandt not owned by the Rijksmuseum: it is officially on loan from the City of Amsterdam.

TAKING A BREAK

Sama Sebo, just 160 yards along Hobbemastraat (turn right from the south entrance), serves Indonesian cuisine, and is a much better bet than the museum café.

Rijksmuseum
- ✚ 202 C2
- ✉ Stadhouderskade 42
- ☎ 020 674 7000; www.rijksmuseum.nl
- 🕐 Daily 10–5; closed New Year's Day
- 🍴 Cupyer's café ($$) 🚋 2, 5, 20
- 💶 Moderate; free admission to Museum Year Card holders (except special exhibitions)

RIJKSMUSEUM: INSIDE INFO

Getting in Most visitors line up at one of the **two entrances to the front hall,** which faces northeast (towards the city center) on Stadhouderskade. A **third entrance** is hidden around the back of the south wing, at Hobbemastraat No. 19. The line is usually much shorter, though it may not be possible to buy tickets for special exhibitions here.

Top tip The Rijksmuseum is at its **most crowded on summer weekends.** If you can, visit between Monday and Thursday; if not, arrive a few minutes ahead of opening at 10 a.m.

Hidden gem Don't overlook the **beautiful stained-glass windows** that enliven the stairways and the second floor of the Rijksmuseum. They depict some of the great Dutch artists whose work hangs in the museum.

Vondelpark

If you fly over Amsterdam, you will appreciate the extent of its greenery. No fewer than 220,000 trees line the canals, dot the squares and fill the courtyards – one for every three Amsterdammers. But the larger parks, of which there are 28, are revered – none more so than 111-acre Vondelpark, which attracts 8 million visitors each year.

Vondelpark lies on a limb of land, a patch of ground below sea level. Within the canal ring, there is no room for a substantial open space, so the map shows a long, narrow rectangle, with a pan-handle protruding from the end, pressing up against Singelgracht. The other end rests on Amstelveenseweg, just over a mile away.

It is a robustly proletarian place in which you will find a microcosm of Amsterdam life: families picnicking while rollerbladers race by, prim dowagers walking poodles past a haze of dope-smokers – though these days you are unlikely to find a colony of hippies camping. But this is more than a study in people-watching: you can walk through a rose garden, pose on a cinematic balcony and even commune with llamas.

Another side of Amsterdam – the wide open spaces of Vondelpark

Right: Summer
brings
Amsterdammers
here in their
millions

The layout takes the form of the classic city park.
L. D. Zocher deliberately imposed this fairly plain style,
augmented with plenty of ponds, in his plans for a
"horseback riding and strolling park." When the
Vondelpark opened in 1865, three of its sides faced open
countryside. Soon, though, rich residents moved out to
enjoy the fresher air. The Vondelpark is conveniently
southwest of the city center, the direction from which the
prevailing wind blows.

A Walk in the Park

The best way to approach Vondelpark is through
the entrance that faces Singelgracht. It is most easily
approached from Max Euweplein, the modern complex
just south of Leidseplein. There is a bicycle path cutting
through it, past the giant chess set and over a bridge.
Cross the busy Stadhhouderskade and you are at the
original iron gates to the narrow end of the park.

About 400m (.5-mile) in, **Eerste Constantijn
Huygensstraat** (the name is nearly as long as the
street) leaps across the neck of the Vondelpark. Just
before the bridge on the right (north) is the city's main
official **youth hostel,** which was born from the gaunt skeleton of an old school building. Directly opposite stands the
Flying Pig Palace across the park, a newer and more liberal
competitor.

Beyond the bridge, the park broadens and the first water
feature appears: a serpentine **pond** that snakes for 400m
(.5-mile) to the heart of the park.

Bear right for the **Nederlands Filmmuseum.** This unmistakable, imposing pavilion was designed by P. J. and W. Hamer
in 1881. Embellishments such as the wide-eyed maidens flank-
ing the stairways are theirs, but the "new" interior makes up
the Cinema Parisien. When Amsterdam's first movie house
faced demolition in the 1980s, as much as could feasibly be

resurrected was reassembled within the Netherlands Film Museum. To see the results, you will need to buy a ticket for one of the three or four daily screenings that range from silent classics to contemporary premières. At any time when the box office is open you can wander around the lobby. It contains a venerable film camera and projector, plus a shifting exhibition of stills. Most of the clientele, however, prefer the outdoor veranda, crowded on summer weekends with people who seem more interested in Grolsch and Heineken than Garbo and Hitchcock – except during one of the regular open-air screenings.

Statue of Vondel. The Dutch national poet is commemorated in bronze

Of all the many citizens whose names could be applied to Amsterdam's most ambitious park, it is telling that the one chosen was the poet Joost van den Vondel. He was a contemporary of Rembrandt who is commemorated in the smaller and tackier Rembrandtplein. Vondel was writing plays at the same time as Shakespeare, though with considerably less success and durability. Nevertheless, a grand **statue** has him presiding over his park on the tongue of land opposite the Filmmuseum.

Threading through the center of the Vondelpark, the obvious refreshment stop is the **'t Blauwe Theehuis** (The Blue Tea House, ► 131), a café-turned-flying saucer that has fallen to earth opposite the bandstand (► 131). Next door, the **Openluchttheater** (Open-Air Theater) has a busy summer program of free performances. A second refreshment stop, the **Melkhuis**, is a big self-service place with less style but better coffee and pastries than the Blue Tea House.

Stay on the south side of the park and you will find the **animal enclosure.** Usually it boasts a motley collection of mammals with assorted horses and donkeys and a woolly llama or two. Make your way around to the next bridge along – slightly concealed by the trees – and you can cross to the **Rose Garden.** The succession of hexagonal flowerbeds looks superb in summer, drab in winter. Continue in a westerly direction and you pass the closest thing the Vondelpark has to a waterfall: a sculpture called *Cascade*, with water washing over rocks.

The western end of the park is being allowed to grow wilder, with hopes that the sorts of creatures that inhabited the original marshland will return. Information displays explain

The park is a favorite spot fo romance

the steps being taken and the aspirations of the project.

There is one last opportunity for refreshment at the curious **thatched café** at the southwest corner, before you emerge on to Amstelveenseweg – a world away from the opulence of the rest of the Vondelpark's surroundings.

TAKING A BREAK

Put together a picnic; the nearest supermarket to the eastern end is the branch of **Albert Heijn** on Overtoom, between Stadhouderskade and Eerste Constantijn Huygenstraat.

Nederlands Filmmuseum
🚩 202 A2
✉ Vondelpark 3
☎ 020 589 1400; www.filmmuseum.nl
🕙 Box office/foyer open from 10 a.m. Mon.–Fri., one hour before the first performance on weekends, until the end of the last performance
🎫 $$ 🚋 1, 3, 6, 12 stop at junction of Overtoom and Eerste Constantijn Huygensstraat
🎟 Tickets for screenings inexpensive–moderate

Below: Most people come to the park by bicycle

VONDELPARK: INSIDE INFO

Top tips Given the size of the Vondelpark, you may wish to **rent a bicycle** (▶ 25). Or, in summer you can rent a pair of rollerblades from the hut next to the café at the southwest corner.

• Trams 2, 5 and 20 stop right outside the **eastern entrance;** tram 6 stops at the **western entrance.**

Stedelijk Museum

After the Old Masters of the Rijksmuseum and the 19th-century angst of Van Gogh, the Stedelijk brings art lovers up to date with some of the most exciting and challenging work in Europe. It is well worth saving an hour or two of time and energy for the city's main repository for modern art and to enjoy an interesting building with relatively few crowds.

Sophia de Bruijn-Suasso, a Dutch aristocrat, bequeathed hundreds of clocks, pieces of jewelry and odd-ments to the city. Faced at the same time with calls for a contemporary arts venue, the city decided to combine the two under the same roof, and the Stedelijk was built in 1895, to a design by A. W. Weissmann. Modern art steadily gained the upper hand and the de Bruijn-Suasso collection was gradually dispersed to other collections. Immediately after World War II, William Sandberg took over as curator and placed Amsterdam in general, and the Stedelijk in particular, in the vanguard of modernism.

Seeing the Stedelijk

The entrance takes you into a strange space, suggesting a disused factory or dairy with well-scrubbed tiles and a utilitarian central staircase. Begin on the **ground floor.** The collection starts in the mid-19th century; there are a few Van Goghs left over from the move to the museum next door in 1972, together with a couple of powerful works by Marc Chagall: *Portrait of Madame Chagall* and *The Circus Rider*. The Dutch De Stijl tradition is well represented, but the largest collection of work by a single artist is that of the Russian, Kazimir Malevich. There is also a collection of applied art by lesser-known artists, which bring new dimensions to the usual concepts of objects like chairs and teapots, and a growing number of video installations.

In the **extension,** you could find some adventurous installations of the kind pioneered by the CoBrA group of artists from Copenhagen, Brussels and Amsterdam.

Climb the stairs that take you back in the original building on the **upper level,** through

Don't miss the bold sculptures at the Stedelijk

Left: Exhibit at the Stedelijk, a museum in the vanguard of modernism

Exhibits at the
Stedelijk are
constantly
changing

galleries often set aside for special exhibitions. Some may be occupied by photography, such as Gabrielle Basilico's dehumanized monochrome depictions of living spaces in European cities with not a soul living there.

TAKING A BREAK

In the Stedelijk's café a raised gallery runs along the western wall groaning under the weight of art books and a 1956 mural by Kurt Appel on the north wall that depicts the interaction between man and nature. Unfortunately, the food is the usual uninspiring museum fare. Or you could try the **Cobra** café on Museumplein or the string of restaurants on Van Baerlestraat.

Stedelijk Museum
➕ 202 B1
✉ Paulus Potterstraat 13
☎ 020 573 2737 (recorded information), 020 573 2911
🕐 Daily 11–5 🍴 Café ($$)
🚋 2, 5, 20 💰 Moderate; free admission to Museum Year Card holders (except special exhibitions)

STEDELIJK MUSEUM: INSIDE INFO

Top tips Because everything at the Stedelijk is so fluid, you may wish to check in advance what is being shown. Or, look into the **glass-encased extension** from the street to see if your artistic appetite is whetted.
• The **museum shop is on the upper floor,** directly above the entrance hall, not on the ground floor as is more usual.
• Each Wednesday at noon there is a **free introductory guided tour** to the Stedelijk. Lectures about current exhibitions take place from time to time, also at noon; some of these are in English.

Van Gogh Museum

He died by his own hand after selling just two paintings during a brief and troubled career as an artist. Yet today Vincent Van Gogh's art is sold for record sums – and the museum that boasts the best collection of his work is the most visited attraction in Amsterdam.

Van Gogh began to draw and paint in 1880 after an unpromising career in teaching and preaching. In the next decade he produced 800 paintings, of which the museum contains a quarter. It also has 500 of his drawings and 700 letters (though because of their fragility these are rarely displayed), and 400 Japanese prints from which Van Gogh drew inspiration and solace.

Buy a ticket to the Van Gogh Museum and see *The State Lottery*

After his death in July 1890, the artist's works passed to his brother, Theo, who survived him by only six months, and Theo's widow. Her son, Willem Van Gogh, sold the collection to the Dutch state in 1962.

The Rijksmuseum Vincent Van Gogh, as it is officially known, opened in 1973. The exterior has the look of a drab college building. Gerrit Rietveld's austere, rectangular design jars with its more elegant red-brick neighbors on Museumplein, but it does make the artist's work seem all the more vivid.

The museum includes works by Van Gogh's contemporaries, who at the time were much more illustrious. The **ground floor** (numbered 0) establishes the context in the second half of the 19th century, when Van Gogh was inspired by

*The Langlois
Bridge in Arles
by Van Gogh*

works such as Léon-Augustin Lhermitte's *Haymaking*. He later
said it was "As if made by a peasant who could paint."

Upstairs on the **second floor**, you are confronted first by a
somber self-portrait, the only one featuring an easel. Historical
sources suggest this is the closest likeness of all his self-
portraits. The large number of self-portraits is not a sign of
vanity: Van Gogh could not afford to pay models and therefore
practised on himself.

The exhibition runs clockwise and chronologically, beginning in Brussels and moving to The Hague. A brief spell spent
in the bleak northeast of Holland in the last quarter of 1883
proved unproductive and Van Gogh was soon back with his

The Extension

Amid great ceremony, the much-needed extension to the Van Gogh Museum,
designed by the Japanese architect Kisho Kurokawa, was opened in 1999. Its
plan is an oval, its exterior clad in titanium and disrupted by wayward cubes, in
welcome contrast to the severity of Gerrit Rietveld's original. To view it most favor-
ably, climb the stairs in the main building to the third floor. You reach the extension on an escalator that whisks you below ground from the main foyer into the
"Knot" – the link between old and new. At the foot, glass surrounds a shallow oval
pond. On the far side are the galleries used for temporary exhibitions.

Poverty obliged
Van Gogh to
use himself
as a model

parents in the town of Nuenen, just across the border in
Belgium. His reverence for the integrity of manual labor is
depicted in *The Potato Eaters* (1885), the first painting that he
signed. Nearby, *Still Life with Quinces and Beans* shows an
unusual levity in the way that the image spills out on to the
frame.

In the spring of 1886, Van Gogh moved to the Montmartre
quarter of Paris, where he stayed with his art-dealer brother,
Theo, and drew influence from the Impressionists. His rest-
lessness drove him on to Arles in the south of France in May
1888, where he hoped to set up an artists' colony in the Yellow
House that he rented. Paul Gauguin arrived in October for a
brief, unhappy stay. It was during this stormy visit that Van
Gogh's mental health deteriorated, demonstrated by the self-
mutilation of his left ear.

After Gauguin returned to Paris, Van Gogh suffered a break-
down and was admitted to an asylum at St.-Remy in April
1889. Here, he produced some of his greatest work, including
Irises. Unable to work with models, he resorted to prints of the
Old Masters for inspiration: *The Resurrection of Lazarus*, after
Rembrandt, is a bold embellishment in which the sun replaces
Jesus and Lazarus bears an uncanny resemblance to Van Gogh
himself. *Wheatfield with a Reaper* is the portentous view from
Van Gogh's room at St.-Remy; the artist wrote that "I saw in
him the image of death."

In May 1890, he moved north to Auvers-sur-Oise, near

VAN GOGH MUSEUM: INSIDE INFO

Orientation You have to **line up first for a ticket** (even if you hold a Museum Year Card) to get through the large glass doors into the foyer. Here you can pick up an English-language floor plan (free) and an audio tour, which costs extra but adds considerably to the experience.

Top tips The line for the Van Gogh Museum is depressingly long at times. **Arrive at 9:30 a.m.** and you may get in by 10 a.m.; arrive at 10 a.m., and you will be lucky to get in at 11 a.m.
• The best way to **dodge the crowds** is to visit on Monday morning; if you cannot manage this, try coming after 4 p.m. when people start drifting away. Last admission is at 5:30 p.m.

Vincent's final, tortured work: *Wheatfield with Crows*

Paris. Two months later he shot himself in a wheatfield; he took two days to die from the wounds. The second-floor exhibition closes with three powerful landscapes that show his brushwork at its most expressive. *Wheatfield with Crows* was painted just two weeks before his death.

The **third floor** is devoted to a shifting collection of drawings and prints, while the **fourth floor** returns to the 19th-century milieu with works by Picasso, Monet and Gauguin juxtaposed with more paintings by Van Gogh.

TAKING A BREAK

On a sunny day, take a seat on the terrace of the **Cobra** restaurant (► 131). The name derives from the COpenhagen-BRussel-Amsterdam alliance of modern artists. Or pick up the ingredients for a picnic at the small supermarket on Van Baerlestraat just beyond the Stedelijk Museum.

Van Gogh Museum
🔲 202 B1
✉ Paulus Potterstraat 7
☎ 020 570 5200; www.vangoghmuseum.nl
🕐 Daily 10–6 (last admission 5:30)
🍴 Café open daily 10–5:30 ($$)
🚃 2, 5, 20
🎫 Expensive; children ages 13–17 pay one-third less, under-13s free; free admission to Museum Year Card holders (except special exhibitions)

At Your Leisure

1 Coster Diamonds

One of Amsterdam's leading diamond-polishing factories sits snugly next to the Rijksmuseum and along the road from the Van Gogh Museum, and operates regular tours (every half-hour or hour) devoted to the hardest mineral in the world.

The experience begins in an exhibition space that includes replicas of some of the world's most celebrated diamonds, such as the Koh-i-Noor and the Cullinan. There's also a somewhat tacky copy of Vincent Van Gogh's

Amsterdam maintains a long tradition of expertise in cutting diamonds

Sunflowers, whose stamens are set with 660 diamonds. By far the most interesting part of the tour, though, is seeing the craftspeople at work cutting diamonds. You can peer right over their lathes to watch the intricate process, which uses a mix of oil and diamond dust to grind each facet.

Each tour group (you will be assigned to one even if you arrive by yourself) is then ushered into one of

Diamond Life

Most of the world's diamonds are mined in equatorial regions or well inside the southern hemisphere, but trade in the gems is largely controlled by the London office of De Beers. When the first diamonds from India arrived in Europe in the 15th century, they were cut in Bruges. But with that city's decline the industry moved to Antwerp, where the center of the trade remains. Amsterdam became significant after the Habsburg Spanish took Antwerp in 1589 and thousands of Protestant and Jewish merchants fled north. Even when Antwerp's diamond trade was re-established, enough traders stayed in Amsterdam to develop a considerable industry. For a time the diamond trade was one of few businesses open to Jews in the Netherlands. Today, the city is a distant second to Antwerp – with India, source of many of the rough diamonds, also developing a trading role.

he "private rooms" for an explana-
ion of the way that diamonds are
ssessed and graded. Trays of rings are
brought out for inspection. This provides the opportunity for you to ask
questions – and for the guide
o sell.

If you get there a few minutes
before it opens at 9 a.m., you are
ikely to get on the first tour well
ahead of the bus groups.

🚉 202 C1 ✉ Paulus Potterstraat 2–8
☎ 020 305 5555;
www.costerdiamonds.com 🕐 Daily 9–5
🚊 2, 5, 20 🎫 Free

The somewhat uninspiring exterior of
the Hollandse Manege

🛈 Museumplein

The apron of green
that spreads out south-
west from the
Rijksmuseum is more
than just a patch of
open space with muse-
ums scattered around –

and much more than it was in the
early 1990s, when a wide, fast road
sped straight down the middle of the
park on the axis of the Rijksmuseum
tunnel. Much to the relief of locals
and tourists, the road has been
replaced with a long, narrow pond
that provides splendid phtotographic
reflections of the Rijksmuseum on
sunny afternoons and plenty of lawn
studded with sculptures such as the
fierce *Fists* creation near the southern
corner. Life is also returning to
Museumplein, thanks to the ambitious extension to the Van Gogh
Museum and a makeover in 2000 that
rejuvenated the greenery.

🚉 202 B1 🚊 2, 5, 20 (northern corner); 16 (southern corner); 3, 5, 12, 20
(Van Baerlestraat, on southwest edge)

🛈 Hollandse Manege

The design of these fine stables by
A. L. Van Gendt was heavily influenced by the Spanish Riding School
in Vienna. They were built in 1882,
when the location was positively
rural. Gradually Amsterdam has
expanded around them, but their
character has remained intact.
From the street the entrance looks
forbidding, but you are free to wander
in and survey the arena from the
balcony (look for the sign saying
"Tribune"), or to watch the horses
from the opulent café (marked
"Foyer").

🚉 202 A2 ✉ Vondelstraat 140 ☎ 020
618 0942 🕐 Mon.–Fri. 9 a.m.–midnight, Sat.–Sun. 9–6 🍴 Café ($) 🚊 1,
6 (Overtoom, one block north) 🎫 Free

The magnificent
neo-Renaissance
Concertgebouw is
renowned for its
acoustics

6 Hilton Hotel

Like other properties belonging to
the multinational hotel chain,
Amsterdam's version is visually uninspiring: a 1960s block awkwardly
parked on a bend of the otherwise
attractive Noorder Amstelkanaal. The
plan of the hotel mirrors the kink in
the canal, which at least breaks what
would otherwise be a drab rectangle.

People do not come here to look at
the architecture, however. They are
here either to stay in one of the 271
rooms or to make a pilgrimage to an
important venue on the John Lennon
trail. Here, in March 1969,
Lennon and Yoko Ono
checked into what is
now room 1902 (origi-
nally a combination of
suite 902 and lounge
904), and arranged for
all the furniture except
the bed to be removed.
They then invited the
world's media to witness
their "bed-in for peace." The
event was later immortalized
in The Beatles' hit *The Ballad of
John and Yoko*, whose lyrics were
written here.

The bed has been left more or less
where it was, but the rest of the room
has been turned into something of a
shrine to Lennon, with drawings on
the ceiling supposedly inspired by the
lyrics to *Imagine*. To see it, you need
to reserve it – at a cost of 2,750
guilders per night.

🚹 206 C1 ✉ Apollolaan 138–40
☎ 020 710 6000 🚊 16 (De
Lairessestraat, two blocks north)

9 Concertgebouw

Amsterdam has always
had a problem with
monuments – or,
rather, the lack of
them. Toward the end
of the 19th century
efforts were made to
add grandeur to the city: the
Rijksmuseum and Centraal Station
were two results, and another was the
Concertgebouw, the first substantial
performance venue in the city.

P. J. H. Cyupers, who built the first
two icons, also chaired the design
committee for the Concertgebouw.
This explains why the design of the
chosen architect, A. L. Van
Gendt, comple-
mented that of
the

Rijksmuseum. In place of the stained-
glass windows showing great artists,
the Concertgebouw features busts of
notable composers.

To appreciate the superb acoustics
of the Grote Zaal (Great Hall), you
will need to buy a ticket for an
evening performance, but you could
call in for a free lunchtime recital in
the Kleine Zaal (Small Hall).

🚹 202 B1 ✉ Concertgebouwplein 2–6
☎ 020 671 8345; www.concertgebouw.nl
🚊 3, 5, 12, 16, 20

Where to...
Eat and Drink

Prices

Expect to pay per person for a meal, excluding drinks
$ under 35 guilders $$ 35–70 guilders $$$ more than 70 guilders

CAFÉS

't Blauwe Theehuis $

This 1930s blue-and-white, pagoda-like structure is in a lovely spot in the heart of the Vondelpark, surrounded by mature trees and waterways. You can sit outside on its large terrace munching pastries and decent sandwiches, or check out its surprisingly stylish licensed top-floor bar (it even has a DJ on Sunday evenings). The café is toward the eastern end of the park, just west of Van Baerlestraat.

➕ 202 A1 ◻ Vondelpark ⊠ 020 662 0254 ◉ Daily 9 a.m.–11 p.m.

Cobra $

This light, modern addition to Museumplein takes its name from a late-1940s expressionist art movement in which painters from Copenhagen, Brussels and Amsterdam played a leading role. Everything from the pattern on the floor to the crockery is inspired by the movement. However, if the weather's nice you may prefer to sit outside and be entertained by the ubiquitous street musicians. Sandwiches, interesting salads, sushi and sashimi are available.

➕ 202 B1 ◻ Museumplein ⊠ 020 470 0111 ◉ Daily 10–10

Ebeling $

A former bank (the restrooms are in the vaults) near the Leidseplein end of Overtoom is now a trendy hangout for 20-something Amsterdammers. It combines funky, eclectic decor and loud music in the evenings with more conventional features such as candlelit tables, a reading area with newspapers and magazines, and maybe a cat snoozing in a corner. The menu includes everything from pasta to burritos.

➕ 202 A2 ◻ Overtoom 52 ⊠ 020 689 1218 ◉ Mon.–Thu. 11 a.m.–1 a.m., Fri., Sat. 11 a.m.–3 a.m., Sun. noon–1 a.m.

Enorm Food Company $

An ultra-modern café on Amsterdam's most fashionable shopping street – just the place for a club sandwich washed down by a half-bottle of Moët & Chandon. You enter via a tunnel of international fashion magazines. In the minimalist eating area behind, watch your shares go up and down on the

TV screen, go on the Internet, or just tuck into soups, salads, sandwiches, pastries or ice-cream.

➕ 202 B2 ◻ 87 PC Hooftstraat ⊠ 020 670 9944 ◉ Mon.–Sat. 8–8, Sun. 9–7

Vertigo $–$$

The café, in the pavilion housing the Nederlands Filmmuseum (▲ 119), takes its name from a famous Hitchcock film. A head for heights is not needed as it's tucked away in a vaulted, candlelit basement. However, in summer one of its big draws is the large terrace overlooking the Vondelpark's joggers and ducks. Trendy young things come here to drink; you can also dine on salads, pastas and steaks. On Monday evenings, meals are themed on that night's film.

➕ 202 A2 ◻ Vondelpark 3 ⊠ 020 612 3021 ◉ Daily 11 a.m.–1 a.m.

Welling $

A slow-paced, slightly genteel brown corner café that is behind, and derives much of its trade from, the Concertgebouw. Velvet drapes and net curtains cover the windows, the chairs and sofas are well worn, and the floor, ceiling and walls are all appropriately brown. Note the walking stick hanging from a hook over the bar: it was the property of a regular, now deceased.

➕ 206 D2 ⊠ JW Brouwerstraat 32
☎ 020 662 0155 🕐 Sun.–Thu.
4 p.m.–1 a.m., Fri., Sat. till 2 a.m.

Wildschut $-$$

This off-the-tourist-track art deco grand café is a five-minute walk south of the Concertgebouw. Its long, curved frontage forms part of a 1920s Amsterdam School of architecture square which, weather permitting, you can admire from a large outdoor terrace (though there is considerable traffic). Inside the spacious café are such features as marble wall panels, theater seats salvaged from a period movie theater and a Wurlitzer juke box. Lunches concentrate on good

sandwiches (try the five-layered club sandwich), while more sub-stantial dishes such as steak are available in the evening.

➕ 206 E1 ⊠ Roelof Hartplein 1–3
☎ 020 676 8220 🕐 Daily
9:30 a.m.–1 a.m.

RESTAURANTS

Bark $$

A busy fish bistro close to the Concertgebouw that delivers swift service and takes orders much later than most restaurants in the city. Tables are tiny and so close together that eavesdropping is unavoidable. You could choose a plate of oysters, a platter of *fruits de mer* or a more creative dish such as swordfish with mussels. Its more meat-oriented sister, De Knijp, in the same block at No. 134 (tel: 020 671 4248), is very similar in style.

➕ 206 E2 ⊠ Van Baerlestraat 120
☎ 020 675 0210 🕐 Mon.–Fri.
noon–3, 5:30–12:30 a.m., Sat., Sun.
5:30 p.m.–12:30 a.m.

Bodega Keyzer $-$$$

This much-loved Amsterdam institution, yards from the Concertgebouw, has been up and running since 1905. It's a thoroughly old-fashioned place, with waiters in bow ties and black jackets, and net curtains over the windows. The pricey restaurant at the rear specializes in French and Dutch fish dishes such as *sole meunière*, smoked eel and shrimp croquettes. The snug café at the front, which in traditional fashion uses tiny Persian rugs for table-cloths, offers a large selection of good, light meals.

➕ 206 D3 ⊠ Van Baerlestraat 96
☎ 020 671 1441 🕐 Mon.–Sat.
9–midnight, Sun. from 11 a.m.

Le Garage $$$

Once a backstreet garage, this is now one of the city's most glam-orous restaurants: the chef/owner is a regular on Dutch TV. Behind an open-plan kitchen and sleek bar lies a dining area of mirrored walls and

red banquette seating. Most dishes, such as *fruits de mer* and *rôtisserie* meats, are French and despite the glitzy surroundings, surprisingly down to earth. Other cuisines appear, too – for example, Dutch chicory with smoked eel starter, and a Thai salad. Reserve well in advance, and dress to impress *nou-veau riche* Amsterdammers.

➕ 206 E1 ⊠ Ruysdaelstraat 54–6
☎ 020 679 7176 🕐 Mon.–Fri.
noon–2, 6–11; Sat., Sun. 6–11

Poentjak Pas $-$$

This unpretentious Indonesian restaurant is just minutes from the Leidseplein on a less traveled tourist thoroughfare. The very friendly pro-prietress will talk you though the varied plates offered in the house *rijsttaffel*, which can be adapted for vegetarian tastes. Otherwise, do what the locals do and order the *Nasi Goreng* special, which is a mini-*rijsttaffel* served on one large plate. The *Guli Kambing* (spicy lamb in coconut sauce) is another option, as well as the *Dadar Isi*, a hearty omelette filled with chicken and vegetables. Ask for some home-made *sambal* (hot sauce) to add a little fire.

⊞ 202 B3 ⊠ Nassaukade 366 ☎ 020 618 0906 ◷ Tue.–Sun. 5.30–10 p.m.

Zabar's $$

A short step off busy Van Baerlestraat transports you to a good approximation of the Mediterranean. This light, airy venue, decorated in soft yellows and reds, is split between three levels; the street elevation is the busiest and upstairs the coziest. The bread served with the aperitif sets the tone: it arrives with pots of garlic butter, olive oil with herbs and crushed olives. The strongest influences are Italian and North African. If you ask for wine, you'll be offered a full bottle; you pay only for the amount you drink.

⊞ 202 B1 ⊠ Van Baerlestraat 49 ☎ 020 679 8888 ◷ Tue.–Fri. 11–11, Sat, Mon. 5.30–11

Where to... Shop

The Museum Quarter not only has priceless objects to look at, but also much to buy that would make a serious dent in your wallet. It is *the* place to spend a fortune – or to watch others spend a fortune – in exclusive boutiques dedicated to the creations of Dutch and international fashion designers, or at Coster Diamonds (▶ 128).

P. C. Hooftstraat

The city's answer to Bond Street or Rodeo Drive is named after 17th-century poet Pieter Cornelisz Hooft. However, it is famous names in the world of fashion that draw shoppers to the three compact blocks between Hobbemastraat and Van Baerlestraat. You may regard the boutiques as too intimidating to enter, but their window displays are often as striking, and their items almost as costly, as the art on display in the museums just round the corner.

Gucci (No. 56) often has eye-catching, pared-down displays: maybe, for example, a stuffed snake with a handbag in its mouth. Other stores worth a peek on this (north) side of the street include: **Shoebaloo** (No. 80), for head-turning footwear; **MEXX** (Nos. 118–120), whose jagged windows make it the street's most dramatic frontage; and **Edgar Vos** (No. 134), where you can admire the top *haute couture* of a Dutch designer.

On the south side, check out: **Emporio Armani** (No. 39); **Oger** (No. 81), for ultra-conservative menswear; **Gianni Versace** (No. 89); the sexy silk lingerie in **La Culotte** (No. 111); and **Oilily's** (No. 133) ever-so-cute children's clothes and accessories, such as pink athletic shoes and dainty lunch-boxes. Want a break from clothes? **Hans Winkel Brillen** (No. 73) is the place for designer specs. The upscale china shop **Focke & Meltzer** (Nos. 65–9) stocks not only foreign brands such as Wedgwood but also a large selection of Delft from De Porceleyne Fles factory and more richly colored Makkumware. Portraits of famous people by artist **Peter Donkersloot** hang in Donkersloot art gallery (No. 127), which, unusually, stays open to midnight every night.

Just off the top of P. C. Hooftstraat, **Romeo Vetro** (Hobbemastraat No. 13) has outlandish glassware blown into the shape of musical instruments, dolphins and boats. Off the other (western) end of P. C. Hooftstraat, on Van Baerlestraat, are more trendy clothes boutiques, such as Dutch designer **Sissy Boy** (No. 15 for men, No. 12 for women).

Cornelis Schuytstraat

Well off the tourist path, this street caters to the needs of the neighborhood's well-heeled yuppies. There are flower shops with artistic displays, chic boutiques and several cafés with sidewalk seating to show off your latest purchases. You could put together a great picnic to take to the Vondelpark (at one end of the street) at **Nan** (No. 26), a fabulous deli, and **Van Averzaath** (No. 36), a classy *pâtisserie* in business since 1905.

Museum Shops

The quarter's three big museums all have shops selling art books, posters and postcards. The **Rijksmuseum**'s shop is often horribly crowded; the **Van Gogh Museum** has an excellent selection of posters of the artist's paintings; and the **Stedelijk Museum** also sells modern designer items – dolls'-house-sized pieces of furniture, staplers, nail clippers – at a high price.

There is also a one-stop shop on Museumplein for books, posters and postcards, which also does a good business in Rembrandt and Van Gogh jigsaws, umbrellas and fridge magnets.

Where to... # Be Entertained

The Museum Quarter has a paucity of atmospheric cafés and after dark it is sedate and dull with none of the appeal of the city's more central districts. However, on fine days the Vondelpark, the city's big green lung, and the Museumplein, the large grassy square backing on to the museums, are pleasant places to spend time in. Street musicians usually provide some entertainment.

The area's main cultural attraction is the **Concertgebouw** (Concertgebouwplein 2, tel: 020 671 8345; www.concertgebouw.nl), Amsterdam's most important venue for classical music (▶ 130). Home to the Royal Concertgebouw Orchestra, the grand neo-classical

building was given a tasteful glass-and-steel extension in the 1980s and lords it over the southwestern side of Museumplein. As well as evening performances, you could take in a Sunday morning concert (those who do are given the opportunity to go on a back-stage tour for a small extra charge), or a free half-hour lunchtime concert 12:30 p.m. Wednesdays. These are held in the Kleine Zaal (Small Hall) or Grote Zaal (Great Hall) – the latter has famously good acoustics and a peculiar arrangement of some of its seating behind the stage. The concerts are very popular, so turn up early to secure a seat. Thanks in no small part to the presence of the Concertgebouw, Van Baerlestraat has several good restau-

rants and is the Museum Quarter's liveliest street at night.

On summer evenings, many Amsterdammers hang out in the Vondelpark. On Wednesday and Sunday afternoons and Thursday through Saturday evenings from the end of May through late August, the **Openluchttheater** (Open-Air Theater) presents all sorts of free performances, including jazz, rock and classical music, children's theater and stand-up comedy: more details on www.openluchttheater.nl

The **Nederlands Filmmuseum** (Vondelpark 3, tel: 020 589 1400; www.filmmuseum.nl, ▶ 119), on the park's northeastern corner, is more an art-house movie theater with a trendy café (Vertigo, ▶ 131) than museum. It shows everything from silent classics to *Brief Encounter* (1954) and *The Texas Chainsaw Massacre* (1974), as well as the latest crop of releases. None of the films are dubbed. On some evenings in July and August, there are free outdoor screenings.

Canal Ring – East

Getting Your Bearings

The eastern side of Amsterdam has a different character from the rest of the city – indeed, it feels more like a "normal" city, with a mix of multicultural housing, chic shops and modern developments jumbled together with canals and docks in varying stages of use and decrepitude.

Entrepotdok is being rapidly rejuvenated

Mirroring this divergence, there is a broad spectrum of activities, from the culture of Heineken-A yeast to the cultivation of exotic spices, and from a museum describing maritime might to another that focuses on genocide. In between, you can find some of Amsterdam's less celebrated but fascinating museums, the city zoo and one of its fanciest hotels.

A good reason to spend a day here is to get a deeper appreciation of the city and the way that it interacts with the rest of the world. An equally good motive, though, is to have fun – which is easy to do in this part of Amsterdam.

AM
REMBRAN
PLEIN
Herengracht
VIJZELSTRAAT
Keizersgracht
Reguliersgracht
Prinsengracht
Lijnbaansgracht
HENDRIK
M VAN
RANDWIJK-
PLANTSOEN
WETERINGSC
STADHOUDERSKADE
Singelgracht
FERDINAND
BOLSTRAAT
Heineken Brouwerij

Left: The "Skinny Bridge" attracts more photographers than any other in Amsterdam

Previous page: The "Skinny Bridge" by night

Canal Ring – East in a Day

From beer to boating, you can enjoy a full range of the district's attractions in one busy day's sightseeing.

9:00 a.m.

Be first in the line at the **Heineken Brewery** (➤ 140–141) for an introduction to the art and science of brewing, and a glass or two to set you up for the day.

11:00 a.m.

Back on the street, wander just over half a mile east through the quiet streets of the eastern Canal Ring to the Amstel River to see the prosaic sluice gates and the pretty **Magere Brug** (above, ➤ 150).

12:00 noon

Back toward the center, admire the Blauwbrug (Blue Bridge) and check out the new developments around Waterlooplein. Then explore the old Jewish Quarter, including the **Joods Historisch Museum** (right, ➤ 142–143), the museum devoted to the Jewish community and the **Portuguese synagogue** (➤ 151). Have lunch at a kosher café.

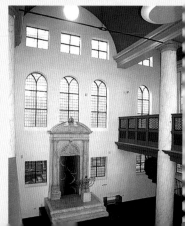

2:30 p.m.

Take a break to explore the collection of flora at the **Hortus Botanicus** gardens (above, ➤ 144–145) or the fauna at **Artis Zoo** (left, ➤ 152–153).

4:00 p.m.

North toward the docks, you can learn about the myth of the Flying Dutchman and the reality of Dutch mastery of the seas at the **Scheepvaart Museum** (➤ 146–149).

6:00 p.m.

Change direction and head west for a slice of traditional Amsterdam. Take a stroll down Reguliersgracht, the "canal of Seven Bridges." There are plenty of places to grab a meal and a drink along the way.

8:00 p.m.

Enjoy a performance at the Tuschinski Cinema, near some of Amsterdam's neater nightlife, or go east to the civilized Carre Theater on the Amstel.

Heineken Brouwerij

Every weekday morning, the Dutch organize a splendid party in a brewery. The Heineken experience is designed to explain the techniques of brewing and give an insight into the history of one of the Netherlands' most successful companies. If you are planning a busy day, though, you may prefer not to avail yourself too freely of the beer dispensed generously at the conclusion of the visit.

In December 1864, Gerard Adriaan Heineken bought a decrepit 16th-century brewery called De Hooiberg ("the Haystack"), which stood behind the Royal Palace. Over the next four years, he moved production to a new site which was, at the time, in open fields south of the city center. (The present production locations are well away from the metropolitan area.) Mr. Heineken introduced the Czech technique of bottom fermentation and oversaw the development of a robust strain of yeast, He also established rigorous quality control and innovative marketing techniques – not least the instantly recognizable red star logo – that created the conditions for successful mass production. Today, the main Heineken brewery can produce one bottle of beer for each inhabitant of Amsterdam every 45 minutes.

The red star symbol on a 19th-century beer mug

The (former) brewery (*brouwerij*) is the plain building dominating the corner of Stadhouderskade and Ferdinand Bolstraat on the south side of Singelgracht. This was where Heineken lager was brewed until 1988, when production moved out and public relations moved in.

The tour begins inside a fermentation tank – now converted into an exhibition area where the story of beer, from its origins in Mesopotamia in the fourth millennium BC, is told with a polished multimedia presentation. It continues through echoing chambers with well-scrubbed white walls and gleaming stainless steel equipment and leads through the stables, whose residents – Shire horses from Britain – haul the brewery's image around Amsterdam. Finally, in a barn of a bar, cheerful waiting staff dispense Heineken by the trayful, along with snacks.

Some visitors find the whole experience too slick, a feeling reinforced by the glib "entertainment" at the end of the tour, where one of the guides jollies along the crowd. But it's a painless way of contributing to charity: your modest 3-guilder entry fee goes to worthy causes.

TAKING A BREAK

If you need some more substantial food or a non-alcoholic drink, you could choose from the wide range of ethnic restaurants on Van der Helststraat, which begins just behind the Heineken brewery and continues south past Albert Cuyp Markt.

Heineken Brewery

To avoid battling with the crowds admiring the Heineken memorabilia, turn up early

➕ 203 D1
✉ Stadhouderskade 78
☎ 020 523 9666
🕐 Tours at 9:30 a.m. and 11 a.m. Mon.–Fri., duration 2 hours
🍴 Café, restaurant, refreshment facility ($–$$$)
🚌 16, 24, 25
🎟 Inexpensive

HEINEKEN BROUWERIJ: INSIDE INFO

Top tips Go on your birthday, or – better still – with someone else who is celebrating theirs. Part of the patter in the bar area involves **giving prizes** (usually a Delft beer tankard) **to someone who is celebrating their birthday** in exchange for some mild humiliation.

• There are, in theory, **two tours Monday to Friday,** at 9:30 and 11 a.m. In practice, these are just the times that the line may start moving. On busy days there can be as many as 10 tours in a morning, setting off at 5- or 10-minute intervals and meeting up in the tasting room.

• Anyone arriving even a few minutes after 11 a.m. **risks being turned away.** The best plan is to arrive at 9 a.m. or shortly afterward, to ensure you are on the first tour of the day. Tours are only for those over 18.

Hidden gem While waiting **in the entrance area,** look for the old hand pumps. They are of heroic dimensions and topped by intricate sculptures.

Joods Historisch Museum

Steel and glass have been employed to combine four neighboring synagogues – dating from 1670 to 1778 – into a complex, the Jewish Historical Museum, which does everything from explaining the tenets of Judaism to outlining the importance of the Jewish community to business life in Amsterdam. The motto of the museum is taken from the Babylonian Talmud: "Seeing leads to remembering, remembering leads to the doing."

Pause outside on Nieuwe Amstelstraat to take in the fine structures that go to make up the museum. Outside, two large yellow triangles have been hoisted high on a frame. Their shapes combine to form a golden Star of David, the symbol that Jewish people were obliged to wear by the occupying Nazis in World War II.

You enter up a narrow stairway, once an alleyway. The designers managed to incorporate aspects of the original street layout in their plans: the entrance and foyer are on the line of the old street of Shulgass, which links the four synagogues together.

The prescribed route around the museum begins in the **New Synagogue**, and this is where you should spend most time on a short visit. It was built in 1752 to replicate what was believed to be the design of the Second Temple in Jerusalem, and the glorious dome was restored in 2000.

The exhibits begin with elements of Dutch-Jewish identity:

The buildings that make up the museum are among the finest in Amsterdam

The Holy Ark is central to Jewish heritage in the city

religion, ties with Israel and the life of the Jewish community in the Netherlands. The museum also looks at the growth of the Zionist movement, which began in the 19th century to work for a permanent Jewish homeland in Israel.

A large proportion of the museum deals with the growth of Nazism, the German occupation and the deportation of 100,000 Amsterdam Jews: few of them returned. Mirroring the testimony of Anne Frank (► 94–97), the paintings of Charlotte Salomon tell the story of one young Jewish woman's experience of Nazi oppression. Like Anne Frank, she perished in a death camp.

The other main part of the complex is the 18th-century **Great Synagogue.** It was designed by Elias Bouwman and contains an introduction to Judaism and Jewish beliefs from cradle to grave. In a side room from the Great Synagogue, a ritual bath is on display to explain the tradition of regarding women as unclean or impure while menstruating, banning sex during this time and for seven days thereafter, and sometimes requiring ritual immersion.

TAKING A BREAK

The **museum café** is a small, often crowded place close to the entrance; you can visit without paying to go into the museum. It does a good line in kosher food and snacks, such as cream cheese and smoked salmon bagels and gefilte fish matzos, washed down with Maccabee or Goldstar Israeli beer.

Joods Historisch Museum
✚ 204 B2
✉ Jonas Daniël Meijerplein 2–4
☎ 020 626 9945; www.jhm.nl
🕐 Daily 11–5. Closed Jan. 1, Yom Kippur, Dec. 25–6
Ⓜ Waterlooplein
🚌 9, 14, 20. The Canal Bus stops adjacent to the Blue Bridge, about 200m (220 yards) west of the museum
🎟 Moderate; free admission to Museum Year Card holders

JOODS HISTORISCH MUSEUM: INSIDE INFO

Top tips Beyond the cash desk, you can pick up the **optional audio tour** for a nominal fee; this will add greatly to the experience.
• To find out more about the Jewish community in Amsterdam, you are free to use the **Resource Center,** open Monday to Friday 1–5 p.m.

Hortus Botanicus

The calm of the garden, coupled with the intensely pleasurable smell, will lift you gently out of the city – though if you are expecting an explosion of color, you should perhaps try the tulip fields instead.

The city's Botanical Garden began as an herbal collection – the Hortus Medicus – for pharmaceutical purposes in 1638 and moved to its present location in 1682. It expanded rapidly when the East India Company brought flora from expeditions across the globe.

The collection is divided into an outdoor garden occupied by temperate or Arctic plants and a series of greenhouses. On your left as you go in is the **Hortus Medicus** itself, the Herb Garden that has been cultivated for medicinal use since the 17th century. Just beyond it is the **Mexican/Californian Desert House**, a nursery for **orchids** and a **butterfly house**. Just south, an elegant 17th-century semicircular plot ripples out from the administration building.

Heading clockwise, you reach the beautiful **Palm House**, a large and ornate 19th-century structure whose highlight is a 300-year-old palm that's still producing cones.

On the far side, the **Three Climates Greenhouse** is a late 20th-century addition that is expertly constructed to allow you to weave from the tropical rainforest via the subtropics to the desert on a sequence of paths. A highlight of the desert section is the *Weltwitschia mirabelis*, the plant known as the "living fossil" because it can live for 2,000 years yet produces only two leaves in its entire life. The tropical section displays a Wardian

Hortus Botanicus is a mix of outdoor gardens and indoor greenhouses

Right: The Three Climates Greenhouse covers climates from desert to rainforest

Garden Tours

An Amsterdam garden-designer, Andre Ancion, leads tours around the **hidden gardens of the city,** exploring styles from Renaissance to baroque. Each walk begins at Herengracht 605. The tour lasts three hours and ends with lunch in a private canal house – included in the price.

✉ Urban Garden Tours, PO Box 15672, 1001 ND Amsterdam ☎ 020 688 1243; www.urbangardentours.nl 🕐 Tours begin at 11 on Mon., Fri. and Sat.; tickets must be collected between 15 and 30 minutes before the walk 🍴 Lunch included 🚌 4 and 12 to Rembrandtplein 💰 Expensive

Below: The Palm House

chest, an airtight wood-and-glass frame invented in 1829 by Englishman Nathaniel Ward to enhance the survival of rare tropical plants. Before its introduction, most plants died on the long sea journey to Amsterdam; afterward, the survival rate increased to 99 percent.

For a different view of the garden, follow the walkway about 16 feet above the ground to explore the canopy of the rainforest.

TAKING A BREAK

Escape the heat of the greenhouses at the **Orangery** café.

Hortus Botanicus
✚ 204 C2
✉ Plantage Middenlaan 2
☎ 020 625 8411; www.nl/-hortus.amsterdam
🕐 Summer (May–Oct.) daily 9–5; winter (Nov.–Apr.) daily 9–4. Closed Jan. 1, Dec. 25
🚌 9, 14 and 20 stop outside
🍴 Orangery café ($)
💰 Moderate (reduced in winter)

HORTUS BOTANICUS: INSIDE INFO

Top tips The **garden entrance** is difficult to spot: it's concealed behind a gatehouse on the corner of Plantage Middenlaan and Dr. D. M. Sluyspad, opposite the Herengracht.

• **Pick up a plan** in English at the door when you go in; labeling is mostly in Dutch and Latin.

• On Sundays there is a **tour at 2 p.m.,** for which you pay 1 guilder extra.

• Summer weekends are very busy. The **last hour of the day** is usually quieter, though the plants are not at their best on a hot summer's day.

Scheepvaart Museum

The superb Maritime Museum tells the story of how Amsterdam, with few natural advantages and many obvious disadvantages, became the most important port in the world the hub of a merchant fleet that instigated – and controlled – large proportion of global trade.

The location of the museum is a telling indication of the decline of Amsterdam as a working port: the ex-naval dockyard it occupies is hidden by the newMetropolis Science and Technology Center (➤ 69), a futuristic building standing over the mouth of the IJ Tunnel, and access to open water is obstructed by new roads and railways. Resourceful as ever, the Dutch have turned a handsome but obsolete naval depot into one of the most popular and impressive tourist attractions in Amsterdam. And beyond the museum, the startling "aircraft wing" design of the ultra-modern Cruise Terminal shows that the city's maritime fortunes are not yet finished.

The building itself is most attractive and is worth admiring from the newMetropolis to appreciate the simplicity and sym-metry of the former naval arsenal that houses the museum.

Inside, the museum layout can be confusing, with an absence of clear signposting for new arrivals. Once you have paid, explore the courtyard, which sports some impressive can-non and occasionally holds special exhibitions. The main part

An ex-naval depot now houses one of Amsterdam's most interest-ing museums

of the collection is actually on the second floor: to reach the start of it, cross into the foyer opposite the entrance and go up the stairs to your right, beneath the figure-head. There is a short introductory film with a Dutch soundtrack – but you can plug into an English translation if you collect a pair of headphones from the counter opposite the movie theater.

The **second floor** is devoted to 17th- and 18th-century shipping, the golden age of Amsterdam's merchant fleet as well as its cultural life. Often the two combine: on the circuit around this level, there are several paintings of famous Dutch naval victories – more interesting as records of historical events than as works of art. There are many more compelling exhibits, such as a map of the world drawn in 1648 (intriguingly, Australia is noted as *"Hollandia Nova, detecta 1644"*). There are also impressive models of ships – plus some real ones, including an 18th-century barge in fine condition. The rapid rise and gradual fall of the East India Company is explained in a video presentation and by means of dozens of exhibits, and the presentation does not shy away from the awfulness of life for the average sailor. The next two centuries are dealt with on the **third floor.**

The Dutch maritime tradition is encapsulated at the moorings outside the museum

By the 19th century, commerce and technology were racing ahead. There were highly effective workaday sailing vessels, nicknamed "butter boxes," in action and techniques for high-speed, wind-powered shipping were being perfected. The era of the clipper was about to begin. The arrival in Amsterdam harbor of an English steamer in 1816 was treated as the sort of novelty that would never catch on.

For about half a century, the sailing ship enjoyed its own brief golden age. The steamship was in development, but was proving slower than the clipper. The completion of the Suez Canal in 1869 changed all the rules, and soon sank – in commercial terms – the clipper fleets.

The Netherlands re-emerged rapidly as a maritime force with the development of shipping companies such as the Holland-America Line. A network of routes sprang up: some of them linked the Dutch colonies with the mother country, while others exploited gaps in the global market for links between other nations.

A full-sized replica of **De Amsterdam**, a tall ship belonging to the East India Company, is usually moored outside the museum. If it is off on one of its occasional visits to other parts of Europe, you will have to make do with the less enthralling collection of smaller vessels, notably a lifeboat bobbing around in the harbor. The original De Amsterdam had a checkered career: on its first voyage to Asia, it ran aground on a sandbank off the coast of England. Unlike its contemporary, the *Cutty Sark* in London's maritime heritage center at Greenwich, the Dutch vessel is a replica (built in the 1980s). But at least it is afloat and able to sail far and wide; it is much in demand all over the Netherlands and elsewhere. You can crawl all over the bridge, the hold and (what many people find most interesting) the living quarters. The trip to the captain's cabin requires the skills of a limbo dancer.

More modest vessels than the clipper now shelter in the museum's haven

TAKING A BREAK

Besides the unremarkable and mediocre **museum café** ($$), there are baguette vendors on the ground floor ($), but there are few alternatives nearby.

Scheepvaart Museum
🕂 205 D3
✉ Kattenburgerplein 1
☎ 020 573 2222; www.scheepvaartmuseum.nl
🕐 Tue.–Sun. 10–5 (also Mon. mid-Jun.–mid-Sep. and during school holidays). Closed Jan. 1, Apr. 29 and Dec. 25
🚌 Nos. 22 and 32 run from Centraal Station to the museum
🚢 The best way to reach the museum is by the Museumboot, which calls at a small wharf close by. See page 39 for more details
🚉 Centraal Station is a brisk 15-minute walk away
💶 Moderate; free admission to Museum Year Card holders

ctors re-enact
aritime tales
board the ship
e Amsterdam

SCHEEPVAART MUSEUM: INSIDE INFO

Top tips Call in advance to find out whether any **special activities** are planned. Often, particularly at summer weekends, actors are brought in to enliven the place or to sing shanties on *De Amsterdam*.
• Aboard the ship, **mind your head** unless you are less than 3 feet tall.
• The shop on the ground floor has an **excellent collection of postcards,** maritime and otherwise, that make a change from the standard canal views of Amsterdam.

Hidden gem The **occasional exhibitions** are well worth seeking out: as inspired offshoots of the main museum theme, they give insights into all kinds of maritime life – for example, tracing the history of KLM, which claims to be the world's oldest operating air transportation company.

How to avoid the crowds Unless it's full of schoolchildren on field trips, you should have the place much to yourself. Summer weekends are the only times when the place becomes crowded with tourists.

At Your Leisure

2 Magere Brug

The "Skinny Bridge" is the most photographed bridge in Amsterdam. According to local legend, it was built for two sisters who were reluctant to take a circuitous route from their home on Kerkstraat, the west end of the present bridge, to the stables on the far bank of the Amstel River. One account says their surname was Mager, which means "skinny," and

The slimline "Skinny Bridge"

gave the bridge its name; another attributes the title to the design of the original bridge.

Either way, the first Skinny Bridge on this site was considerably skinnier than the present version. This is a 20th-century replacement, but its graceful proportions are none the less appealing. From the south side, you can look along the river to the sluice gates that are an essential part of the water management system in Amsterdam. These allow the canal network to be regularly flushed out, keeping the city fragrant.

➕ 204 A1 🚊 4 to Utrechtsestraat, one block west

➍ Portugees Israëlitische Synagoge

The year 1492 was a highly significant one for Spain – not simply because Christopher Columbus, sailing on behalf of the Spanish Crown, landed in the New World, but because the country expelled its Jewish population. Some became Maranos ("crypto-Jews"), which allowed them to stay, but many of the Sephardic victims of the Inquisition moved to neighboring Portugal.

When increased persecution forced Jews from both Iberian countries to seek sanctuary in Amsterdam, they called themselves "Portuguese Jews" – Spain was at war with the Netherlands at the time. Hence their capacious new place of worship was called the "Portuguese Synagogue."

The designer was Elias Bouwman, who also built the Great Synagogue, now one of the components of the Jewish Historical Museum, which stands opposite. Unlike the museum, the Portuguese Synagogue is a functioning place of worship. There is tight security, and male visitors are expected to wear a *yarmulke* (head covering). You can borrow one from the cash desk.

The best way to begin a visit is with the instructive **video,** which explains the growth of the Sephardic community in Amsterdam (in English as well as Dutch), in one of the single-story rooms that completely enclose the synagogue.

The main structure is a substantial, light and airy venue. When it was completed in 1675, it was the largest in Europe. Its wooden roof is supported by four massive stone columns; the only lighting is from four large brass chandeliers. The

Holy Ark is made from Brazilian jacaranda wood.

➕ 204 B2 ✉ Mr Visserplein 3 ☎ 020 624 5351 🕐 Daily 10–4 except Sat. and Jewish holidays 🚇 Waterlooplein 🚊 9, 14, 20 💶 Moderate

➏ Nationaal Vakbondsmuseum

Trade unionism developed slowly in the Netherlands, which never experienced an industrial revolution on the scale of that in Britain or Germany. Diamond-workers were at the forefront, and at the start of the 20th century their union commissioned H. P. Berlage to build new headquarters on what is now Henri Polaklaan (Mr Polak was the chairman of the union). In keeping with the notion that museum staff should enjoy proper leisure time, the Vakbondsmuseum (Trade Union Museum) is closed at weekends. The design of the venue is arguably more appealing than its contents, with an impressive exterior and opulent interior full of grand designs by leading artists of the day. The exhibits themselves are mostly of interest to students of labor history or active trade unionists keen on an international perspective.

➕ 204 C2 ✉ Henri Polaklaan 9 ☎ 020 624 1166 🕐 Tue.–Fri. 11–5, Sun. 1–5 🚊 6 and 20 counterclockwise (toward Centraal Station) stop nearby on Plantage Parklaan; from the opposite direction, the closest stop is on Plantage Middenlaan, one block south 💶 Inexpensive; free admission to Museum Year Card holders and discount for card-carrying union members

7 Verzetsmuseum

The Nazi occupation of the
Netherlands lasted five days short of
five years, a desperately traumatic
time for the Dutch people.
Amsterdam, with easily the largest
population of Jews, was the city that
saw most suffering – and the greatest
resistance against the German forces.
The Resistance Museum's central purpose is to deal with the fight against
the Nazi occupation from 1940 to
1945, but it encompasses much more,
including the growth of Fascism
before World War II and the fight
against racism since then.

The location is the Plancius
Building, built in 1876 as a social club
for the Oefening Baart Kunst, a Jewish
choral society. Inside, the space has
been transformed into a dark, moody
series of exhibits.

The museum is an important
complement to Anne Frank's House,
describing the wider context of the
grim game of "hide and seek" that
took place during the occupation.
Thousands of Jews were hidden by
fellow citizens, while others were
spirited out of the country or given
false identities. The stirring events
that took place in February 1942,
when a general strike was called in
protest against a Nazi crackdown on
Jews, are covered – as are the terrible
"Hunger Winter" of 1944–45 and the
incentives given to the Dutch who
collaborated with the occupation
force. Revealing a hiding place earned
a reward of 7 guilders per person
apprehended.

🔢 204 C2 ✉ Plantage Kerklaan
61a ☎ 020 620 2535;
www.verzetsmuseum.org 🕐 Tue.–Fri.
10–5, Sat.–Sun. noon–5. Closed Jan. 1,
Apr. 30 and Dec. 25 🚋 6 and 20 counterclockwise (toward Centraal Station)
stop just outside Artis Zoo, diagonally
across the road; from the opposite
direction, the closest stop is on
Plantage Middenlaan, one block south
🎫 Moderate

8 Artis Zoo

The curious name of Amsterdam's zoo
derives from the Latin "Artis Natura
Magistra," meaning "Nature, Mistress
of the Arts." The concept of locking
up exotic creatures in small cages in
chilly northern cities is considered
questionable today, but the zoo's
popularity is indisputable. This is
partly thanks to a program of
continual improvements: a
rejuvenated segment of **"African
Savannah"** opened in 1999, giving
more space to zebras, wildebeest and
a variety of birdlife. Work is continuing to enhance the living conditions
of the elephants and giraffes.

The area that most fascinates
children (who make up the majority
of visitors here) is the **wolf
enclosure,** where the powerful
canines can roam around some sort of
approximation to the primeval forests

The aquarium at Artis Zoo

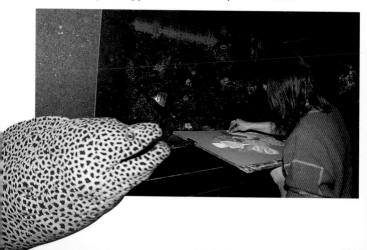

of Europe while spectators gawk from a footbridge. The zoo also has a certain style that adults may appreciate: its noble 19th-century aims are evident from the naturalistic motifs that adorn the library and aquarium.

➕ 205 D2 ✉ Plantage Kerklaan 38–40
☎ 020 523 3400; www.artis.nl ⏰ Daily
9–5 🍽 Café ($$$) 🚊 6 and 20 counterclockwise (toward Centraal Station) stop immediately outside; from the opposite direction, the closest stop is on Plantage Middenlaan, one block south 💲 Expensive

territory. During the 19th century it became the richest

Old dock, new prospects: the Entrepotdok is drifting upscale

❾ Entrepotdok

In the 20th century, Amsterdam's docks, in the east of the city, fell into dereliction; but they are now being reclaimed by cafés, artists' studios and upscale housing. The best example is Entrepotdok, with a southwest-facing quayside that is especially convivial on summer afternoons.

The solid-looking gatehouse leading from Rapenburgerplein hints that this was no ordinary dock lined with warehouses. It was designed as Amsterdam's own "free port," a zone beyond the reach of the Customs authorities where goods could be shipped in and out as long as they were not actually "landed" in Dutch

dock in the city. Today, it is a peaceful corner where you can escape the crowds and traffic noise that prevail in eastern Amsterdam. Entrepotdok stretches for more than half a mile, extending to the back end of Artis Zoo. The construction of a new footbridge gives access to the zoo, the **Resistance Museum** (➤ 152) and the **Trade Union Museum** (➤ 151).

➕ 205 E2 ✉ Entrepotdok ⏰ Access at any time 🍽 Several cafés ($$–$$$) 🚊 6 and 20 counterclockwise (toward Centraal Station) stop just outside Artis Zoo; from the opposite direction, the closest stop is on Plantage Middenlaan, one block south of the zoo entrance 💲 Free

The Tropenmuseum is politically and environmentally correct

exhibition begins on the **ground floor** above the entrance hall with a display on Man and Environment that focuses on the desecration of the rainforest.

The **second floor**, which you reach via a sweeping staircase, concentrates on Asia and Oceania. Indonesia features strongly, and there is an exhibition devoted to a Toraja funeral – an exceedingly ceremonial affair from the island of Sulawesi. From the **third floor**, the striking design of the Tropenmuseum is evident, with an arc of glass sweeping over the hall. The most impressive area on this floor is the section on Latin America, covering the Caribbean islands and Surinam (on the South American mainland), plus much more about the Hispanic world.

➕ 205 E1
✉ Linnaeusstraat 2
☎ 0202 568 8215;
www.kit.nl/tropenmuseum ⏰ Mon.–Fri. 10 a.m.–5 p.m., Sat.–Sun. and holidays (except Jan. 1, Apr. 30, May 5 and Dec. 25) noon–5 🍴 Ekeko Restaurant features world food; the café features an outdoor terrace ($) 🚊 7, 9, 10, 14 💶 Moderate; free admission to Museum Year Card holders

🔟 Tropenmuseum

Tucked away beyond Singelgracht in the southeastern suburbs, this grand edifice is easily missed. Even the entrance is hard to locate – on the eastern-facing side, at basement level, and with a sign announcing it to be the **Kindermuseum (Children's Museum),** which is just a small part of the whole Tropical Museum.

The building is an eclectic, early 20th-century structure by J. J. and M. A. van Nieukerken, with the predictable Gothic overtones seen in Centraal Station and the Rijksmuseum. It opened in 1923 as home to the Vereeniging Kolonial Instituut, now the Royal Tropical Institute, which is funded by the Dutch development ministry. One of its duties is to run the most politically correct museum in Amsterdam.

Making up for the excesses of colonialism, the vast **Light Hall** has been opened up to influences from all over the world – not just the parts of the tropical world that fell under Dutch rule. The

Where to...
Eat and Drink

Prices
Expect to pay per person for a meal, excluding drinks
$** under 35 guilders **$$** 35–70 guilders **$$$ more than 70 guilders

CAFÉS & BARS

Backstage $
Larger-than-life Gary Christmas used to be half of the Christmas Twins' cabaret act with his brother Greg, who died a few years ago. Gary now dispenses chat and astrological advice to strangers and his dedicated local clientele in his tiny, garish and camp café, which has become something of an Amsterdam institution. His home-made knitwear is for sale; the john, with centerfold pin-ups of both sexes, is not for the prudish. The specialty of the house is the toasted tuna sandwich, made from a secret recipe.

🚹 203 F2 ◻ Utrechtsedwarsstraat 67 ☎ 020 622 3638 🕐 Mon.–Sat. 10–5:30

Bagels & Beans $
This popular daytime café is an ideal spot for breakfast or lunch if you're visiting the Albert Cuyp market, which starts just across the road. Its superb bagels come with cream cheese, Dutch cheese or combinations such as banana and maple syrup. Other specialties of the house include muffins, coffee and heavenly fruit juices such as forest fruits (mixed berries) or kiwi. When the weather allows there is a large outdoor terrace.

🚹 203 off 01 ◻ Ferdinand Bolstraat 70 ☎ 020 672 1610 🕐 Mon.–Fri. 8:30–6, Sat. from 9:30 a.m. Sun. from 10 a.m.

Brouwerij 't IJ $
The windmill in Amsterdam's eastern part of the city, just a 10-minute walk from the Maritime Museum and practically around the corner from the Tropenmuseum, is worth paying a visit to if you're thirsty. The in-house brewery has at least four beers on tap, alcoholic content ranging from five to nine percent in strength. The interior is basic beer hall with a no-frills bar and a few wooden benches and a view of the giant beer kettle at the rear; in warm weather, many choose to sit outside on the waterfront. Although the only snacks available are peanuts, the café next door does *tapas*.

🚹 205 E2 ◻ Funenkade 7 ☎ 020 622 8325 🕐 Wed.–Sun. 3–8 p.m.

Café Schiller $$
The best feature of the Hotel Schiller is this café/bar, which adds a touch of civility and sophistication to Rembrandtplein. It is famous for its original art deco fittings – marble walls, ornate lamps, a curvaceous bar, booths upholstered in gold and black stripes. An interesting short dinner menu features such dishes as oxtail soup and lamb sweetbreads.

🚹 203 E3 ◻ Rembrandtplein 26 ☎ 020 624 9846 🕐 Sun.–Thu. 4 p.m.–1 a.m., Fri., Sat. till 2 a.m.

De Druif $
"The Grape" brown café has been here since 1631: the mustard-colored walls, tiers of old liqueur barrels and antique *jenever* pump on the bar all indicate its age. It's very much a locals' haunt. The café overlooks the Entrepotdok's entrance, where you can watch barges chugging past at the back.

🚹 204 C3 ◻ Rapenburgerplein 83 ☎ 020 624 4530 🕐 Sun.–Thu. 11 a.m.–1 a.m., Fri., Sat. till 2 a.m.

Hooghoudt $$

The cellar-like ground floor of this 17th-century warehouse has a double identity. At the front is the tasting house for the Hooghoudt distillery in Groningen, with its *jenevers* and liqueurs racked behind the bar. Behind lies a stylish little dining-room area, where you can have filling Dutch dishes such as beef stew in a red wine and *jenever* sauce. Whether you come for a drink or to eat, you'll find a very civilized atmosphere.

🚇 203 E3 ✉ Reguliersgracht 11
☎ 020 420 4041 🕐 Thu.–Tue.
4 p.m.–midnight

De Kroon $–$$

Adding a welcome touch of sophistication to tacky Rembrandtplein, this is one of the city's grandest and trendiest grand cafés. Situated on the second floor, it has a glassed-in balcony overlooking the square. The decor takes the form of modern paintings by local artists, plush velvet furnishings and natural history artifacts around the bar. The eclectic food is quite ambitious and not always successful, but it's a great place for a cocktail or coffee.

🚇 203 E3 ✉ Rembrandtplein 17
☎ 020 625 2011 🕐 Sun.–Thu.
10 a.m.–1 a.m, Fri, Sat. till 2 a.m.

Oosterling $

The Oosterling's pedigree is indisputable: it occupies a building dating from 1735 that was once owned by the Dutch East India Company, and the Oosterling family has been selling drinks here since 1879. Old barrels are used for table tops, others are racked up behind the long granite-topped bar. Unusually, the café doubles as a liquor store.

🚇 203 F2 ✉ Utrechtsestraat 140
☎ 020 623 4140 🕐 Mon.–Sat.
11 a.m.–1 a.m, Sun. from 1 p.m.

Pata Negra $

An authentic, usually packed *tapas* bar that is cramped, frenetic and noisy. Iberian hams hang over the bar and bullfighting posters and tiled murals of nostalgic Hispanic scenes cover the walls. Sangria and sherries are available, plus a long *tapas* menu that covers all the classic dishes, from meatballs to *calamares*. Reserve in the evening if you want to sit down at the communal tables.

🚇 203 F2 ✉ Utrechtsestraat 124
☎ 020 422 6250 🕐 Daily
1 p.m.–midnight

De Wetering $

A down-to-earth, cosy old brown corner café full of slightly bohemian locals, despite the fact that it is just around the corner from the chic antiques shops of the Spiegelkwartier and the Rijksmuseum. Downstairs by the bar is standing room only; on the upper level, sand covers the floorboards and a log fire burns in winter.

🚇 203 D2 ✉ Weteringstraat 37
☎ 020 622 9676 🕐 Sun.–Thu.
4 p.m.–1 a.m, Fri, Sat. 4 p.m.–2 a.m.

RESTAURANTS

Amstel Intercontinental $–$$$

Amsterdam's most fashionable hotel is a little too far from the center for a convenient base, but it's just the place to live it up for a couple of hours. Choose between a substantial afternoon tea with delicious sandwiches and pastries in its conservatory lounge or a meal in the less welcoming, library-styled Amstel Brasserie. If you really want to push the boat out, reserve a table in La Rive (jacket required). This restaurant has the feel of a dining room of a grand country-house hotel. Until recently, its was regarded as the best in the city. The lounge and restaurants all bask in views of the river.

🚇 204 off B1 ✉ Prof Tulpplein 1
☎ 020 622 6060 🕐 Afternoon tea
Mon.–Fri. 3–6, Sat, Sun. 1–3, 4–6;
Amstel Brasserie Mon.–Fri. noon–3,
5–1 a.m, Sat, Sun. noon–1 a.m.; La
Rive Mon.–Fri. noon–2, 6:30–10:30,
Sat. 6:30 p.m.–10:30 p.m.

An $

An inexpensive, few-frills Japanese café squeezed into a long, narrow space, where diners sit at wooden tables or wait for take-out. The long menu ranges from authentic *sushi* to *teriyaki*, with a good choice of vegetarian options. Japanese tea is served free.

➕ 203 E1 ✉ Weteringschans 199 ☎ 020 627 0607 🕒 Mon.–Sat. 11:30–8

Artist Libanees Restaurant $–$$

This unpretentious restaurant is run by two brothers (Ralpho and Simon) who were former cabaret artists. They now serve authentic Lebanese cooking at reasonable prices. If you come with four guests, you can make a meal of the *mezes* (warm and cold appetizers), which smaller parties need to order *à la carte*. You can choose from several variations of eggplant, lamb and even okra. But don't miss the *baba ghanouj*, or garlicy eggplant puree with warm pita as an appetizer.

Lebanese wine is available, and in warm weather the terrace is *the* place to be.

➕ 203 F1 ✉ Tweede Jan Steenstraat 1 ☎ 020 671 4264 🕒 Daily 5–10 p.m.

Cambodja City $

Deceptively simple surroundings include photos of food in the window, a few paper dragons, a take-out counter and vinyl-topped tables. But this basic *eethuis*, one of many in the De Pijp neighborhood, produces some of the best Asian food anywhere in Amsterdam. The menu is a jumble of Cambodian, Thai and Vietnamese dishes, or you can order "special dinners" that stick to one of the cuisines.

➕ 203 off D1 ✉ Albert Cuypstraat 58/60 ☎ 020 671 4930 🕒 Tue.–Sun. 5–10 p.m.

Dynasty $$–$$$

This seductive, upscale Southeast Asian restaurant fills the ground floor of a handsome old gabled house on a street well-known for its

gay bars. You dine by candlelight under a ceiling entirely covered in upturned paper umbrellas – or, weather permitting, in the pretty garden at the rear. The kitchen's repertoire covers Thai, Vietnamese and Chinese dishes.

➕ 203 D3 ✉ Reguliersdwarsstraat 30 ☎ 020 626 8400 🕒 Wed.–Mon. 5.30–11 p.m.

Inez IPSC $$$

This is one of Amsterdam's most voguish restaurants. Its exclusivity is underlined by the fact that there is no sign suggesting its existence on the street. The second-floor dining-room has large windows overlooking the Muntplein. The "freestyle" cuisine might include lobster ravioli and leg of goat in a truffle sauce.

➕ 203 E3 ✉ Amstel 2 ☎ 020 639 2899 🕒 Daily noon–3, 7–11:30

Kort $$

Kort's shady outdoor terrace overlooks houseboats and old gabled buildings. Not surprisingly, this is

one of the most desirable places to eat in Amsterdam when it's warm. Otherwise, you dine in the simply but attractively furnished crypt of a 17th-century wooden church. The fusion food – such as pear and mozzarella salad, or salmon in a seaweed sauce – is light and tasty.

➕ 203 E2 ✉ Amstelveld 12 ☎ 020 626 1199 🕒 Wed.–Mon. 11:30–11

Okura Hotel $$$

This Japanese-owned hotel has acquired a well-deserved reputation for serving the best Japanese food in Holland at its Yamazato and Teppanyaki restaurants. Yamazato specializes in *sushi* and *tempura* prepared to a much higher level than most restaurants outside Japan. Their changing theme menus, which might feature lobster and, in season, game, are worth the stiff price not only for their quality but for their unusual interpretations. The Teppanyakis tables are always filled with Dutch businessmen entertaining Japanese guests. Before or after

Where to...
Shop

The essential shopping highlights in this part of the city are the art and antiques of the Spiegelkwartier, the touristy but colorful Flower Market and the down-to-earth Albert Cuypmarkt, which has all the flavor of a traditional street market.

Spiegelkwartier

The 80 shops of Amsterdam's premier fine art and antiques district deal in everything from Old Masters to antiquities, Russian icons to Chinese prints, and Delftware to modern art. At its heart is Nieuwe Spiegelstraat, which runs from Herengracht's Golden Bend down toward the Rijksmuseum. The rarified shops opened up here because they knew they would enjoy a cap-

dinner, go up to the 24th floor for a drink with a panoramic view.

✠ 203 off D1 ☒ Ferdinand Bolstraat 333 ☎ 020-678 8351 ☒ Yamazato daily noon–2, 6-9:30; Teppanyaki daily noon–2 p.m., 6:30 p.m.–10 p.m.

Tempo Doeloe $$

If asked to pick one Indonesian restaurant, many Amsterdammers would choose this intimate, chic yet informal establishment. Its only drawback is its popularity; it's invariably full and service can be stretched to the limit. Ring the doorbell to enter. The cuisine is authentic (dishes marked "*pedis*" will blow your head off if you're not used to spicy food), and the *rijsttafels* are generous and varied.

✠ 203 F2 ☒ Utrechtsestraat 75 ☎ 020 625 6718 ☒ Daily 6–11:30 p.m.

Trez Restaurant $$

Down in the De Pijp neighborhood near the Albert Cuyp market, this alluring bistro focuses on delicious

southern European tastes from Spain, Italy, Portugal and France. The cozy interior is decorated with candles and fresh flowers and the kitchen is open, so you can see the chef in action. In warm months, you can also sit outside. Start off with a Trez platter for two, which features a wide range of the house *tapas* and antipasti, or order anything from garlicy snails, shrimps or *soup du jour*. Tempting main courses feature duck, lamb, chicken or fish.

✠ 203 off D1 ☒ Saenredamstraat 39 ☎ 020 676 2495 ☒ Daily 6–10 p.m.

Warung Marlon $

De Pijp is the area to go for down-to-earth ethnic eating, and on 1e Van der Helststraat nowhere is less pretentious than this spartan yet lively little Surinamese place. Since Surinam is in South America, you may wonder at the amount of Asian food on the menu, particularly Indonesian dishes such as satay and fried rice. The reason is that most restaurants in Surinam are Asian-

run. For lunch, you will probably find that one of the large soups, served with a boiled egg, rice and bean sprouts, is a meal in itself.

✠ 203 E1 ☒ 1e Van der Helststraat 55 ☎ 020 671 1526 ☒ Wed.–Mon. 11–8

Le Zinc...et les Dames $$

This is an engaging pastishe of rural France in an old, shuttered canalfront warehouse. Downstairs is a candlelit wine bar with a zinc-topped bar, chunky cafeteria-tables, French wines by the glass and carafe posted on a blackboard and nibbles such as *rillettes* and *tapenade*.

Upstairs is a romantic restaurant, hung with paintings of nude women (*les dames*). Dishes such as *charcuterie* from Lyons, a veal stew from Burgundy and *tarte au citron* from Provence reflect the diversity of French regional cooking.

✠ 203 E2 ☒ Prinsengracht 999 ☎ 020 622 9044 ☒ Tue.–Sat. bar 4 p.m.–1 a.m., restaurant 5:30–11 p.m.

tive market of art-lovers. With its old-gabled buildings and ornate window displays, Nieuwe Spiegelstraat is perhaps the city's prettiest canal-free thoroughfare and ideal for a wander and browse even if you have no intention of making a purchase – note that bargains are in short supply. Starting at the Herengracht end, it's worth checking out what's showing at **De Appel** (No. 10), a major center for contemporary art exhibitions. **Umbria** (No. 20) deals in giant new and old urns from Spain and Italy, while **Van Dreven & Toebosch** (No. 33) specializes in clocks, barometers and music boxes. **Eduard Kramer** (No. 64) has a vast selection of old Delft tiles, most of which have been salvaged from kitchens in canal houses, as well as Dutch trinkets and jewelry.

Nieuwe Spiegelstraat runs into to Spiegelgracht, where you'll find many of the quarter's modern art galleries and also, at No. 10, **Bell Tree**, an excellent children's toy shop.

More intriguing shops can be found just off Spiegelgracht and Nieuwe Spiegelstraat on the streets facing or parallel to the canals. **Songlines** (Prinsengracht 570) is dedicated to aboriginal art; **Anton Heyboer** (Prinsengracht 578) deals in antique toys such as scooters, dolls and rocking horses.

Meulendijk & Schuil (No. 45a Kerkstraat) is stocked with model planes, telescopes and globes. The wonderfully arcane and tiny **Thom & Lenny Nelis** (541 Keizersgracht) is devoted to antique pharmaceutical paraphernalia such as old scales and dispensary jars.

Other Shopping Streets

The shops on the section of the Singel alongside the Bloemenmarkt (Flower Market) sell amusing tourist tat such as singing and dancing Father Christmases and ties decorated with cows and windmills. **Maranon** (Singel 488–490) has a vast and colorful collection of hammocks.

Utrechtsestraat, with its old-fashioned delis and its flower and herring stalls set up on the bridges that cross it, feels partly like a neighborhood main street. At the same time, it's one of Amsterdam's more chic shopping streets, with several upscale boutiques and art galleries. Worth a look is **Concerto** at Nos. 52–60, a music store with great second-hand collections filling half a block.

On Vijzelstraat, watch for **Holtkamp** at No. 15, which, with its handmade chocolates and swan-shaped meringues, bills itself as a luxury bakery. **Peter Doeswijk**, two doors down at No. 11, sells telephones and lavatory seats painted with original designs – maybe in tartan or of Amsterdam canal scenes.

MARKETS

Bloemenmarkt (Mon.–Sat. 9:30–5, Sun. noon–5): the Flower Market projects out over the Singel, but don't take the often-quoted "float-

ing" description too literally. Growers once used to sell flowers from the boats that brought them into the city; but the stalls and garden shops are now very much fixed. Though the street can be horribly overcrowded, the freshly cut flowers look and smell delightful. It's a good place to buy bulbs, which can be mail-ordered, and wooden tulips, a popular souvenir.

Albert Cuypmarkt (Albert Cuypstraat, Mon.–Sat. 9–5): the lifeblood of De Pijp district is the city's biggest and best general market. Running from Ferdinand Bolstraat to Van Woustraat, it's over half a mile long, with 350 stalls. Fruit and vegetables, herring and eels, cheese and olives, underwear and jeans and every item under the heading of general bric-a-brac that you can imagine are available. Just as interesting are all the multicultural shops and cafés along the street; for more salubrious-looking eating and drinking options, head for 1e Van der Helstraat.

Where to...
Be Entertained

Rembrandtplein and its nearby streets are the nocturnal focal point for the eastern canal ring. Named after a 19th-century statue of Rembrandt, the tacky, sometimes rowdy square is lit by neon at night and surrounded by mostly second-rate cafés and restaurants (▶ 155–158 for recommendations). But if you sit on their large outdoor terraces, street musicians and passing trams provide free entertainment. Traditional, folksy Dutch sing-alongs take place in cafés such as Hof van Holland and Popular.

To the west, Reguliersdwarsstraat (beyond Vijzelstraat) is one of the city's main focal points for Amsterdam's happening gay scene, with explicit sex shops, a gay coffee shop (**The Otherside**, at No. 6) and gay clubs, restaurants and cafés. One of the most civilized cafés is **April** (No. 37), though you could say that it still performs its original role as a working men's club as the night progresses; at other times it's not at all cruisy.

NIGHTCLUBS

Just east of Rembrandtplein, **iT** (Amstelstraat 24, tel: 020 625 0111) is a flamboyant, sometimes outrageous high-energy dance club housed in a former movie theater that gets consistently good reviews. Some nights are mixed, others gay. **Escape** (Rembrandtplein 11, tel: 020 622 3542), on Rembrandtplein,

is the largest disco in town, though not as universally acclaimed as iT. Its big night, called Chemistry, is on Saturdays; be prepared to line up and dress up if you want to get past the doormen. High-tech, trendy **Exit** (Reguliersdwarsstraat 42, tel: 020 625 8788) is one of the best-known gay clubs. **Club Arena** (sGravesandestraat 51, tel: 020 694 7444), a 10-minute tram ride from the city center and open only Fridays and Saturdays, plays dance music from specific decades. The complex, which includes a budget hotel and café, used to be a Catholic orphanage.

MOVIE THEATERS

If you decide to go to the movies when you're in Amsterdam, be sure to make it the **Tuschinski Theater** (Reguliersbreestraat 26–28, tel: 020 623 1510). Built in 1921 in the most over-the-top art deco style, Amsterdam's showcase movie theater would look more at home on Los Angeles' Hollywood Boulevard. The original gaudy fittings have been restored. Have a peek at them in the lobby, but better still buy a ticket for whatever is showing in Screen 1, the main (giant) auditorium. The priciest tickets are for double seats and include a glass of champagne. Guided tours are conducted in July and August on Sundays and Mondays at 10:30 a.m. Expect lines on weekends if you haven't reserved in advance.

THEATER AND CHAMBER MUSIC

Down by the Amstel, the **Koninklijk Theater Carré** (Amstel 115–25, tel: 020 622 5225), built in the 19th century as a circus, now hosts large-scale musicals along with opera and ballet. Farther south, **De IJsbreker** ("The Icebreaker," Weesperzijde 23, tel: 020 668 1805; www.ysbreker.nl) is a leading venue for innovative modern chamber music and has a pleasant riverside café.

Excursions

Excursions

One great advantage of the Netherlands is that almost anywhere in the country is quick and easy to reach from Amsterdam. In just a few minutes the free ferry north across the IJ River will deposit you on the edge of Waterland – the start of a tranquil region steeped in tradition.

Heading west instead, within 15 minutes you can exchange the bustle of Holland's biggest city for the much calmer and more manageable town of Haarlem – and, on a hot summer's day, join the Amsterdammers at play on the beach at Zandvoort.

To the east, the ancient capital of Utrecht is only 30 minutes away. Although it has long since relinquished political power to Amsterdam, it retains a certain majesty. The core of the city, carved through by a unique pair of "sunken canals," is one of the most alluring in Europe. Go southwest and, at the right time of year, you drift through swaths of color en route to Leiden. The university city of Leiden is both handsome and historic, with traces of the Pilgrim Fathers who sought religous freedom here before crossing the Atlantic aboard the *Mayflower*.

Finally, the airport at which you may well have arrived is a notable attraction in its own right. Schiphol is the most visitor-friendly of all Europe's major airports.

Previous page:
Windmills at
Zaanse Schans

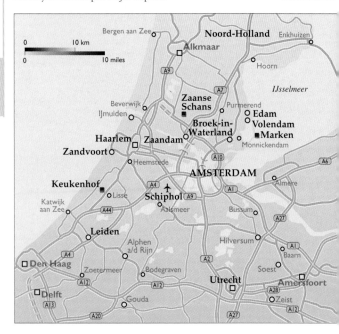

Noord-Holland

Noord-Holland (North Holland) is the name for the tongue of
land poking north from Amsterdam, with the North Sea on
one side and the IJsselmeer (created by damming the Zuider
Zee) on the other.

Skaters on a
frozen lake
at Broek-in-
Waterland

As soon as you leave
Amsterdam behind, the countryside looks and feels very
different from the busy land-
and cityscapes farther south.
In blustery, gray weather, the
windswept fields can epitomize the bleakness depicted
by Van Gogh. But on sunny
days, they resemble his most
optimistic landscapes. The
coast and waterways still bear
evidence of the ocean-going
tradition that ended when the
Afsluitdijk cut off the Zuider
Zee from the North Sea. On
weekends, the area is a play-
ground for Amsterdammers.
North Holland is also a
sanctuary for birdlife.

Trains will take you to
some of the places of interest
and buses fill in many of the
gaps: 111 runs from
Amsterdam's Centraal Station
to the island of Marken, and
116 goes to Volendam and
Edam.

But this is one part of the
country where your own
transportation, whether on
two or four wheels, can be a real advantage by conferring the
freedom to create your own route. If you are on foot or cycling,
a good way to begin is with the free ferry across the IJ from the
rear of Amsterdam's Centraal Station: this operates every few
minutes from early morning to late at night. On the northern
bank, there are buses and cycle paths to take you through the
undistinguished suburbs of Amsterdam-Noord to Broek-in-
Waterland, well-marked for motorists emerging from the tunnel under the IJ.

Broek-in-Waterland

A pretty patchwork of cottages amid a tapestry of serene waterways, Broek-in-Waterland sets the tone for the region. A 16th-
century church stands primly at the heart of the village.

Marken

A minor road northeast takes you to the causeway leading to Marken, an island with this single tenuous road connection. Cars and buses are obliged to stop at the south end of the settlement. The quiet and relative isolation makes this the loveliest of all North Holland villages, a quaint collection of wooden houses linked by venerable bridges.

Above: The lovely village of Marken

For a while, it was one of the busiest ports in the region, thanks to the fishing and whaling fleet; now its main industry is tourism, and there are plenty of cafés and restaurants on the waterfront. From here, there are regular ferries shuttling across to the lively port of Volendam.

Cyclists may decide to turn around and head for home after Marken, while motorists must first retrace their steps to continue farther north, hugging a coastline that is protected by a formidable dike.

Volendam and Edam

The road along the shore passes through Monnickendam, then winds around the coast to Volendam, whose wharf is a frenetic collusion of boats painted in primary colors, cafés and souvenir shops. The "real" town that lies immediately behind it has considerable charm.

Above: The wharf of Volendam is always busy

Volendam merges with Edam, a place much less bland than the cheese that shares its name. When the tourist buses have gone for the day, usually by around 4 p.m., it is a delight to wander around the quiet streets, heavy with history (and cheese shops). Bus 116, a fast main road or a handy cycle path will take you directly back to Amsterdam from Edam. But to complete a rustic tour, you could head west to take in a couple of extra sights.

Zaanse Schans

The Zaan River has, like others in the area, become a commercial backwater. During the 17th and 18th centuries, however, the town of Zaandam was an important ship-building center. Most visitors to **Zaandam** these days come to see Zaanse Schans, a collection of houses and windmills to the north of the town. In 1960, a plan was devized to turn the area into a living folk-museum, and the houses were contructed accordingly to give a more villagey feel.

The mills that parade along the east bank of the Zaan are the survivors of around 600 that used to dominate the horizon.

The most interesting is the **Verfmolen**, the Color Mill. Wood, plants and roots were ground here for textile-makers, and chalk was crushed for painters. The mill still earns its keep supplying naturally made colors to artists. As well as the standard collection of lovely houses painted in deep greens and dotted beside gentle canals, a motley selection of farm animals is distributed across some small fields. Museums on the site are devoted to such specialties as clocks and costume.

✉ Zaandam ☎ 075 616 2221 (Zaandam VVV) for information 🕐 Site open at all times. Individual attractions Nov.–Feb., weekends 9–5; Mar.–Jun., Sep.–Oct., Tue.–Sun. 9–5; Jul., Aug., daily 9–5 🍴 De Hoop Op d'Swarte Walvis restaurant (tel: 075 616 5540), open daily for dinner, Mon.–Fri. for lunch ($$$) 🚉 Koog-Zaandijk, four trains each hour 💶 Site free; attractions inexpensive–moderate

Czar-gazing

It is a long mental leap from this placid part of Holland to the Winter Palace in St. Petersburg, but some of the origins of Russia's finest city can be traced to the town of **Zaandam.** Early in his reign, Peter the Great toured Western Europe to study the techniques that would enable him to modernize the then-primitive Russian Empire. He came to Holland at the tail end of the 17th century to study the latest maritime technology, meeting accomplished shipbuilders and cartographers. His home, **Czaar Peterhuisje (Czar Peterhouse)** in the town is now a museum: you may be surprised at the modest scale of the small wooden house, now enclosed in a more permanent stone building. The museum describes shipbuilding on the Zaan and the life of the Czar.

While based here, the Czar also learned a great deal about land reclamation, which proved invaluable when creating his new capital, St. Petersburg, from the marshland fringing the Baltic.

Czaar Peterhuisje

✉ Krimp 23, Zaandam ☎ 075 616 0390 🕐 Apr.–Oct., Tue.–Sun. 1–5; Nov.–Mar., Sat.–Sun. 1–5 🚉 Zaandam 💶 Inexpensive; free admission to Museum Year Card holders

After the tourist buses depart around 4 p.m., Edam is no longer clogged

Haarlem and Zandvoort

On a sunny day, this pretty town and lively resort make a great combination.

Haarlem

Just 15 minutes from Amsterdam, Haarlem is the perfect anti-
dote for anyone who feels
overwhelmed by the city.
Small, manageable and
friendly, it offers the feel of a
"real" Dutch town combined
with a strong historical and
cultural character of its own.

There is an easy and
absorbing circular walk to be
made, starting at one of the
principal sights, the splendid
1908 art nouveau **railway
station.** In the main ticket
hall there is a pair of large
tiled murals designed to
inspire the working classes:
one showing a plowman, the
other two blacksmiths. At the
west end of the station (away
from the main hall) there is a
VVV tourist office.

Start walking south,
directly away from the VVV,
on Kruisweg, which turns
into Kruisstraat halfway
along. After 10 minutes or so,
you will encounter an antiques shop, **De Spiegelwinkel** (Open
Mon. 1–6, Tue.–Fri. 10–6, Sat. 10–5, late opening Thu. 7:30–9)
housed in a sumptuous mansion. Almost directly opposite, the
Hofje van Oorschot is a rare thing: a *hofje* (➤ 90) that is open
to the street rather than being cloistered away.

Continuing south along Barteljorisstraat, you pass on your
left the **Corrie ten Boomhuis.** The ten Boom family were evan-
gelists who played an important part in the Resistance during
World War II, providing shelter for Jews.

A little farther on, the **Grote Markt** opens up – a broad and
beautiful jumble of buildings. The market square is dominated
by **Sint Bavokerk,** also known as the Grote Kerk or Great
Church. This 15th-century late Gothic brute exceeds in sheer
bulk anything in Amsterdam. It has been under repair for several years, but has remained open – the entrance is hidden

Haarlem offers
a comfortable
alternative to
Amsterdam

around the back on Oude Groenmarkt. Inside, the highlight
is the extravagant baroque organ, installed in 1738 and later
played by 10-year-old Wolfgang Amadeus Mozart. Head south
along Warmoesstraat, which turns into Schagchelstraat and
Grote Heiligland, a street endowed with some lovely houses.
Near the end is the **Frans Halsmuseum**, set in a refuge built in
1608. Return the way you came or head east and follow the
canal system back to the station. Along the way, at Spaarne 91,
you pass the **Global Hemp Museum** and **Internet Café** – an
interesting combination.

Corrie ten Boomhuis

✉ Barteljorisstraat 19 ☎ 023 531 0823; www.corrietenboom.com
🕐 Apr.–Oct., Tue.–Sat. 10–4; Nov.–Mar., Tue.–Sat. 11–3. Visit is by guided tour
💶 Free; donations appreciated

Sint Bavokerk

✉ Grote Markt ☎ 023 532 4399 🕐 Apr.–Aug., daily 10–4 except Sun.;
Sep.–Mar. daily 10–3:30 except Sun. 💶 Inexpensive

Frans Halsmuseum

✉ Groot Heligland 62, Haarlem ☎ 023 511 5775; www.franshalsmuseum.nl
🕐 Mon.–Sat. 11–5, Sun. noon–5. Closed Jan. 1 🍽 Peter Cuyper restaurant,
on Kleine Houtstraat, open Tue.–Fri. 11:30–3, Tue.–Sat. 5:30–11 💶 Moderate

The Dutch like
to be beside
the seaside,
if the weather
co-operates

Zandvoort

The average Dutch seaside resort is brash and unpretentious,
and certainly Amsterdam's local beach makes no pretentions
to sophistication. The original settlement of Zandvoort was a
fishing village established at a gap in the dunes that run along
the North Sea shore west of Haarlem. It's been transformed into
a strip of hotels and apartment buildings, though there is still
some evidence of the old port.

A few miles north, Zandvoort's more upscale sibling,
Bloemendaal, caters for a wealthier clientele.

Many trains from Amsterdam continue through Haarlem
direct to the resort.

Utrecht

A cathedral cut in two, a pair of canals that have sunk well below street level and a monstrous shopping mall slapped along one side of the city center. From this description Utrecht may sound unpromising; in fact it is a beautiful, friendly and surprising place.

The Rhine once flowed through this part of the Netherlands, and the Romans established an important crossing point here. By the time the fickle river shifted its course south of the city, Utrecht was an important political base, its bishop one of the most important figures in the Low Countries. His grant of a charter to the young settlement of Amsterdam in 1300 is often taken as the date of that city's founding. As power ebbed away, Utrecht was in danger of becoming something of a backwater, but its university has long provided a dynamic edge and the city's central location has attracted plenty of business.

The city arms reflect the heritage of Utrecht

There are four trains each hour from Amsterdam, taking 30 minutes. Follow the sign for "Centrum" and you should emerge on Lange Elisabethstraat; any of the side streets on the other side of this thoroughfare should take you to the main canal, **Oudegracht.**

A great trench has been dug for the Oudegracht and its parallel partner, the **Nieuwegracht.** Each is flanked by canalside paths well below the streets, and cafés have sprung up in the cellars that line them. Oudegracht temporarily disappears in the area of the **Stadhuis,** an imposing if glum structure, then reappears to head south. A 10-minute walk along the east bank provides a good way to acquaint yourself with the city. Stay at street level: you'll see more.

Just after the street becomes Twijnstraat (which has a profusion of good cafés and restaurants) and separates from the canal, you will find yourself at the corner of Nicholaasstraat. Turn left along it to visit the **Centraal Museum's** collection, which covers the origins of the city, the Golden Age and large quantities of contemporary art. Nearby, just along **Agnietenstraat,** there is a row of lovely cottages. You pass them on your way to the foot of the Nieuwegracht; turn left (north) along it, and after 300m (330 yards) you reach on your left the **Catharijne Convent Museum,** one of the most imaginatively created museums in the country. Its collection of religious art – including works by Frans Hals and Rembrandt – threads through the old convent and into St. Catharijnekerk behind it.

Continuing north, you pass through a calm and beautiful quarter to reach the **Dom** (cathedral) – one of the strangest sights in the Netherlands. Its construction took more than two centuries, finishing in 1517, but a hurricane in 1674 took out the nave like a battering ram. As a result, Domplein boasts a fine 364-foot tower with a carillon, plus a much-truncated cathedral with the west face bricked over. To see how magnificent the original must have been, look for the plan on the south side, near the ancient boulder brought here from Denmark. It dates from the 10th century and bears runes devoted to King Harald.

Centraal Museum

✉ Nicholaaskerkhof 10 ☎ 030 236 2362; www.centraalmuseum.nl
🕐 Tue.–Sun. 11–5. Closed Jan. 1, Apr. 30, Dec. 25 💶 Moderate; free admission to Museum Year Card holders

Catharijne Convent Museum

✉ Lange Nieuwstraat 38 and Nieuwegracht 63
☎ 030 231 7296; www.catharijneconvent.nl
🕐 Tue.–Fri. 10–5, Sat., Sun. and public holidays 11–5 🍴 Café, restaurant, refreshments ($–$$$) 💶 Moderate

Vismarkt, one of the busiest corners of the city

Leiden and the Bulbfields

The university town of Leiden has lovely canalside walks, attractive cottages and first-rate museums, any one of which would be quite enough for a provincial city. And there is no shortage of places to eat, drink and relax.

From the railway station, find your way out along Stationsweg and you can begin sightseeing almost at once. The **Rijksmuseum voor Volkenkunde (National Ethnological Museum)**, at Steenstraat 1 (tel: 071 516 8800), is a huge old 19th-century hospital filled with the gatherings of Dutch explorers. The best exhibits are those from Asia, particularly Java and Japan. Substantial renovations were due to finish in 2001. Until then, exhibits are restricted (Tue.–Fri. 10–5, Sat.–Sun. noon–5; inexpensive).

Follow the canal past the museum to the florid **Morspoort**, one of the original city gates. This opens on to a street filled with restaurants and takes you along to one of the most photographed sites in the city: the chunky bridge that spans the **Oude Vest** waterway. Immediately to your right is another bridge across the Rhine – or at least the course cut by that great river long ago, when it used to flow through Leiden after Utrecht. Now it is known as the **Oude Rijn,** or Old Rhine.

The walk south along Rapenburg takes you to the loveliest part of the city. On the left (east) is the **Rijksmuseum van Oudenhede (National Museum of Antiquities).** This has also been undergoing repairs for years; at present the entrance is hidden around the back (Tue.–Fri. 10–5, Sun. noon–5).

The mighty **Pieterskerk** dominates this area. Inside near the north entrance is a mummified body from around 1700,

Above: Illuminating bulbfields near Leiden

Top left: The old course of the Rhine runs through Leiden

The colors of Keukenhof attract thousands of visitors

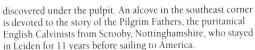

discovered under the pulpit. An alcove in the southeast corner is devoted to the story of the Pilgrim Fathers, the puritanical English Calvinists from Scrooby, Nottinghamshire, who stayed in Leiden for 11 years before sailing to America.

Immediately to the west of the church is **Pieterskerkchoorsteg,** with plenty of eating possibilities plus, on the left (north), a sign at the start of **William Brewster Steeg** noting that this was the site of the Pilgrim's Press.

Beyond it is the **Stadhuis (town hall),** with a richly decorated stairway, and behind that an artificial mound with views across the city. If you look towards the northwest, you should see a windmill – a handy beacon for the walk back to the station, and a museum in its own right (open Tue.–Sat. 10–5, Sun. 1–5).

For a couple of months each spring, the unremarkable fields between Leiden and the small town of Heemstede dazzle with color. This is the center of tulip cultivation in Holland and at its heart is **Keukenhof,** near the village of Lisse. Keukenhof means "kitchen garden." The location was used for market gardening until a consortium of bulb-growers realized the tourist potential of a site close to Amsterdam. A Summer Garden opens for six weeks in August and early September.

Keukenhof

✉ Stationsweg 166a, Lisse ☎ 0252 465 555; www.keukenhof.nl 🌐 Spring Garden: late Mar.–late May, daily 8–7:30; Summer Garden: mid-Aug.–mid-Sep., daily 9–6 🍴 Refreshment facilities ($$) 🚉 Leiden; sign at main exit directs you to platform 1 of bus station; bus 54 to site 💶 Expensive; Summer Garden moderate

Schiphol Airport

From a tiny airfield on the reclaimed land of Haarlemermeer, Schiphol has grown to become the fourth-busiest airport in Europe (after Heathrow, Frankfurt and Paris Charles de Gaulle). A high proportion of travelers are here simply to change planes, and there is plenty to keep them occupied when they do.

The **Panoramaterras (Spectators' Gallery)** covers much of the roof area, allowing unparalleled views of the aprons and runways (Apr.–Sep., 9–9; Oct.–Mar. 9–6, free). The **Nationaal Luchtvaartmuseum (National Aviation Museum)** is devoted mainly to Dutch aviation, but there is an excellent introduction to the subject with a replica of a Flyer designed by Wilbur and Orville Wright, together with black-and-white archive footage explaining how they mastered powered flight. You can, for an extra charge, sample a "virtual reality" parachute jump, getting strapped into a harness about 6 feet above the ground.

Schiphol World Tour is a one-hour bus ride showing you the workings of the airport from the inside, driving around the apron and getting the inside story on how everything from catering to cargo functions (departures from Schiphol World Hal: mainly afternoons in winter, 10:30–3:30 at least hourly Jul., Aug., moderate. Minimum age 18, passport required).

Should your flight be delayed, there are plenty of options **"airside"** (after the security check). You can improve your golf at a computer-simulated range or take a gamble at the Holland Casino (minimum age 18, reasonable dress and passport or driving licence required), where clocks and screens show departure times.

Trademark tulips outside the terminal at Schiphol

National Aviation Museum
✉ Westelijke Randweg 201, Schiphol ☎ 020 406 8000; www.aviodome.nl
🕐 Apr.–Sep., daily 10–5; Oct.–Mar., Tue.–Fri. 10–5, Sat.–Sun. noon–5.
Closed Jan. 1, Dec. 25 🚉 Schiphol, then a signposted walk for 10 minutes
💲 Expensive

The story of flight is encapsulated in the National Aviation Museum

Walks

1 THE IDEAL CANAL WALK

Walk

There are many candidates for the loveliest canal in Amsterdam. But for a fascinating and fun introduction to the city, the walk around the Herengracht is hard to beat. Preceding it with Brouwersgracht and ending with Nieuwe Herengracht gives an ideal, balanced walk; or, if you are feeling fit, this walk can easily be combined with Walk 2 (▶ 178–180), to provide a complete circuit of the city center.

DISTANCE 3 miles **TIME** 2–3 hours
START POINT Haarlemmerplein ✚ 200 C4
END POINT newMetropolis Science and Technology Center ✚ 204 C4

north bank of Brouwersgracht. Most of the canalside buildings are warehouses converted to apartment buildings: there is no longer any sign of the two dozen breweries that gave the canal its name.

1–2
Tram 3 will drop you off at Haarlemmerplein, or you can walk there in 20 brisk minutes from Centraal Station. Follow the tram tracks back south for 50m (55 yards), until just before they cross a bridge over **Brouwersgracht**. This is your cue to turn left and follow the

2–3
To avoid a detour, cross the Oranjebrug here. As soon as you are over, look to the left at **No. 133**: the ground floor is level, but the top three are leaning madly. Passing a statue of educator Theo Thijssen perching on the edge of a schoolboy's desk, you reach the first of many good views

Above: View along Prinsengracht from Brouwersgracht
Previous page: Gabled house, Brouwersgracht

from a bridge: this one, the crossing of **Prinsengracht** – "Prince's canal." Continue along and across **Keizersgracht** ("Emperor's canal"). At

3–4

Cross Brouwersgracht and walk around to the next bridge, near half a dozen gabled houses. This is the dainty **Melkmeisjesbrug** for pedestrians (and the odd illicit bicycle). Almost anywhere you look along Herengracht, there is something to delight the eye. Even where the 20th century intervenes, as in the new building

sides of a square to get to the far (eastern) bank. Pause to take in a definitive Amsterdam scene of water, trees and crowds of buildings.

Brouwersgracht boasts extravagant apartments

at Nos. 105–107, the effect is softened by the addition of an energetic tablet on an otherwise plain wall.

4–5

At the point where **Leliegracht** sets off to the right (west), there is a rare opportunity to see a canal along its length from close to water level while remaining on dry land. Cross Herengracht if you want to visit the **Theatermuseum** (▶ 99). Otherwise, stay on the east side and admire the **Bartolotti Huis**, a particularly fine mansion, from afar. The 20th century intrudes at the intersection with Raadhuisstraat, "Town Hall Street," which runs to the Royal Palace – formerly the town hall. In the other direction, an elegant early 20th-century terrace draws the eye toward the tower of the **Westerkerk** (▶ 92–93). Nearby, the **Ajax Fan Shop** sells merchandise from Amsterdam's favorite soccer team. At Oude Spiegelstraat you enter the area known as 9 Straatjes (▶ 105). Wijde Heisteeg marks its end and the point where you should cross Herengracht to continue south on the other bank. Just past the **Bijbels (Bible) Museum**, No. 380 with its intricate stonework is the **Netherlands Institute for War Documentation.**

Some canalside houses acquire a distinct lean

5–6

At the point where Herengracht swerves to the left, **Leidsegracht** sets off to the right. This stretch of the canal is busy with tour boats, people and vehicles, but subdues once you are across Leidsestraat and on to the **Golden Bend (Gouden Bocht)**, once full of wealthy residents (hence the "golden"), now occupied by business and foreign consulates. The bend itself takes place at the point Nieuwe Spiegelstraat begins, lined with art and antiques shops.

6–7

Vijzelstraat marks the end of the Golden Bend and the beginning of another lovely stretch, despite the proximity of exuberant Reguliersdwarsstraat. The only time you will be conscious of this is at **Thorbeckeplein**, facing you at the point where Reguliersgracht begins. Tour boats pause here to give their passengers the chance to gaze at the Seven Bridges (only properly visible at water level). This is also the point where you cross Walk 3. The calm resumes for the last 300m (330 yards) of Herengracht. Just before you cross Utrechtsestraat, a flamboyant St. George appears on the building that houses the Italian consulate on the opposite (north) side. The patron saint of England originally patronized

Taking a Break

A lovely, if pricey, place to lunch before the walk begins properly is **De Bellhamel** at Brouwersgracht 60 (▶ 103). At Leidsestraat, you could head 200m (220 yards) to the right (southwest) to have a coffee and drink in the view from the top floor of the **Metz & Co.** department store.

7–8

The Blue Bridge marks the end of the Herengracht proper. You can end the walk here – trams 9, 14 and 20 cross the bridge, and Waterlooplein Metro station is 200m (220 yards) northeast. Otherwise, turn right immediately across the Blue Bridge along the east bank of the Amstel. Cross the first bridge and turn left on to Nieuwe Herengracht.

Genoa. Just ahead is the Amstel River, and to the right the **Magere Brug**, the "Skinny Bridge" (▶ 150). The walk heads left (north) to the **Blauburg ("Blue Bridge")**, constructed in cast iron in 1874. Some say it is a copy of Pont Alexandre III in Paris, though that was actually built later. There has been a crossing here for centuries, and from here you can gaze at the scene as Rembrandt did.

replica of the Magere Brug, is named **Walter Susskindbrug** after the German who helped hundreds of Dutch children escape the Nazis during World War II. Alongside is the neat terracing of the **Amstelhof**, the first of the city's refuges for older people. Head along the south bank of Nieuwe Herengracht, which cuts through part of the old Jewish quarter and skirts the three-climates greenhouse of the **Hortus Botanicus** (▶ 144–145).

8–9

Across bustling Plantage Middenlaan, you enter **Wertheim Park**, a pleasant open space with a memorial at the far end to the thousands of Dutch people of Jewish descent who died in the Nazi death camps at Auschwitz-Birkenau.

Cross the canal to reach Anne Frankstraat; once across, turn right down the path. Look across the **Entrepotdok** (▶ 153), one of the original free ports. The

The "Blue Bridge"

very last stretch of canal is called **Shippersgracht**. Cross Prins Hendrikkade to reach the statue of Neptune. From here, you can skirt the edge of the entrance to the IJ road tunnel as you aim for the new**Metropolis Science and Technology Center** (▶ 69). Once you reach it, just keep walking – up the building. Usually the stairway to the crest of the building is open and provides a 21st-century sense of space in stark contrast to the crowded 17th-century beginnings of the walk. The view is superb across the city, Centraal Station and the IJ River – and close enough almost to touch the **Scheepvaart Museum** (▶ 146–149), which is where Walk 2 begins.

2 ALONG THE WATERFRONT

Walk

Amsterdam's old waterfront is full of maritime history, from the museum that celebrates the achievements of the East India Company to the headquarters of the West India Company and beyond. It is relentlessly busy with traffic and people,

DISTANCE 1.25 miles **TIME** 1 hour
START POINT Scheepvaart Museum ✛ 205 D3
END POINT Haarlemmplein ✛ 200 C4

between the end point and start point on Walk 1, allowing you to complete a circle if you wish. It also places you close to the start of Walk 4.

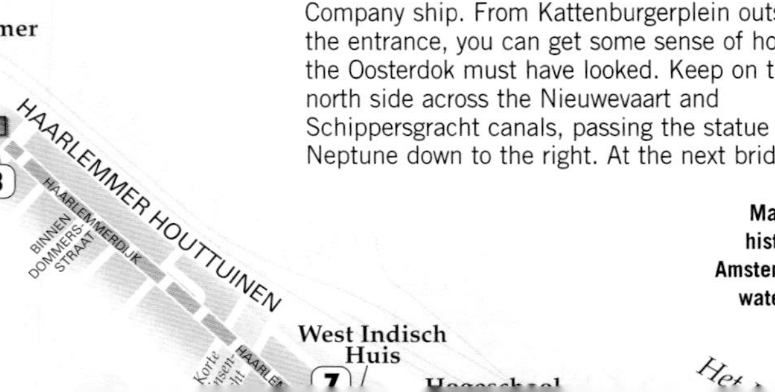

1–2

The **Scheepvaart Museum** (➤ 146–149) has a number of vessels bobbing around outside, notably *De Amsterdam*, a replica of an East India Company ship. From Kattenburgerplein outside the entrance, you can get some sense of how the Oosterdok must have looked. Keep on the north side across the Nieuwevaart and Schippersgracht canals, passing the statue of Neptune down to the right. At the next bridge,

but there are some real treasures to be discovered along the way. This walk takes the "short cut"

Maritime
history at
Amsterdam's
waterfront

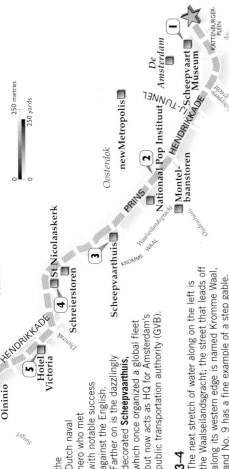

admire the view of **newMetropolis** (▶ 69), then cross the road and look along **Oudeschans** – schans means "moat," and was one of the city's defenses. The tower on the right, **Montelbaanstoren,** acted as part of those fortifications.

2–3

Stay on the landward side of Prins Hendrikkade. At No. 142, the **Nationaal Pop Instituut** is the center for Dutch popular musical culture (open Mon.–Thu. 10–5). Just along at No. 131, a plaque marks the home of Admiral de Ruyter,

the Dutch naval hero who met with notable success against the English. Farther on is the dazzlingly decorated **Scheepvaarthuis,** which once acted as HQ for Amsterdam's public transportation authority (GVB).

3–4

The next stretch of water along on the left is the Waalseilandsgracht; the street that leads off along its western edge is named Kromme Waal, and No. 9 has a fine example of a step gable. Rounding the next bend to the left suddenly reveals a splendid vista, from the easternmost turret of the Centraal Station ensemble to **St. Nicolaaskerk,** and in the middle of it, the **Schreierstoren** ("Weeping Tower"), where it is said women gathered to give their menfolk a tearful farewell. These days the tower is home to the Café VOC. A plaque relates how English

navigator Henry Hudson (c.1550–1611) set sail from here on April 4, 1609, aboard the *Half Moon* to discover the harbor of what is now New York and the river that bears his name.

This walk is a mix of ancient and modern

4–5

Keep to the landward side of Prins Hendrikkade (and watch out for traffic, especially bicycles). St. Nicholas is the patron saint of sailors and his church, to the left, was the last many mariners saw of the city as they set off on their voyages. These days, the city is cut off from the water by **Centraal Station** (▶ 68), and the church bids farewell to rail travelers. Past the tour boats moored in Damrak, the **Hotel Victoria** appears ahead. On its north side, two 17th-century houses seem have been embedded in the facade. The story is that the hotel wanted to demolish a string of houses to allow it to expand west along Prins Hendrikkade, but the adjacent landlords refused to sell out. The expansion went ahead, but had to detour around the back of the two awkward abodes.

5–6

The most notable sight along the next stretch is the grand location for **Oininio**, a trendy café closed for refurbishment. When the road crosses Singel just ahead, you get a superb view straight ahead: on the right, the flourishing, French Renaissance-style **Hogeschool van Amsterdam** (**Amsterdam High School**); in the center, the wonderfully lopsided **Spanse Gevel Eetcafé**; and on

West India House used to rule half an empire

6–7

Aim for the warehouse with Gabriel on top and a cheese shop below and turn right at it onto Haarlemmerstraat. From the **West Indisch Huis** (**West India House**), the well-proportioned mansion along on the left, Dutch maritime activities in the Caribbean and South America were con-

Gabriel standing on a globe. At ground level, a ship's propeller donated by a shipping company is fixed to a brick plinth.

7–8

After a slight kink in the road, two chimneys appear in the distance, while in the foreground you can enjoy an impressive array of gables. There is a good canal view at the bridge over **Korte Prinsengracht**, where Haarlemmerstraat turns into Haarlemmerdijk. Three blocks later, at the intersection of Binnen Dommersstraat, a trio of foghorns is on display, while diagonally across there is a modern tablet showing a decorator's brush. The walk ends where Haarlemmerstraat broadens out into the square that bears its name. On the far side is the closest Amsterdam has to a triumphal arch, the **Haarlemmer Poort**, which provides a view of the primary-colored sculpture that marks the entrance to the Westerpark. From Haarlemmerplein, you can take tram 3 back to the center, start Walk 1 (▶ 174–177), go a short distance east to the start of Walk 4 (▶ 184–186) or wander around the Jordaan (▶ 88–91).

Taking a Break

Highlights along the route include the **Café VOC** in the "Weeping Tower" (10–1 daily, lunch on terrace 11–3) and the **1e Klasse** in Centraal Station (▶ 68).

3 A Slice of Amsterdam

Walk

DISTANCE 2 miles **TIME** 1½ hours at a gentle pace
START POINT Golden Tulip Barbizon Palace Hotel, southeast of Centraal Station ✚ 204 A1
END POINT Rijksmuseum ✚ 202 C2

Almost any walk in Amsterdam that takes you around the city's arc of canals is bound to be enjoyable. The same cannot be said, though, for those that cut against the watery grain – for example, finding a pretty way to cover the ground from Centraal Station to the Rijksmuseum is tricky. This itinerary is the most pleasant way to walk between two of the city's great nodes, avoiding much of the traffic and sleaze that afflict other routes, though not entirely free of either.

1–2

Begin just southeast of Centraal Station, where Zeedijk branches from Prins Hendrikkade. The name **Zeedijk**, "sea dike," was correct when it was first built: it provided essential protection when the Zuider Zee was open water and Amsterdam was thus connected to the North Sea. On your right, **St. Olofkerk** has an alarming tablet above the door – a skeleton reclining among skulls. Built in 1415, St. Olof served as

the city's stock exchange in the 16th century. You will shortly see a fine view as Zeedijk crosses the water, with the narrow finger of **Oudezijds Kolk** to the left and the broader expanse of **Oudezijds Voorburgwal** to the right.

2–3

Known as a seedy, depressing and sometimes dangerous street, Zeedijk is recovering some of its old respectability: among the garish snack-bars are excellent places to eat. Still, it's hard to forget that this is the eastern boundary of the **Red Light District** (➤ 63–65). The southern portion also borders on Amsterdam's modest **Chinatown**. Both are left behind when Zeedijk expands into Nieuwmarkt, dominated by the large, squat **Waag** (➤ 72). On the south side of the market-place is a sculpture of a man planting an unwanted kiss on a woman; on the north, wood-and-ceramic street furniture allows people (mainly all-day drinkers) to sit and reflect on the canal ahead.

Reguliersgracht, also known as "Seven Bridges Canal"

3–4

Take the right (west) side of Kloveniersburgwal. A short way along the canal you can look across to the **Trippenhuis**, the original location for the collection now hanging in the Rijksmuseum. The headquarters of the **Oostindisch Huis (East India House)**, around the corner on Oude Hoogstraat, is now part of the University of Amsterdam; on weekdays you can admire the beautifully proportioned courtyard.

the right and left you should find yourself on the short pedestrian street named Halvemaansteeg. This takes you across a busy tram line into **Rembrandtplein**, a square now devoted to serving tourists with food, beer, drugs and porn. Rembrandt occupies a plinth in the middle, wearing an expression of disapproval.

6–7

This open space consists of two discrete squares, the southern of which is **Thorbeckeplein**, named after the man whose statue stands on the southern side facing Herengracht (see Walk 1). The square is the closest Amsterdam gets to a Parisian feel, though places such as Mister Coco's Food Factory (motto: "Lousy Food and Warm Beer") do their best to spoil the effect.

Look due south along **Reguliersgracht,** which begins here, and you will see the first couple of crossings in the series that gives this canal the nickname **Seven Bridges.** Stay on the left (east) bank and continue south, watching for fine woodwork on a bay window poking out of No. 57 Reguliersgracht. Soon you reach Kerkstraat, named after the beautiful 17th-century **Amstelkerk,** on the left-hand side, now occupied by the Café Kort.

A statue of Thorbecke overlooks Thorbeckeplein

4–5

Heading south, you are moving into hotel territory: across the canal, on the east side, is the downtown **Youth Hostel.** Near the end of Kloveniersburgwal, reach the Balmoral "Scottish Pub," part of the Doelen Hotel. Unless you are desperate for one of the extensive range of malt whiskies that it sells, cross the structure to your left: the first lifting bridge to be built in the city.

5–6

Continuing south along Kloveniersburgwal, the waterway opens up into a broad basin, the Binnenamstel. Cross it on Halvemaansbrug, continue across the road, and with

250 metres
250 yards

Centraal Station

HENDRIKKADE

St Olofkerk

PRINS

Red Light District

Chinatown

De Waag

NIEUWMARKT

Oostindisch Huis

Trippenhuis

Taking a Break

Recommended options are **Bird** (Zeedijk 77, ► 73), **In de Waag** (► 72), in the middle of Nieuwmarkt, or, for something more substantial, **Le Zinc...et les Dames** at Prinsengracht 999 (► 158).

Weteringschans and Singelgracht, you approach the **Rijksmuseum** (► 114–117) as the architect intended: straight at the handsome facade. If you're heading for the **Van Gogh Museum** (► 124–127) or **Stedelijk Museum** (► 122–123), continue straight on underneath one of the four arches. Even if you're aiming only as far as the Rijksmuseum, you should still do this, and turn right for the quiet south entrance to the museum.

Worth the walk: the grand facade of the Rijksmuseum

7–8

Cross bridge five, heading west along the south side of **Prinsengracht**, the outer canal of the three concentric arcs. Just before you start along it, look out for the stork planted above the door of the handsome house on the corner. There are a few houseboats strung out along here, but the main attractions are the houses and their

6 Rembrandtplein
Thorbeckeplein

7 Amstelkerk

8 WETERINGSCHANS
Rijksmuseum

9 Van Gogh Museum
Stedelijk Museum

elaborate gables. Cross the busy Vijzelgracht; calm is restored as you continue to the next crossing along, Nieuwe Spiegelstraat. If you have an hour or two to spare, browse among the art and antiques shops down on the

right (north). The walk heads left (south) over Prinsengracht to one of the prettiest and liveliest intersections in the city.

8–9

Head along **Spiegelgracht** toward the twin towers of the Rijksmuseum rising ahead. Pause on the bridge over the Lijnbaansgracht for a tranquil canal view. After negotiating the busy

4 THE WESTERN ISLANDS

Walk

DISTANCE 1.25 miles **TIME** 1 hour
START POINT/END POINT South end of Grote Bickersstraat ✚ 201 D4

Nowhere on this short walk are you more than a mile from Centraal Station, yet it takes you to a part of Amsterdam that feels very different from the rest of the city: a series of small islands that have something of the atmosphere of provincial Holland.

1–2

Going west from Centraal Station, the railway line marks what was the northern shore of the IJ until a succession of islands was created in the 17th century. The walk begins on the north side of the tracks at the foot of Grote Bickerstraat where it meets the busy Haarlemmer Houttuinen at Hendrik Jonkerplein. A good landmark is the **Blaauwhooft Café**, which occupies the acute angle of a triangular building. From here, head right (east) for a short distance along **Blokmakerstraat**, named after the craftsmen who made the pulleys that helped keep the mercantile fleet moving. Nowadays

supposed to resemble the silhouette of a whale.

2–3

Turn left (north) along Hollandse Tuin, flanked by some 1970s housing, and admire the sailing barges and well-kept houseboats moored across on the far side of **Westerdok**; you pass Zeilmakerstraat to your left. Bear left and head along Touwslagerstraat; take the first right from here on Grote Bickersstraat. You soon reach a typical lifting canal bridge over Realengracht; on the far side, you can see the first striking pair of warehouses converted into apartments, **De**

Zandhoek has plenty of fine examples of biblical gable stones

the **Westelijke Eilanden (Western Islands)** are residential. Close to the water's edge, you will find a large sculpture rising from the wharf. This slab of black granite is

3–4

Continue over the bridge and straight on along **Zandhoek**. Three houses proclaim their loyalties with beautifully decorated tablets. No. 3, De Eendracht, is guarded by the image of a fierce lion; No. 4 features Noah's Ark; and No. 6 has a white horse. Just beyond them stands **De Gouden Reael**, a café-restaurant which specializes in French regional cuisine and is named after the "golden real," a Spanish coin. Across another bridge, over Zoutkeetsgracht, you reach an island devoted to **Willem Barentsz**, the ill-fated Dutch explorer who sought a Northeast Passage between Europe and Asia in the 16th century. He reached the island of Novaya Zemlya in the sea that now bears his name, but perished in the Arctic winter.

4–5

Turn left at Barentszplein along Barentszstraat past a coffee shop named after the explorer. Barentszstraat ends at the **Westerkanaal**, one of the main maritime gateways to the web of canals in Amsterdam, and a

snap right turn off to **Houtmankade**.
Continue to the penultimate turning on the right.

5–6

Go east along **Roggeveenstraat**, a pedestrianized street with an imposing school building on the left and handsome 19th-century housing on the right. At the end, skirt around Barentszplein and go south back over the bridge to Realeneiland. Turn right along Taandwaarsstraat and left past modern residential developments – with two large warehouses, sagging with age, at the far end.

Het IJ

A placid scene in the Western Isles

6–7

Turn right along Realengracht (the name of the canal and the waterside street) to **Drieharingenbrug,** one of Amsterdam's loveliest and youngest – bridges. The present narrow, graceful structure replaced the 18th-century original in 1983, and is just wide enough to allow two bicycles to pass. The "three herrings" alluded to in the name are carved above a door on the north side of the bridge.

The serenity of the Western Isles is much sought after

7–8

On the south side of the bridge, you are on **Prinseneiland,** the smallest of the Western Islands. Bear right past a particularly fine house, built in 1629, and proceed to circumnavigate counterclockwise along the street that wraps around the isle. The line of buildings on the western flank have their shutters painted with mercantile slogans such as *D'Koren beurs* and *Schel Visch*. At the bend in the road, look for No. 24A – formerly the studio of the artist George Breitner.

8–9

Follow Prinseneiland around through an interesting mix of new and old housing to the bridge over Bickersgracht. Cross it, and turn right down the street of the same name. The garden at No. 29 is lovely, and if you look across the canal you can see the tracks running down to the water where ships were once launched. A short way south toward the main railway line that marks the abrupt conclusion of the Western Isles, you soon reach **Hendrik Jonkerplein,** the starting and finishing point of the walk.

Taking a Break

The halfway point (5) is at the **Café Noordester,** at Houtmanskade 7 (tel: 020 624 2904) – named after the Northeast Passage – where a conservatory filled with wicker chairs spills on to the sidewalk.

If you are taking an evening stroll, you could stop in at the **Restaurant Carline Schluumter** at Barentszstraat 242 (tel: 020 422 7880, open daily 5–10).

Otherwise, settle for one of the cafés of Jordaan, across on the south side of the tracks, at any time, though on a fine evening the light on the islands is particularly appealing.

Practicalities

GETTING ADVANCE INFORMATION
Websites

- Amsterdam tourist advice www.visitamsterdam.nl English-language site with comprehensive info

- www.amstel.com offers a city guide that addresses the concerns of people who come to Amtserdam to indulge

- Dozens of links and information on everything from history to property can be found, in Dutch, at www.dds.nl

BEFORE YOU GO

WHAT YOU NEED

- ● Required
- ○ Suggested
- ▲ Not required
- △ Not applicable

	U.K.	Germany	U.S.A.	Canada	Australia	Ireland	France	Spain
Passport/National Identity Card	●	●	●	●	●	●	●	●
Visa	▲	▲	▲	▲	▲	▲	▲	▲
Onward or Round Trip Ticket	▲	▲	▲	▲	▲	▲	▲	▲
Health Inoculations (tetanus and polio)	▲	▲	▲	▲	▲	▲	▲	▲
Health Documentation (► 192, Health)	●	●	●	●	●	●	●	●
Travel Insurance	○	○	○	○	○	○	○	○
Drivers' License (national)	●	●	●	●	●	●	●	●
Car Insurance Certificate	○	○	△	△	△	△	○	○
Car Registration Document	●	●	△	△	△		●	●

WHEN TO GO

Amsterdam

High season   Low season

JAN	FEB	MAR	APR	MAY	JUN	JUL	AUG	SEP	OCT	NOV	DEC
41°F	43°F	48°F	55°F	63°F	68°F	72°F	72°F	68°F	57°F	46°F	41°F

Sun   Cloud   Wet   Sun/Showers

Temperatures are the **average daily maximum** for each month. "Damp and mild" sums up the climate in Amsterdam. The ideal month to visit is May, when both the rain and the crowds are less intense than in June, July and August.
September, though wetter, is also a good bet.
The weather is often miserable – chilly and drizzly – between October and March, though **rarely do the canals freeze.**
Strong winds in winter can **increase the chill factor,** and fog can blot out the sunlight for days.
During December, Amsterdam is **crowded with Christmas shoppers** and with foreign visitors spending the festive season in the city.

In the U.K.
- Netherlands Board
  of Tourism
  PO Box 523
  London SW1E 6NE
  ☎ 020 7734 0860

In the U.S.A.
- Netherlands Board
  of Tourism
  355 Lexington Avenue
  New York, NY 10017
  ☎ 888/GO HOLLAND

In Canada
- Netherlands Board
  of Tourism
  25 Adelaide Street East
  Toronto, Ontario M5C
  1Y2
  ☎ 416/363 1577

GETTING THERE

By Air **Schiphol airport** has excellent flight connections from all over the world. From the U.K., there are **non-stop flights** from more than 20 airports. The main airline is **KLM** (tel: 08705 074 074; www.klm.com). From Ireland, **Aer Lingus** (tel: 01 886 8888; www.aer-lingus.ie) has frequent departures from Dublin and one flight a day from Cork. From the U.S., there are **daily non-stop flights** from Atlanta, Boston, Chicago, Detroit, Houston, Los Angeles, Miami, New York, San Francisco, Seattle and Washington D.C. The Canadian cities with **non-stop links** are Montreal, Toronto and Vancouver. There is one **direct non-stop service** from Sydney; from other Australian and New Zealand cities the best connections are in Singapore, Bangkok, Hong Kong and Los Angeles.
Typical flying times to Amsterdam: U.K. (1¼ hours), Dublin (1½ hours), New York and Toronto (8 hours), Vancouver and Los Angeles (11 hours), Sydney (22 hours).

By Rail **Centraal Station** has direct connections from major cities in western Europe, including high-speed Thalys links from Paris, Brussels and Cologne. From Britain, there are connections at Brussels with trains operated by Eurostar (tel: 0990 186 186; www.eurostar.com), with bargain fares to Amsterdam.

By Sea **Stena Line** (tel: 0990 707070; www.stenaline.co.uk) operates a link between Harwich in the U.K. and Hoek van Holland; its fast ferry takes four hours. There are rail connections from London and to Amsterdam. **P&O North Sea Ferries** (tel: 01482 377177; www.ponsf.com) has a nightly service from Hull to Rotterdam with a bus connection to Amsterdam. **DFDS Seaways** (tel: 08705 333 000; www.dfdsseaways.co.uk) sails from Newcastle to IJmuiden, with a bus connection to Amsterdam.

TIME

Holland is on Central European Time. one hour ahead of GMT in winter, two hours ahead in summer. The clocks change at the end of March and October.

CURRENCY AND FOREIGN EXCHANGE

Currency The monetary unit is the **guilder,** written as Fl, and divided into 100 cents. **Coins** are issued in denominations of 5, 10 and 25 cents, and 1, 2.50 and 5 guilders. Although supermarket prices are quoted in units smaller than 5 cents, there are no coins smaller than this, so prices are rounded up or down. **Bills** are issued in denominations of 10, 25, 100, 250 and 1,000 guilders. The Euro single currency will be introduced on January 1, 2002; the guilder will cease to be legal tender six months later. Some smaller shops/restaurants may not accept credit cards; others accept them only for transactions more than 50–100 guilders.

Exchange The **most economical way to obtain guilders** is to use a bank credit or debit card in one of the many automatic teller machines (ATMs) outside most banks, and at the airport and main station. There are plenty of currency exchanges at the airport, station and in tourist areas, as well as bank exchange facilities. Some automatic change machines are being installed, but give poor rates of exchange.

TIME DIFFERENCES

GMT	Amsterdam	New York	Germany	Spain	Sydney
12 noon	→ 1 p.m.	← 7 a.m.	→ 1 p.m.	→ 1 p.m.	→ 10 p.m.

WHEN YOU ARE THERE

CLOTHING SIZES

U.K.	Rest of Europe	U.S.A.	
36	46	36	Suits
38	48	38	
40	50	40	
42	52	42	
44	54	44	
46	56	46	
7	41	8	Shoes
7.5	42	8.5	
8.5	43	9.5	
9.5	44	10.5	
10.5	45	11.5	
11	46	12	
14.5	37	14.5	Shirts
15	38	15	
15.5	39/40	15.5	
16	41	16	
16.5	42	16.5	
17	43	17	
8	34	6	Dresses
10	36	8	
12	38	10	
14	40	12	
16	42	14	
18	44	16	
4.5	38	6	Shoes
5	38	6.5	
5.5	39	7	
6	39	7.5	
6.5	40	8	
7	41	8.5	

NATIONAL HOLIDAYS

Jan. 1	New Year's Day
Mar./Apr.	Good Friday, Easter Monday
Apr. 30	Queen's Day
May 5	Liberation Day
6th Thu. after Easter	Ascension Day
May/Jun.	Whit Monday
Dec. 5	St. Nicholas's Day
Dec. 25	Christmas Day
Dec. 26	Tweede Kerstdag ("Second Christ's Day")

On St. Nicholas's Day, businesses close early; on other holidays, most businesses close all day, though tourist facilities usually remain open.

OPENING HOURS

○ Shops   ● Post Offices
● Offices   ● Museums/Monuments
● Banks   ● Pharmacies

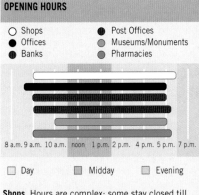

8 a.m. 9 a.m. 10 a.m. noon 1 p.m. 2 p.m. 4 p.m. 5 p.m. 7 p.m.

☐ Day   ▨ Midday   ☐ Evening

Shops Hours are complex: some stay closed till late on Monday and open late on Thursday; many downtown stores open on Sundays (▶ 46). On the main shopping streets in the city center, stores typically open Mon. 11–6, Tue., Wed. and Fri. 9–6, Thu. 9–9, Sat. 9–5 and Sun. noon–6.
Museums While the big attractions are usually open 10–5, smaller ones may keep shorter hours, such as 11–5, and often remain closed on Sunday morning (typically open 1–5). There is no general policy of closing on Monday, though a few of the minor museums do.

POLICE 112 or 020 559 9111 for non-emergencies

FIRE 112

AMBULANCE 112

TELEPHONES

There is a multiplicity of types of public phones in Amsterdam accepting a variety of pre-paid or credit cards and coins, depending on the operating company and age of the pay phone. As a general principle, the least expensive way to make calls either within Holland or abroad is with a pre-paid card (available at tobacco shops, supermarkets and

currency exchanges). The most expensive method is from a hotel bedroom.

International Dialling Codes from Amsterdam
U.K.: 44
U.S.A./Canada: 1
Ireland: 353
Australia: 61
New Zealand: 64
Germany: 49
Spain: 34
France: 33

PERSONAL SAFETY

The official website www.visitamster-dam.nl does not mince its words about places to avoid: after dark, it says, the alleyways of Nieuwendijk are "a mugger's delight, and pretty foul," and the south end of Zeedijk and the streets off it are "sleazy and riddled with miserable-looking junkies."

The whole Red Light District – in which these areas are included – attracts dozens of thieves who target visitors befuddled by drink or drugs. Outside this area, most parts feel safe, even at night.

POST

Mail boxes are red. Finding a post office can be frustrating; they are thinly scattered and none keep extended hours. Schiphol airport keeps longer hours than most. Newsstands, some supermarkets and tobacco shops sell stamps.

ELECTRICITY

Plugs have two round pins, with an optional earth pin, requiring an adaptor for U.K.,

North American, Asian and Australasian

appliances. The power supply is 220 volts. Some North American appliances on 110 volts may need a transformer.

TIPS/GRATUITIES

In restaurants and cafés the custom is to leave a few coins or round up the bill.

Yes ✓   No ✗

Hotels (service included)	✓	change
Tour guides	✓	5–10 guilders
Hairdressers	✓	round up
Taxis	✓	round up fare
Usherettes	✗	
Porters	✓	5–10 guilders
Cloakroom attendants	✗	

EMBASSIES AND CONSULATES

U.K.	**U.S.A.**	**Canada**	**Australia**	**Germany**
020 676 4343	020 664 4661	070 311 1600	070 310 8200	070 342 0600
		(The Hague)	(The Hague)	(The Hague)

HEALTH

Insurance E.U. citizens with the right documentation are entitled to emergency medical treatment at reduced rates, but still have to meet some of the cost. Travel insurance is recommended for Europeans and is essential for other visitors.

Dental Services Emergency treatment is available at reduced cost for E.U. citizens with the relevant documents, but fees can be high. Other visitors should have medical insurance covering dental treatment.

Weather Amsterdam is farther north than Warsaw and Winnipeg, but the summer sun can still burn. Use sunscreen in June, July and August and drink plenty of fluids. Carry a bottle of mineral water rather than stopping at sidewalk terraces for a beer.

Drugs Pharmacies can provide a wide range of remedies over the counter. The recreational narcotics available in Amsterdam should not be treated lightly: the effects on mind and body can be severe, and are often exacerbated when mixed with alcohol.

Safe Water Tap water is safe to drink and usually palatable. Canal water is unpalatable in the extreme with more than 2,000 houseboats discharging raw sewage directly into the canal system. Don't fall in! Bottled mineral water, often called by the generic name "spa," after a popular Belgian label, is readily available everywhere.

CONCESSIONS

Students/Children Very few discounts are offered by museums, cafés and restaurants, but there are special deals for air travel. On the rare occasions when "student discounts" are advertized, they are usually restricted to people studying in Amsterdam.

Senior Citizens Visitors age 65 or over qualify for discounts at museums and other tourists attractions. Proof in the form of a passport or identity card may be required.

TRAVELING WITH A DISABILITY

Positive steps have been taken to make Amsterdam a disabled-friendly destination, with lifts and ramps installed in many public buildings and easy access to public transportation. But the unique geography of Amsterdam, with cobbled streets, recklessly parked cars and awkward canal bridges, can be difficult for wheelchair-users.

CHILDREN

There is no common agreement on what age qualifies them for free or reduced-rate entry into museums and other attractions. Baby-changing facilities are widely available.

RESTROOMS

Men's urinals are easy to find but allow little privacy. The more discreet type consist of a wrap-around steel frame; but in busy central areas such as the Red Light District, urinal "pillars" are provided that have no screening and may be used by four men at once. Women can use facilities in cafés, though sometimes it may be necessary (or polite) to buy a drink.

LOST PROPERTY

If you lose luggage at Schiphol airport, tel: 020 601 2325; on trains, tel: 020 557 8544; on trams, buses or the Metro, tel: 020 460 5858.

SURVIVAL PHRASES

Yes/no **ja/nee**
Hello **hallo**
Good morning **goedmorgen**
Good afternoon **goedemiddag**
Good evening **goedenavond**
Goodbye **tot ziens**
How are you? **Hoe gaat het met u?**
Fine, thank you **Goed, bedankt**
Please **Alstublieft**
Thank you **Dank u** or **Bedankt**
Excuse me **Pardon**
Sorry **Sorry**
Do you have ...? **Heeft u ...?**
I'd like ... **Ik wil ...**
How much is it? **Hoeveel is het?**
Open **Open**
Closed **Gesloten**
Push/pull **duwen/trekken**
Women's restrooms **Dames**
Men's restrooms **Heren**

TRAVEL

Airplane **Vliegtuig**
Airport **Luchthaven**
Bicycle **Fiets**
Bus **Bus**
Taxi **Taxi**
Train **Trein**
Tram **Tram**
Arrivals **Aankomst**
Departures **Vertrek**
Non-smoking **Niet roken**
Platform **Spoor**
Seat **Plaats**
Reserved **Gereserveerd**
Ticket **Kaartje**
Ticket office **Loket**
Timetable **Dienstregeling**
First class **Eerste klasse**
Second class **Tweede klasse**
Single/round trip **Enkele reis/retour**

OTHER USEFUL WORDS & PHRASES

Yesterday **Gisteren**
Today **Vandaag**
Tomorrow **Morgen**
I don't understand **Ik begrijp het niet**
Do you speak English? **Spreekt u Engels?**
I need a doctor **Ik heb een dokter nodig**
Do you have a vacant room? **Zijn er nog kamers vrij?**
    - with bath/shower **met bad/douche**
    - with balcony **met balkon**
Single room **Eenpersoonskamer**
Double room **Tweepersoonskamer**
One/two nights **Een/twee nachten**
Rate **Prijs**

DIRECTIONS & GETTING AROUND

Where is...? **Waar is...?**
    - the tram stop **de tramhalte**
    - the telephone **de telefoon**
    - the bank **de bank** (note: bank also means seat)
Turn left/right **Ga naar links/rechts**
Go straight on **Ga rechtdoor**
Here/there **Hier/daar**
North **Noord**
East **Oost**
South **Zuid**
West **West**

DAYS OF THE WEEK

Monday **Maandag**
Tuesday **Disndag**
Wednesday **Woensdag**
Thursday **Dondersdag**
Friday **Vrijdag**
Saturday **Zaterdag**
Sunday **Zondag**

NUMBERS

1	**een**	13	**dertien**	30	**dertig**	102	**honderd twee**
2	**twee**	14	**veertien**	31	**een en dertig**	200	**twee honderd**
3	**drie**	15	**vijftien**	32	**twee en dertig**	300	**drie honderd**
4	**vier**	16	**zestien**			400	**vier honderd**
5	**vijf**	17	**zeventien**	40	**veertig**	500	**vijf honderd**
6	**zes**	18	**achttien**	50	**vijftig**	600	**zes honderd**
7	**zeven**	19	**negentien**	60	**zestig**	700	**zeven honderd**
8	**acht**	20	**twintig**	70	**zeventig**		
9	**negen**			80	**tachtig**	800	**acht honderd**
10	**tien**	21	**een en twintig**	90	**negentig**	900	**negen honderd**
11	**elf**	22	**twee en twintig**	100	**honderd**		
12	**twaalf**			101	**honderd een**	1,000	**duizend**

EATING OUT

Have you got a table for two? **Heeft u een tafel voor twee?**
I want to reserve a table **Ik wil een tafel reserveen**
I am a vegetarian **Ik ben vegetariër**
Could I have the check, please? **De rekening alstublieft**
This is not what I ordered **Dit is niet wat ik besteld heb**
Can we sit by the window? **Mogen wij bij het raam?**
Is the kitchen still open? **Is de keuken al open?**
What time do you close? **How laat gaat u open?**
Do you have a highchair? **Heeft u een kinderstoel?**
Is this spicy/highly seasoned? **Is dit gerecht pikant/gekruid?**
The food is cold **Het eten is koud**
Enjoy your meal! **Eet smakelijk!**

Service included **Bediening inbegrepen**
Service not included **Exlusief bediening**

Appetizer **Voorgerecht**
Bottle/glass **Fles/glas**
Breakfast **Ontbijt**
Café **Café**
Cold **Koud**
Cover charge **Couvert**
Dessert **Nagerecht**
Dinner **Diner/avondeten**
Dish of the day **Dagmenu** ,
Drink **Drank/drankje**
Dry **Droog**
Fork **Vork**
Fried **Gebakken**
Hot **Warm**
Hot (spicy) **Scherp**
Knife **Mes**
Lunch **Lunch/middageten**
Main course **Hoofdgerecht**
Medium **Medium**
Menu **Menukaart**
Rare **Rare**
Restaurant **Restaurant**
Set menu **Menu**
Specialties **Specialiteiten**
Spoon **Lepel**
Table **Tafel**
Waiter **Ober**
Waitress **Serveerster**
Well done **Doorbakken**
Wine list **Wijnkaart**

MENU A–Z

Aardappelen Potatoes
Ansjovissen Anchovies
Appeltaart (met slagroom) Apple cake (with whipped cream)
Azijn Vinegar
Biefstuk hollandse Steak
Biefstuk duitse Hamburger
Bier or Pils Beer
Bonen Beans
Boter Butter
Boterham Sandwich
Bouillon Consommé
Brood Bread
Broodje Bun or roll
Carbonade Pork chop
Champignons Mushrooms
Chocola Chocolate
Citroen Lemon
Eend Duck
Ei Egg
Erwten Peas
Forel Trout
Garnalen Shrimp
Hachée Stew
Ham Ham
Haring Herring
Hertenvlees Venison
Honing Honey
Hutspot Hot-pot
Ijs Ice cream
Jenever Gin
Jus Gravy
Kaas Cheese
Kabeljauw Cod
Kalfsvlees Veal
Kalkoen Turkey
Kip Chicken
Knoflook Garlic
Koffie Coffee
Kreeft Lobster
Lamsvlees Lamb

Makreel Mackerel
Melk Milk
Mineraal water Mineral water
Mosterd Mustard
Oesters Oysters
Olie Oil
Paling Eel
Pannekoeken Pancakes
Patates/frites french fries
Peper Pepper
Rijst Rice
Rode wijn Red wine
Rookworst Smoked sausage
Room Cream
Rundvlees Beef
Salade or Sla Salad
Saus Sauce
Schaaldieren Shellfish
Schelvis Haddock
Schol Plaice
Sinaasappelsap Orange juice
Soep Soup
Spek Bacon
Stamppot Sausage stew
Suiker Sugar
Thee Tea
Tong Sole
Tosti Cheese on toast
Uien Onions
Uitsmijter Fried egg on bread with ham
Varkensvlees Pork
Vis Fish
Vlees Meat
Vruchten Fruit
Water Water
Wild Game
Witte wijn White wine
Worst Sausage
Wortelen Carrots
Zalm Salmon
Zout Salt

Picture credits

The Automobile Association wishes to thank the following photographers and libraries for their assistance in the preparation of this book:
Front and back cover: (t) AA PhotoLibrary/Ken Paterson; (ct) AA PhotoLibrary/Ken Paterson; (cb) AA PhotoLibrary/Ken Paterson; (b) AA PhotoLibrary/Ken Paterson

AMSTERDAMS HISTORISCH MUSEUM 2iii, 49; © ANNE FRANK HOUSE 94cl, 94cr, 95c, 96t, 96c; ANTHONY BLAKE PHOTO LIBRARY 32 (Anthony Blake), 33t (Joy Skipper), 33b (Gerrit Buntroch); ART DIRECTORS AND TRIP PHOTO LIBRARY 91c, 92, 150, 168, 169; BRIDGEMAN ART LIBRARY 3i, 109 *An Englishman in Moscow*, 1913–14 by Kazimir Severinovich Malevich (1878–1935), Stedelijk Museum, Amsterdam, 21 *Titus Reading*, c 1656 by Rembrandt Harmensz. van Rijn (1606–69), Kunsthistorisches Museum, Vienna, Austria, 116 *The Night Watch* c 1642 (oil on canvas by Rembrandt Harmensz van Rijn (1606–69), Rijksmuseum, Amsterdam, 124 *The State Lottery* (w/c) by Vincent van Gogh (1853–90), Rijksmuseum Vincent van Gogh, Amsterdam, 125t *The Langlois Bridge in Arles*, March 1888 (oil on canvas) by Vincent van Gogh (1853–90), Rijksmuseum Vincent van Gogh, Amsterdam/Roger-Viollet, Paris, 126 *Self Portrait before his Easel*, 1888 by Vincent van Gogh (1853–90), Rijksmuseum Vincent van Gogh, Amsterdam, 127 *Wheatfield with Crows*, 1890 (oil on canvas) by Vincent van Gogh (1853–90) Rijksmuseum Vincent van Gogh, Amsterdam; COSTER DIAMONDS BV 128; JAMES DAVIS TRAVEL PHOTOGRAPHY 15t, 31cbl, 164, 164/5, 164, 171; MARY EVANS PICTURE LIBRARY 13t, 16/17, 17; EYE UBIQUITOUS 3v, 28cr, 31ctr, 187; GETTY ONE/STONE 2iv, 60, 61, 79, 163, 170/1; ROBERT HARDING PICTURE LIBRARY 10/11, 18, 80c, 83, 97, 170; HULTON GETTY PICTURE COLLECTION 18/19; JOODS HISTORISCH MUSEUM 142; MUSEUM AMSTELKRING/GORT JAN VAN ROOY 65c; MUSEUM HET REMBRANDTHUIS 20cr, 20bl, 66t, 66c; NATIONAAL LUCHTVAARTMUSEUM-AVIODOME, SCHIPHOL 172b; NEWMETROPOLIS/JAN DERWIG 9t; PICTURES COLOUR LIBRARY 30t, 30cl, 63c, 63ctr, 63bc, 64, 182; REX FEATURES LTD 19b; RIJKSMUSEUM 114, 115; SCHEEPVAART MUSEUM AMSTERDAM 146; SKYSCAN/MARCO VAN MIDDELKOOP 10, 13b, 31tr; TROPENMUSEUM 154c; WORLD PICTURES 3iii, 161, 166, 167, 172.

The remaining photographs are held in the Association's own photo library (AA PHOTO LIBRARY) and were taken by ALEX KOUPRIANOFF with the exception of: 3ii, 14t, 14b, 19t, 23, 30cr, 30br, 31bl, 31br, 51t, 52t, 52b, 54c, 54b, 56/57, 56, 57t, 57c, 58t, 58b, 59c, 59b, 62, 65tl, 67, 80b, 82, 86, 93t, 93b, 95t, 113t, 117, 119, 120b, 122, 123, 130, 135, 136bl, 138c, 138b, 140, 141, 143, 147, 148, 149 which were taken by KEN PATERSON and 122/123 which was taken by WYN VOYSEY.

Abbreviations for terms appearing above: (t) top; (b) bottom; (l) left; (r) right; (c) center.

Streetplan

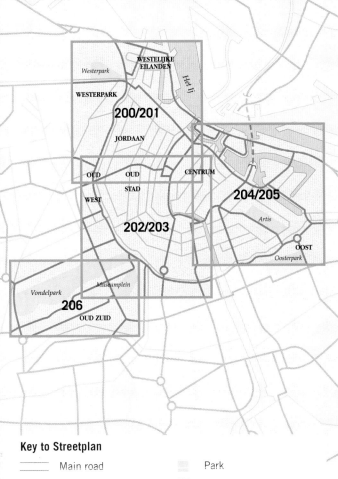

Westerpark

WESTELIJKE EILANDEN

Het Ij

WESTERPARK

200/201

JORDAAN

OUD

OUD

STAD

CENTRUM

WEST

204/205

Artis

202/203

OOST

Oosterpark

Museumplein

Vondelpark

206

OUD ZUID

Key to Streetplan

Main road		Park	
Other road		Important building	
Footpath		Featured place of interest	
Pedestrian street		•	Metro station
Rail line		*i*	Information

0	100	200	300	400	500 metres
0	100	200	300	400	500 yards

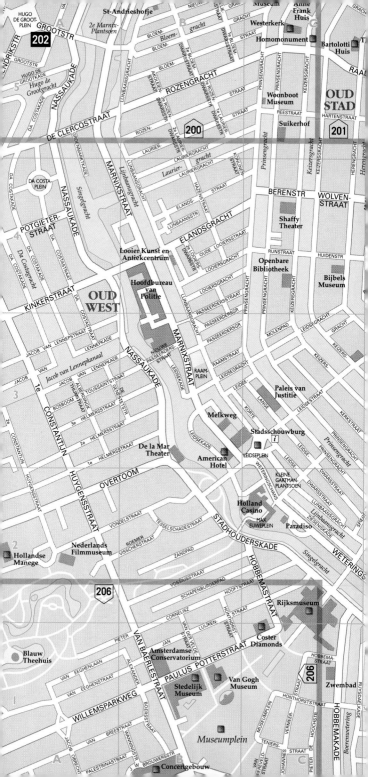

202

Rijksmuseum

MASTRAAT

HOBBE STR

HOOCHSTRA

PIETER DE

JOHANNES

VERHAEF STRAAT

VERHAEF STRAAT

VAN

MEERELVELD

TENIERS

STRAAT

METSUSTRAAT

GABRIEL

METSUSTRAAT

ROELOF

HARTSTRAAT

Coster
Diamonds

NICOLAAS MAESSTRAAT

RUYSDAELSTRAAT

CORNELIS ANTHONISZ STRAAT

ROELOF HARTPLEIN

BALTHASAR FLORISZ ST

GERARD TERBI

HONTHORST
STRAAT

Amsterdamse
Conservatorium

POTTERSTRAAT

PAULUS

Van Gogh
Museum

Stedelijk
Museum

Museumplein

VAN

BAERLESTRAAT

202

GABRIEL

MORELSESTRAAT

RUYSDAELSTRAAT

NICOLAAS MAESSTRAAT

FRANS VAN MIERISSTRAAT

JAN LUYKENSTRAAT

BARTHOLOMEUS RULOFFSSTRAAT

VAN DER VELDE
STRAAT

Concert-
gebouw

CONCERT-
GEBOUWPLEIN

VAN BAERLESTRAAT

BOERSSTRAAT

BROWERSTRAAT

JAN WOLKERSWEG

WONDERCOETESTRAAT

NICOLAAS

MAESSTRAAT

FRANS

HEINZE

STRAAT

JACOB OBRECHT PLEIN

REIJNIER VINKELESKADE

Noorder

Amstelkanaal

PIETER

ALEXANDER

VAN
EEGHENLAAN

VAN
EEGHENSTRAAT

WILLEMSPARKWEG

VAN

BREESTRAAT

WANNINGSTR

VAN

PALESTRINASTRAAT

JACOB

OBRECHTSTRAAT

JACOB OBRECHTSTRAAT

VERHULSTRAAT

DE LAIRESSESTRAAT

ZUID

BANSTRAAT

BANSTRAAT

OUD

BREITN

Blauw
Theehuis

202

JACOB
OBRECHT
PLEIN

CORNELIS SCHUYTSTRAAT

JOHANNES

J J VIOTTASTRAAT

HACQUARTSTRAAT

Hilton
Hotel

WILLEM WITSENSTRA

Vondelpark
Openlucht
Theater

VAN
EEGHENSTRAAT

WILLEMSPARKWEG

VAN

BREESTRAAT

VALERIUSSTRAAT

VAN

VERHULSTSTRAAT

EMMASTRAAT

DUFAYSTRAAT

J J VIOTTASTRAAT

Melkhuis

Revalidatiecentrum
Amsterdam

KONINGSLAAN

KONINGINNEWEG

DUFAYSTRAAT

JOHANNES

VERHULSTSTRAAT

LASSUS

STRAAT

DE LAIRESSESTRAAT

VALERIUSSTRAAT

GOETHEKADE

VAN

HET

kanaal

KATTENLAAN

JOHANNA
PARK

Het

VALERIUS
PLEIN

OKEGHEM

STRAAT

Vondelpark

SCHOOL
STRAAT

SAXENBURGER
STRAAT

REYER ANSLO
STRAAT

VONDELKERK
STRAAT

FREDERIKS
STRAAT

EMMALAAN

EMMA
PLEIN

PRINS

HENDRIKLAAN

ORANJE

NASSAULAAN

SOPHIALAAN

HENDRIK JACOBSZ

KONINGINNEWEG

HEIJE STR

HELMERSSTR

RHIJNVIS
FEITHSTRAAT

OVERTOOM

J CREMER
PLEIN

HUEISTRAAT

BUSKEN

KONINGS

LAAN

EMMALAAN

ORANJE
NASSAULAAN

SOPHIALAAN

SOPHIALAAN

STRAAT

WALDECK PYRMONTLAAN

SAXEN WEIMARLAAN

Kostverlorenkade

Baarsjesweg

De Kostverlorenkade

ZOCHERSTRAAT

AMSTELVEENSEWEG

Questionnaire

Dear Traveler

Your comments, opinions and recommendations are very important to us. So please help us to improve our travel guides by taking a few minutes to complete this simple questionnaire.

Send to: Spiral Guides, MailStop 66, 1000 AAA Drive, Heathrow, FL 32746–5063

Your recommendations...

We always encourage readers' recommendations for restaurants, nightlife or shopping – if your recommendation is added to the next edition of the guide, we will send you a FREE AAA Spiral Guide of your choice. Please state below the establishment name, location and your reasons for recommending it.

_____

_____

_____

_____

_____

Please send me AAA Spiral_____

(see list of titles inside the back cover)

About this guide...

Which title did you buy?

_____ **AAA Spiral**

Where did you buy it? _____

When? __ __ / __ __

Why did you choose a AAA Spiral Guide? _____

_____

_____

_____

Did this guide meet your expectations?

Exceeded ☐   Met all ☐   Met most ☐   Fell below ☐

Please give your reasons _____

_____

_____

_____

continued on next page...

Were there any aspects of this guide that you particularly liked?

Is there anything we could have done better?

About you...

Name (Mr/Mrs/Ms) ______

Address ______

______ Zip ______

Daytime tel nos. ______

Which age group are you in?

Under 25 ☐ 25–34 ☐ 35–44 ☐ 45–54 ☐ 55–64 ☐ 65+ ☐

How many trips do you make a year?

Less than one ☐ One ☐ Two ☐ Three or more ☐

Are you a AAA member? Yes ☐ No ☐

Name of AAA club ______

About your trip...

When did you book? m m/ y y When did you travel? m m/ y y

How long did you stay? ______

Was it for business or leisure? ______

Did you buy any other travel guides for your trip? ☐ Yes ☐ No

If yes, which ones? ______

Thank you for taking the time to complete this questionnaire.

All information is for AAA internal use only and will NOT be distributed outside the organization to any third parties.